Catalogue Foster and Partners

D0724422

PRESTEL
MUNICH · BERLIN · LONDON · NEW YORK

Contents

Introduction
Norman Foster

When I lecture, I often say to an audience that I want to share with them some of my experiences and those of my colleagues – our combined endeavours. That ambition is the foundation for this new catalogue of our work – a book that spans almost exactly forty years of practice. Looking back over those four decades one sees a period of huge social and technological transformation. That is as true of the practice of architecture as it is of the world at large. One sees also that this pattern is accelerating rather than diminishing, and that is reflected in the buildings and projects illustrated here.

I established my independent practice – then known as Foster Associates – in 1967. The office then was very small, really only a handful of people. Over the years it has grown and its horizons have expanded. Today, Foster and Partners is a global practice with a staff of 650 people and projects in fifty countries. My close colleagues – Spencer de Grey, David Nelson and Graham Phillips, together with a wider group of younger partners – have helped to guide the practice's evolution. Alongside them, both personally and professionally I am fortunate to have had so many generous collaborators – the architects who have contributed to the life of the studio, the consultants, particularly engineers and quantity surveyors and, not least, the clients with whom we have worked. This book is in part a reflection of their creative contributions.

Although design is generated in London and management flows out from there, it is impossible to think of the London studio in isolation from our network of overseas offices – in that sense we have a physical presence on the site of every project, wherever it is in the world. The dynamic of Riverside owes much to the interaction and movement between these different places and cultures. The studio is young and cosmopolitan: the average age is a little over thirty and as many languages are spoken there. I have heard it said that it is more like a college than a conventional architect's office and I believe that's true.

It might be said in this context that the only constant is change. However, in reviewing our work, I believe that it is possible to identify a number of themes and concerns, which have guided us consistently over the years. When I entered the architectural profession in the early 1960s, there was a common demarcation between what was considered 'architecture' – a high art – and what was regarded as mere 'building'. I have always rejected such distinctions. Design for me is all

encompassing. It is about values. I believe one has a moral duty to design well and to design responsibly – whether that is at the scale of a door handle or a city masterplan. To design is to question and to challenge. Design can explore the new and build on the past. It can transform patterns of health, living and working. Above all, design is a human act – a response to the needs of people, both material and spiritual.

Tracing a line from my early passions and influences to my work today, I found myself writing down a few key words. The first of these was 'inspiration'. There is so much that inspires design. For me there have been people and places, the work of other architects and artists, as well as natural forces and the achievements of technology. Being affected by what we see, and then moved to create is the starting-point for all original work at any stage in a career. 'Fascination' was the word that next came to mind, suggesting curiosity and the urge to learn and understand. The fascination I felt as a student is the same as I experience now when I come across new ideas. Then came the word 'motivation' – the passion, the constant search for satisfaction that drives the designer. That mix of inspiration, fascination and motivation can be complex and contradictory, so perhaps in the end 'integration' is the key word and the first of the themes I would highlight. Integration, for me, can mean bringing disparate elements into harmony, or breaking down conventional social and spatial boundaries.

Our early buildings were mostly for industry, for clients such as Reliance Controls and Fred Olsen. I saw those projects as an opportunity to challenge preconceptions and stereotypes: for example, about how one accommodated 'white-collar' and 'blue-collar' staff. Traditionally in the workplace they had been kept apart, using 'clean and dirty', 'us and them' distinctions. Instead, we brought them together and in doing so tried to raise standards for everyone. Similarly, in the late 1960s I envisaged a school building that would be open-planned, filled with light, democratic and flexible, without corridors or institutional barriers. Today, we have realised such a school in the Bexley Business Academy (2001-2003) and a related series of new City Academies.

We have applied the same rationale in university buildings for scientific and medical research, first at Imperial College in London, and again at Stanford University in California. In this context communication is one of the most valuable commodities. One hears tales of brainwaves

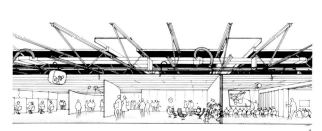

1

2

3

4

or breakthroughs being achieved not in the rarefied atmosphere of the laboratory but by people getting together for a coffee. In the Center for Clinical Science Research at Stanford (1995-2000) and again in the Clark Center (1999-2003), the social spaces are as important as the laboratory spaces. They are designed for social interaction, which means breaking down barriers between the different specialities and dissolving professional boundaries.

That process of challenging accepted responses or formulae is something that continues to underpin the work of the practice across a range of building types. It means trying to ask the right questions, allied with a curiosity about how things work – whether they be organisations or mechanical systems. I have characterised that tendency to reconfigure a building type entirely from first principles as 'reinventing'. Often that is a process that can be seen to unfold through a series of projects. For example, our office building for Willis Faber & Dumas in Ipswich (1971-1975) developed thoughts about the nature of the workplace first explored with Reliance Controls and Fred Olsen. The atrium, with its escalators, and the social dimension of the roof garden and restaurant all help to engender a sense of community, while the achievement of such 'luxuries' as a swimming pool within a tight commercial budget presented a special kind of design challenge. Above all, we were concerned with the quality of life and light, with introducing a little joy into the workplace. While Willis Faber 'reinvented' the office building, it also focused ideas that would be re-explored in low-rise projects such as our European Headquarters for Electronic Arts (1997-2000), the McLaren Technology Centre (1998-2004) and a family of high-rise office projects.

We took an equally radical approach with the Sainsbury Centre for Visual Arts (1974-1978). All the varied functions and user groups – galleries and teaching spaces, students, academics and the public – are brought together in a single unified space. It is a gallery without walls in the conventional sense. Traditionally, this range of facilities would have produced a collection of four or five separate buildings. But by integrating everything under one roof in this way we encouraged creative interaction and cross-fertilisation between different departments and activities. It is also a celebration of light and space. The use of natural toplight is an important part of the energy equation, but it goes beyond that to impact on the spirit of the place. In that respect, we would

probably not have conceived our terminal building at Stansted Airport (1981-1991) without the experience of the Sainsbury Centre.

With Stansted, we took the accepted concept of the airport and literally turned it upside-down. We went back to the roots of air travel, to try to recapture the clarity of the early terminals and to celebrate the act of flying. At Stansted, gone are the labyrinthine routes of the typical airport terminal. Instead, passengers proceed from the set-down point to the check-in area, passport control and on to the departure lounges, where they can see the planes – all on a single level. All the heavy services that usually clog the roofspace are instead placed in an undercroft so that the roof can become a lightweight canopy, admitting daylight. Looking forward again, Stansted undoubtedly provided the springboard for our terminal buildings at Chek Lap Kok in Hong Kong (1992-1998) and Beijing (2003-2007). Significantly, it also provided a model since adopted by airport planners worldwide.

One of the things that most excites me about practising architecture today is the dynamic mobility we enjoy, not just in moving around the world, but also in our ability to respond quickly to new challenges. Chek Lap Kok and Beijing illustrate this in both senses, moving very fast indeed. In the case of Beijing, we received official confirmation that we had won the competition in November 2003; a week or so later we had a team in place, and by early January the first tender package was ready for ground breaking to commence a month later. Consider that this is a building of over a million square metres, capable of handling up to 60 million passengers per annum. Yet it will have been commissioned and completed in three years: the time taken to conclude the public inquiry for Heathrow Terminal 5 – and was the outcome of that ever in doubt?

Although Chek Lap Kok is the largest airport in the world – soon to be overtaken in terms of passenger numbers by Beijing – like Stansted, the experience of the traveller is paramount. We strove to make the building friendly and accessible, easy to navigate, and thus to reduce the dependence on signage. Departing, you do not have to have zones or colours to guide you. You can see the land on one side or the sea on the other, and the aircraft you are moving towards. Interestingly, although it is very large – providing under one roof all the facilities and passenger-handling capacity provided by Heathrow's four existing terminals, together with part of the new Terminal 5 – Chek Lap Kok is also very efficient in energy terms because it is very compact.

5

6

1. Hong Kong International
Airport, Chek Lap Kok
(1992-1998). The Stansted
model was developed and
expanded by Chek Lap Kok.

2. Beijing International
Airport, Beijing, China
(2003-2007). Chek Lap Kok
in turn informs the design
of Beijing – the world's
largest and most technically
advanced airport building.

It has a relatively small footprint, which is a major consideration when land is scarce. Chek Lap Kok is also an example of how political will can produce a long-term solution to a problem, on an unprecedented scale, and achieve it quickly.

When the time came to select the site for a new airport there was no land available. The site itself had to be created. But far from being an obstacle to development, it became the catalyst for one of the largest construction projects of modern times. In 1992 Chek Lap Kok was a small mountainous island off the South China coast. In an ambitious reclamation programme that involved moving 200 million cubic metres of rock, mud and sand, the island's 100-metre peak was reduced to a flat 7 metres above sea level and the land area expanded to four times its original size. At 6 kilometres long and 3.5 kilometres wide, it is as large as the Kowloon peninsula. In one tenth of the time that it has taken London's Heathrow Airport to grow piecemeal, Hong Kong has overtaken it by realising far more capacity in a single integrated building.

Hong Kong is an astonishing place, where the 'can do' approach overcomes almost any obstacle. It is also significant in terms of the history of the practice in that it gave us our first opportunity to build overseas. The headquarters for the Hongkong and Shanghai Bank (1979-1986) was conceived during a sensitive period in Hong Kong's history, and was intended as a statement of confidence, created without compromise. Our brief was to create 'the best bank building in the world'. In the process we reinvented the high-rise office building. We took the unusual step of pushing the services and circulation cores to the perimeter to create flexible, open office floors. Vertical movement combines high-speed lifts with escalators – a connection to Willis Faber. A mirrored 'sunscoop' directs sunlight down through the heart of the building, and the banking hall is elevated to create a sheltered public plaza at ground level – a space that has unexpectedly become a lively weekend picnic spot for the city's Filipino community.

From the outset the Hongkong Bank placed a high priority on flexibility and it has attributed a measure of its continued strength as a company to the ability to reconfigure the building to suit its changing needs. Similarly, the Willis Faber building was far sighted in incorporating a custom-designed access floor throughout, anticipating the revolution in information technology by more than a decade; so much so that – alone among insurance companies – Willis Faber was able to introduce

computerisation without having to build a new facility. Shifting technological, social and economic patterns mean that the work styles and lifestyles of building occupants are continually evolving. Being aware of those changes and being able to predict future trends is fundamental to the way that we work as designers. To help us to explore alternative working and living patterns we have a specialist Workplace Consultancy team in the studio that explores and analyses these trends. As these two projects demonstrate, gaining a clear understanding of a client's needs at the outset can lead to dramatic improvements in an organisation's long-term effectiveness and the welfare of a building's occupants.

Connections can be made between Willis Faber and the Hongkong Bank and some of the practice's more recent high-rise office buildings. For example, the Commerzbank in Frankfurt (1991-1997) stemmed from a desire to reconcile work and nature within the compass of an office building. That is a theme explored both in the design of Willis Faber, which attempted to bring the 'park' into the office, and in the Hongkong Bank, where we proposed 'gardens in the sky'. The Commerzbank is significant in that it gave us the opportunity to design a building that is symbolically and functionally 'green'. Although the climate is controlled, it uses natural ventilation for energy reduction, making it the world's first ecological high-rise building. It is also responsive to its city-centre location, emerging as it does from the centre of a large traditional urban block. We developed a strategy that allowed us to place such a tall building in the city and yet to break down its scale. By preserving or rebuilding the smaller-scale perimeter buildings in the block, we were able to restore the grain of the neighbourhood at street level. We were also able to enhance local amenities by providing a covered public arcade through the site, which provides a social focus, with cafés and spaces for exhibitions and other events.

Our headquarters tower for Swiss Re at 30 St Mary Axe in the City of London (1997-2004) is rooted in a radical approach – technically, architecturally, socially and spatially – and takes forward many of the ideas explored in the Commerzbank. The building's profile can be likened to a cigar – a cylinder that widens as it rises from the ground and then tapers towards its apex. This form responds to the specific demands of the small site. It appears less bulky than a conventional rectangular block of equivalent floor area and reduces down draughts, while the

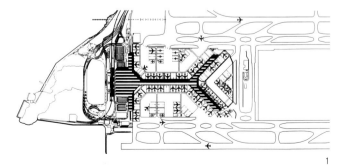

1

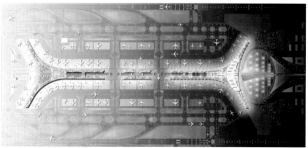

2

3. Hongkong and Shanghai Bank Headquarters, Hong Kong (1979–1986). A reinvention of the high-rise office building, circulation and service cores are pushed to the perimeter of the plan.

4. Commerzbank Headquarters, Frankfurt (1991–1997). With its perimeter service cores and 'sky gardens,' the Commerzbank restates themes explored in the Hongkong Bank.

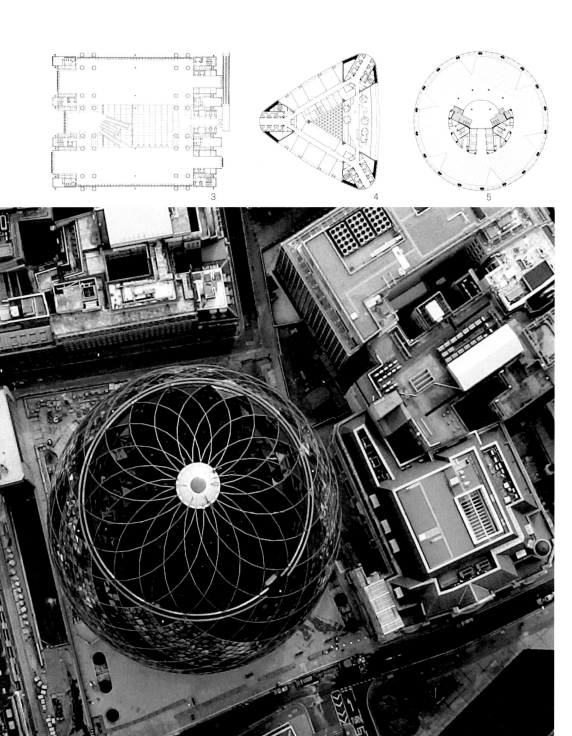

3   4   5

6

5, 6. Swiss Re Headquarters, 30 St Mary Axe, London (1997–2004). With its spiralling gardens and strong environmental agenda, Swiss Re in turn restates themes from Commerzbank – part of a continuing process of reinventing the tall office building.

9

1

1, 2. City Hall, London
(1998-2002). The project
demonstrates the potential
for a sustainable, virtually
non-polluting public building;
natural ventilation and
heating strategies combine
with a form designed
to minimise heat gain.

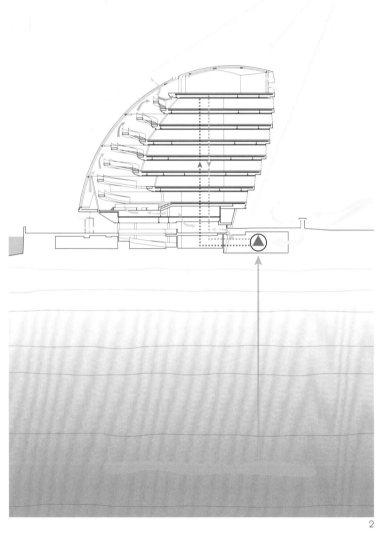

2

Heat exchanger

Natural ventilation

Ceilings chilled by
ground water

Warm air extracted
via ceiling is recycled

Cold water from
underground aquifer

slimming of the building's profile at its base reduces reflections,
improves transparency and increases daylight penetration at ground
level. Our environmental strategy focuses on a series of sky gardens,
which are created by making triangular incisions into the edges of each
circular floor-plate. Each floor is rotated in relation to its neighbour so
that the gardens spiral up around the perimeter of the building. These
spaces are natural social focal points – places for refreshment and
meeting areas – and function as the building's 'lungs', distributing
fresh air drawn in through opening panels in the facade. As with the
Commerzbank, which is naturally ventilated for 80 per cent of the year,
this system reduces the building's reliance on air-conditioning which,
together with other sustainable measures, means that it uses only half
the energy consumed by its environmentally sealed neighbours.

The sustainable design strategies that underpin these two projects
highlight another significant theme in our work. Sustainability is a
word that has become fashionable over the last decade. However,
sustainability is not a matter of fashion, but of survival. The United
Nations, in its *Global Environment Outlook 2002*, outlined a series of
possible environmental scenarios for the next thirty years. At worst, it
foresaw crises triggered by increasing water shortages, global warming
and pollution. It suggested that these trends might be slowed, but only
if nations work together to address radically the global consumption
of natural resources and energy, and to halt man's degradation of
the natural environment.

Scientists predict that the Earth will warm by 1.4 to 5.8 °C by
2100 – more than temperatures are thought to have changed since
the dawn of humanity. It is now generally accepted that this warming
is due to rising atmospheric concentrations of 'greenhouse' gases
– most significantly carbon dioxide. But in my experience few people
are aware that in the industrialised world buildings consume half the
energy we generate and are responsible for half the carbon dioxide
emissions, the remainder being divided almost equally between
transport and industry. Architects clearly have an important role to
play in challenging this equation. Sustainability requires us to think
holistically. The location and function of a building; its flexibility and
life span; its orientation, form and structure; its heating and ventilation
systems and the materials used; together impact upon the amount
of energy required to build and maintain it, and travel to and from it.

3, 4. Chesa Futura, St Moritz (2000-2002). The project fuses state-of-the-art computer design tools with centuries-old construction techniques – including hand-cut and hand-fixed larch shingles – to create a building that is both environmentally sustainable and contextually apt.

3

4

Only by finding new solutions to these problems can we create sustainable forms of building for the future. These are issues that have concerned the practice from its earliest days. The planning study we undertook in the mid-1970s for Gomera, in the Canary Islands, pioneered the exploration of sustainable patterns of tourist development on the island. It was a 'green' project long before the environmental agenda was seriously being discussed. We investigated the use of indigenous building techniques, together with alternative energy sources – wind and solar power, and methane production from domestic waste – to minimise the island's reliance on imported resources and encourage self-sustaining development.

Today within the studio we have a Research and Development Group that includes a Sustainability Forum. The Forum was established to consolidate and develop the practice's knowledge base and help us develop better access to information on new products, materials, and research findings. In many of our projects we have pioneered solutions using renewable energy sources, which offer dramatic reductions in pollution. Examples are not confined to buildings. Working with industry we have created a new generation of super-efficient wind turbines, cladding systems that harvest energy, even a solar-electric vehicle. A central aim is to keep the practice's sustainability policy up to date and ensure that it is applicable at a range of scales, from masterplanning to product design. Beyond that, we also commit resources to obtaining funding for research projects, which can feed back into our built work as well as advance a wider critical debate.

Many of the 'green' ideas that we explored in early projects are only now becoming a reality because of the new technologies at our disposal. Thirty years ago, when we were designing the Willis Faber building, a conversation with the late Buckminster Fuller prompted the idea of wrapping the site in a free-form triangulated glass skin. The 'Climatroffice', as the project was known, suggested a new rapport between nature and the office, its garden setting creating a microclimate within an energy-conscious enclosure. Then, unfortunately, we lacked the technological tools to realise it in the time available. But today we have sophisticated computer-modelling software that allows us to design and build complex structures in a fraction of the time it would have taken in the 1970s. Our London City Hall (1998-2002) is a case in point. Its orientation and formal geometry were guided by a desire

to minimise the building's surface area in relation to its volume, and thus reduce heat loss and gain through the building's skin. The starting point was a sphere, which has 25 per cent less surface area than a cube of the same capacity. As a result of computer analysis, this pure form was manipulated to achieve optimum performance, in particular to minimise the surface area exposed to direct sunlight. This strategy is backed up with a host of passive environmental-control systems. The building is naturally ventilated for most of the year, with openable windows in all the office spaces; heat generated by people, computers and lights can be recycled; and cold groundwater can be pumped up through boreholes from the water-table to cool the building. The combination of these energy-saving systems means that for the majority of the year the building requires no additional heating and overall uses only a quarter of the energy consumed by a typical high-specification London office building.

Another new office building, a headquarters tower for the Hearst Corporation (2001-2005), under construction in New York, takes equally bold steps in terms of sustainability. It uses 90 per cent recycled steel – highly significant in terms of the building's embodied energy – and, among other measures, collects rainwater to irrigate planting. It is the first tower in Manhattan to be awarded a stamp of approval through the US Green Buildings Council's Leadership in Energy and Environmental Design Program (LEED). Environmentally friendly construction is in keeping with Hearst's philosophy as a company. Hearst places a high value on the notion of the healthy workplace and it is not alone in believing that providing such an environment is set to become an important factor in the recruitment process in the future. As a private corporation occupying the entire building, Hearst also had the benefit of making a decision unencumbered by outside interests. It reinforces my experience that it is enlightened owner-occupiers – companies such as Willis Faber and Commerzbank – that can be relied upon to provide a lead for the market to follow.

In a very different context, our Chesa Futura apartment building in St Moritz, Switzerland (2000-2002) married advanced computer-aided design tools with state-of-the-art prefabricated timber construction to create a building that is environmentally benign. It is a building that can be regarded almost as a mini manifesto. It demonstrates that you don't have to build on the edges of towns and cities, consuming precious

5, 6. Gomera Regional Planning Study, Canary Islands (1975). A 'green' project long before the term had gained common currency, the Gomera masterplan explored strategies for sustainable, energy self-sufficient tourist development on the island, including harnessing wind and solar power.

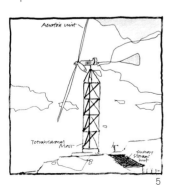

5

6

land and creating sprawl; and you don't have to consume large amounts of energy, even in a cold climate. It is a low-energy structure not just in terms of its consumption, but also in terms of the life-cycle of the materials used in its construction. Wood is an entirely sustainable, renewable resource and it absorbs carbon dioxide during its growth cycle. Additionally, in that part of Switzerland, building in timber is culturally sympathetic, reflecting local architectural traditions; and it contributes to the local ecology of harvesting older trees to facilitate forest regeneration.

Like Chesa Futura, the glasshouse at the National Botanic Garden of Wales (1994-2000) draws lessons from the ecology of its site, in this case to heat and service the building in an environmentally friendly way. It is heated in part by a biomass boiler — a wood-chip combustion plant — that burns timber trimmings from the gardens and prepared waste supplied by landfill contractors. This process is broadly carbon neutral, the carbon dioxide emitted during the combustion process balanced by that absorbed by the plant matter during its lifetime. This environmental approach is continued throughout: rainwater from the roof of the glasshouse is channelled into storage tanks to supply grey water for irrigation and flushing lavatories, while waste from the lavatories is treated naturally using reed beds. Even the ash created by combustion is reused as fertiliser. These are sustainable systems that work with, rather than against nature.

With our transformation of the Reichstag in Berlin (1992-1999) as the new home of the German Parliament, we showed how sustainable strategies could work in the context of an old building — once a huge consumer of energy and a major source of pollution. We developed a radical new energy solution, using wholly renewable bio-fuel — refined vegetable oil from rape or sunflower seeds — which, when burned in a co-generator to produce electricity is remarkably clean and efficient compared to burning fossil fuels. Together with the increased use of daylight and natural ventilation, this has led to a 94 per cent reduction in the building's carbon-dioxide emissions. The building is also able to store and recycle surplus energy, using underground seasonal energy reservoirs.

Before the installation of new services, the building consumed enough energy annually to heat 5,000 modern homes. Raising the internal temperature by just one degree on a mid-winter's day required a burst of energy sufficient to heat ten houses for a year. Today the Reichstag creates more energy than it consumes, allowing it to act as a local power station supplying other buildings in the new government quarter. If a nineteenth-century building can be transformed from an energy-guzzler into a building so efficient that it is now a net energy provider, how much easier is it to design new buildings that make responsible use of precious resources?

The Reichstag illustrates another theme that has become an important part of the practice's work: how new architecture can be the catalyst for the revitalisation of old buildings. An old building on this scale, especially one with a history as complex as that of the Reichstag, is like a city in microcosm, with many layers of intervention over time. Just as the experience of a city can be enriched when old and new elements are brought into a creative dialogue, so too can that of a building.

The Reichstag as we found it had been mutilated successively by fire, war and insensitive postwar rebuilding. Interiors that had weathered the first two onslaughts had been destroyed by the third, the few surviving nineteenth-century fragments concealed beneath a bland plaster lining. Remarkably, when we peeled away this layer we discovered striking imprints of the past, including broken mouldings, masons' marks and graffiti chalked on the walls by victorious Red Army soldiers in 1945. These scars have been preserved and each historical layer articulated to allow the Reichstag to become, in effect, a 'living museum' of German history.

Our reconstruction takes cues from the past in other ways too: for example, we reinstated the original *piano nobile* and courtyards and reopened the formal west entrance. But in other respects it represents a radical departure. Within its massive masonry walls the building has been made transparent, its interiors opened up to the light, and the activity of the chamber revealed to view. It is a public building in every sense — a symbol of both city and nation — with millions of visitors every year. Visitors are invited up to the roof terrace and into the cupola, where ramps spiral up to an observation deck, allowing people to ascend symbolically above the heads of their political representatives.

Like the Reichstag, the British Museum is a historic building that has been reinvigorated by a contemporary architectural intervention. The Great Court (1994-2000) was once one of London's long-lost spaces. Originally an open garden, shortly after its completion in the

1, 2. New German Parliament, Reichstag, Berlin (1992-1999). The scars of history uncovered during the rebuilding have been preserved to allow the Reichstag to function as a living museum.

Right: The Great Court at the British Museum, London (1994-2000). A conscious dialogue between old and new.

Improving access	Security
Private cars	Public transport
Tourists	Londoners
Ceremonial	Everyday
People	Traffic
People still	People moving
Visual clutter	Legibility
Local needs	London wide needs
Design	Management
Old	New

1   2   3

mid-nineteenth century the courtyard became the site of the round Reading Room and its associated bookstacks. It was the departure of the British Library to St Pancras that gave us the opportunity to reclaim the courtyard. By clearing away the bookstack structures and casting a lightweight glazed canopy over the space we were able to 'reinvent' the courtyard as the organisational heart of the Museum and enhance the experience of the nearly six million people who visit it each year. The Great Court is a new kind of civic space – a cultural plaza – that has pioneered patterns of social use hitherto unknown within this or any other museum. And for the first time in its history the magnificent Reading Room is open to all.

As part of a related series of interventions, we freed the forecourt from parked cars and restored it to provide an appropriate formal reception space for the Museum and a herald of the Great Court. Together these two spaces represent a major new amenity for London. A rendezvous for those who live or work in Bloomsbury, the Great Court has also become a popular shortcut, a place to pause and have a coffee on the pedestrian route from the British Library and London University, in the north, to Covent Garden in the south.

Our work at the British Museum is rooted in the belief that it is not only individual buildings but also their wider urban context that affects our well being. In that sense, it relates to our 'World Squares for All' masterplan, which contains detailed proposals for the environmental improvement of Trafalgar Square, Parliament Square, Whitehall and their immediate surroundings in central London. Its goals are to enhance pedestrian access and enjoyment of the area for Londoners and the thousands of people who visit each year, and to create more sympathetic settings for its historic buildings and monuments. I have described that task as a 'balancing act', a search to promote a genuinely integrated solution able to satisfy the often conflicting needs of those who live in, or visit the city: something that holds true for any historical urban environment attempting to sustain contemporary activities. Our first step was an extensive research programme that involved London-wide studies of traffic patterns and pedestrian movement through and around the central area, together with consultations with more than 180 public bodies and thousands of individuals. This led us to develop two possible approaches, which formed the subject of a public exhibition: the public's response was overwhelming support for change.

The first phase of our work to be implemented has seen the transformation of Trafalgar Square. The northern edge of the square, in front of the National Gallery, has been closed to vehicles and paved to create a broad pedestrian plaza in front of the building. Although in architectural terms it is a relatively discreet intervention, its effect has been radical, changing completely the visitor's experience – with a ripple effect that can be felt throughout the surrounding area – and with none of the traffic chaos predicted by the sceptics.

Frequently when I share a project with others I find myself talking about the importance of the social focus, the heart of the building, the way in which it can change the quality of people's lives. As we can see in Trafalgar Square, that applies equally to urban infrastructure – the squares, parks and public spaces, the bridges and transport systems, the 'urban glue' that holds cities together. Indeed, I would argue that the quality of life in a modern city is influenced more by the quality of its infrastructure than by the nature of its individual buildings. Infrastructure can also have a powerful impact in other ways. For example, it is interesting to look at our Millennium Bridge in London or our Millau Bridge in rural France in terms of the prosperity they are bringing to their local communities and their powerful symbolic role – attributes whose value far exceeds that of the connection itself.

Our work in Nîmes is another demonstration of how an individual project, linked to an enlightened political initiative, can help to regenerate the wider fabric of a city. The effect of the Carré d'Art (1984-1993) and its related works in the Place de la Maison Carrée has been to transform an entire urban quarter. We took a space once choked by parked cars and unfriendly to visitors and gave it new life. We re-routed the traffic and repaved the square to create a space that invites people in. Go there today and you find it buzzing with activity. There is a thriving outdoor café life, new shops have opened and the ripple effects can be felt well beyond the site.

A similar objective has driven our Sage music centre in Gateshead (1997-2004), which is both a catalyst in the cultural regeneration of the riverside and a key element in helping to establish Tyneside as a cultural destination in its own right. In each case, a concern for the physical context has produced projects that are sensitive to the culture and climate of their place. What these projects tell us is that the holistic thinking that underpins sustainable strategies for architecture must

5. Millau Viaduct, Gorges du Tarn, France (1993-2004)

6. Millennium Bridge, London (1996-2000).

7-10. A family of Foster masterplans, each of which has explored sustainable patterns of urban development. From left: King's Cross, London (1987); Nîmes, France (1989); Sagrera, Barcelona (1991); and most recently Santa Giulia, Milan (2004).

5   6

1, 2. Trafalgar Square, London (2002-2003). Before and after: the north side of the square has been recreated as a broad pedestrianised terrace that mediates between the National Gallery and the body of the square.

3. Norman Foster's sketch emphasises that such a project is a balancing act.

4. The Sage Gateshead, Gateshead (1997-2004).

4

equally be applied at the scale of the city. Architects are rarely given the opportunity to influence the urban environment on the broadest scale through planning an entire city or neighbourhood, but we can 'think global and act local'. We know that attractive, sustainable localised communities can be created when transport connections, workplaces, schools, shops, parks and recreation spaces are all within walking or cycling distance of home.

The clean nature of much post-industrial work means that workplaces can be combined with housing in mixed-use development – our own studio in Battersea was a pioneer in London in this regard. However, such integrated communities in many cases still conflict with outdated planning guidelines that specify separate zones for residential, commercial or industrial use, or for leisure and culture. In the past, it was the blighting nature of heavy industry that was responsible for many of these zoning policies. Today, in contrast, 'clean' industries, such as microelectronics and new service-sector offices and studios are completely compatible with residential areas. In our work in Duisburg, in the former 'rust belt' of the Ruhr, we have demonstrated that inner cities can be revitalised by introducing these newer industries and locating them alongside housing and schools – even creating more green spaces in the process.

However, while we know that virtually every new building can be designed to run on a fraction of current energy levels, or make use of renewable energy sources, the bigger global picture is dominated by two further crucial issues: population growth and the shift towards living in cities. The world's population stands at 6.4 billion; in ten years it is expected to reach 7.5 billion. By 2015 there will be twenty-three 'megacities' – cities with populations of more than ten million. Nineteen of them will be in developing countries, where up to half the population will be urbanised. But what will those cities look like?

One of the chief problems facing the world today is urban sprawl. As cities grow horizontally rather than vertically, swallowing up more and more land, people are forced to travel greater distances between home and work, bringing consequent increases in energy consumption and carbon dioxide emissions. There is a direct correlation between urban density and energy consumption – denser communities promote walking and cycling rather than driving – and high density does not automatically mean overcrowding or economic hardship. Significantly,

the world's two most densely populated communities, Monaco and Macao, are at opposite ends of the economic spectrum; and in London some of the most expensive areas are also the most densely populated. Mayfair, Kensington and Chelsea, for example, have population densities up to three times higher than those found in many of the capital's poorest boroughs.

Working within the context of existing cities we can increase densities and improve urban quality using both high-rise and low-rise solutions. However, in situations where land is scarce, we have to explore new ways of building. Our Millennium Tower proposed for Tokyo (1989) takes a traditional horizontal city quarter – housing, shops, restaurants, cinemas, museums, sporting facilities, green spaces and public transport networks – and turns it on its side to create a super-tall building with a multiplicity of uses. It would be over 800 metres high with 170 storeys – twice the height of anything so far built – and would house a community of up to 60,000 people. This is 20,000 more than the population of Monaco and yet the building would occupy less than one hundredth of the land. It would be a virtually self-sufficient, fully self-sustaining community in the sky. This sounds like future fantasy. But we have, now, all the means at our disposal to create such buildings.

Architects have a vital role as advocates, encouraging sustainable solutions. But we in turn need more progressive developers and politicians with courage to set goals and incentives for society to follow. Some countries have given a lead. Germany, for example, has long understood the need to reduce consumption and promote renewable energy sources, and that is reflected in building codes. Naturally, it is no coincidence that some of the practice's most advanced environmental thinking has been encouraged by the attitudes of German clients. There are, I believe, no technological barriers to sustainable development, only ones of political will.

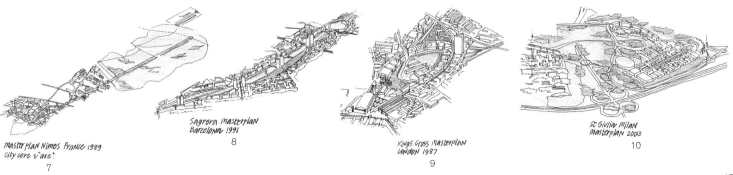

master plan Nimes France 1989
city core d'axe:
7

Sagrera Masterplan
Barcelona 1991
8

Kings Cross Masterplan
London 1987
9

St Giulia Milan
Masterplan 2003
10

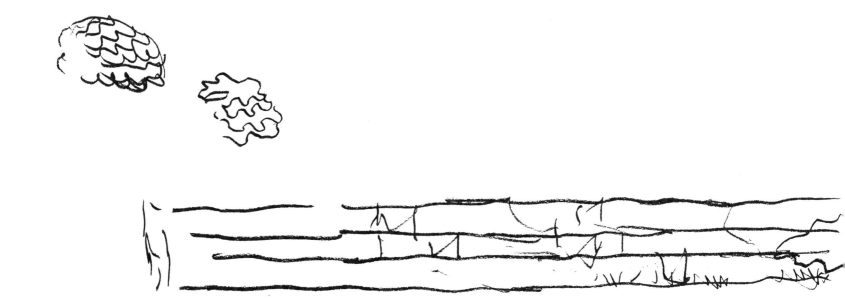

The Berlin Brain

Free University of Berlin

Berlin, Germany 1997 –

Since the end of the Second World War, the Free University has occupied a central role in the intellectual life of Berlin. One of the city's most symbolically important institutions, its foundation marked the rebirth of liberal education there after the war. Today, with more than 39,000 students, it is the largest of Berlin's three universities. This redevelopment scheme includes the restoration of its Modernist buildings and the design of a new library on the campus.

The University's mat-like campus was designed by Candilis Josic Woods Schiedhelm, and when the first phase was completed in 1973 it was hailed as a milestone in university design. The facade was designed in collaboration with Jean Prouvé, following Le Corbusier's 'Modulor' proportional system. It was fabricated from Cor-Ten steel, which when used in appropriate thicknesses, has self-protecting corrosive characteristics. The rusty appearance of these buildings led to the affectionate nickname of 'die Rostlaube' – the 'rust-bucket'. However, in the slender sections used by Prouvé the steel was prone to decay, which by the late 1990s had become extensive. As part of a comprehensive process of renewal, the old cladding has been replaced with a new system detailed in bronze, which as it patinates with age emulates the details and colour tones of the original.

The new library for the Faculty of Philology occupies a site created by uniting six of the University's courtyards. Its four floors are contained within a naturally ventilated, bubble-like enclosure, which is clad in a mix of solid aluminium and glazed panels and supported on steel frames with a radial geometry. An inner membrane of translucent glass fibre filters the daylight, while scattered transparent openings allow momentary views and glimpses of sunlight. The bookstacks are located at the centre of each floor, with reading desks arranged around the perimeter. The serpentine profile of the floors creates an edge pattern in which each floor swells or recedes with respect to the one above or below it, generating a sequence of generous, light-filled spaces in which to work. Amusingly, the library's cranial form has already earned it a nickname of its own – 'the Berlin brain'.

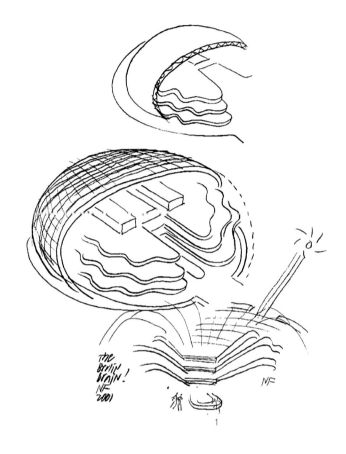

1

2

1, 2. Concept sketches by Norman Foster.

3-5. Progress photographs showing the concrete floor slabs, the domed steel enclosure, and the external skin, with its mix of solid and glass panels.

3

4

5

6

7

8

6. Visualisation showing the library's position within the Free University campus.

7. Detail of the new bronze facade installed on the original campus buildings.

8. A view of one of the refurbished lecture halls, with its acoustic panelling.

Academies
England 2003–

Following the completion of the Brent and Bexley Academies, the practice is building a further seven new schools around the country. The Academies represent a new direction in secondary education. Inspirational and state-of-the-art places of learning, they are designed to create exciting new opportunities for pupils and to play a key role in the regeneration of local communities by establishing after-school social and educational facilities.

Supported by private sponsors working together with the DfES and local education partners, each Academy addresses local needs with highly tailored design solutions for diverse specialist themes, ranging from business and science to sport and the arts. While each project addresses a unique set of requirements, all reflect operational and educational themes based on clear, compact layouts, a well-supervised and secure learning environment and a flexible range of spaces. Of paramount importance is a desire to establish a sense of identity and engender a feeling of community.

Depending upon the site and the programme, the schools vary in plan from simple linear forms to more complex courtyard arrangements. The Djanogly Academy in Nottingham is an example of the former. The smallest school in this group, designed for 810 pupils, it is a lower school only. Its toplit central street serves classrooms on two levels, while double-height spaces at either end of the building accommodate communal activities. In contrast, the largest school, the Thomas Deacon Academy, which will accommodate 2,200 pupils, has a more articulated plan form. The educational brief centres on six colleges that provide a structured tutoring approach. This is reflected in the plan, in which the six V-shaped colleges, each with its own central study space, combine to form a three-storey ribbon of teaching accommodation that weaves around a roofed central courtyard and a media resource centre – the social and visual heart of the school. Other Academies in this group are organised to reflect different tutorial arrangements based on 'houses', 'home bases' or year groups. In each case the buildings are designed for sustainable operation and zoned for out-of-hours access, creating inspiring places in which to teach and to learn.

1, 2. Construction photographs of the West London Academy at Ealing, and (below) the Djanogly City Academy in Nottingham.

3. Comparative sketch plans of all the practice's nine academies at (from left): Brent, Bexley, Nottingham, Ealing, Edgware, Corby, Langley, Peterborough and Folkestone. Classrooms are coloured blue; social spaces pink; circulation yellow; theatres orange; sports facilities green; and plant rooms grey.

4-6. Renderings of the exterior approach to the Djanogly City Academy (left), daylit interiors at Corby Academy (middle), and curving circulation spaces at the Langley Academy (right).

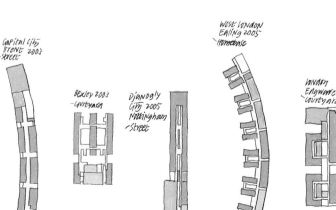

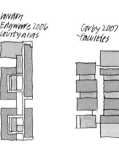

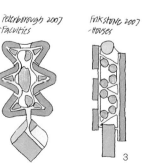

4

5

6

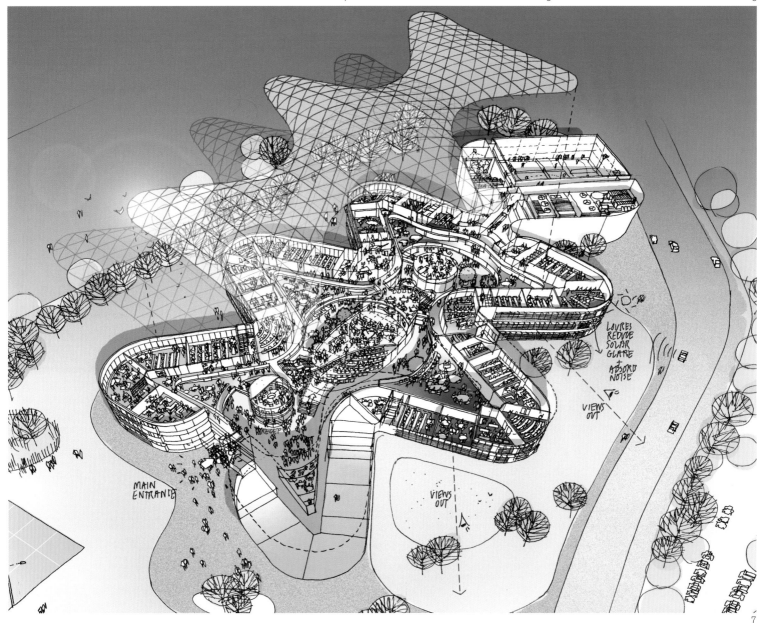

MAIN ENTRANCE

LOUVRES REDUCE SOLAR GLARE + ABSORB NOISE

VIEWS OUT

VIEWS OUT

7

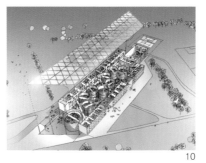

8

9

10

7. Exploded axonometric of the central courtyard and six 'colleges' at the Thomas Deacon Academy in Peterborough.

8-10. External landscaping at Ealing (left), the central atrium in the London Academy, Edgware (middle), and an exploded axonometric of the Folkestone Academy (right).

Wembley Stadium
London, England 1996–

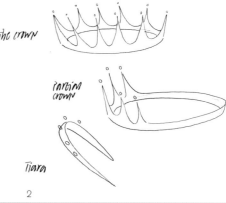

2

6

Originally built for the British Empire Exhibition of 1924, and in turn the main venue for the Olympic Games in 1948 and the football World Cup Finals in 1966, the old Wembley Stadium became the most famous sports and entertainment venue in Britain. The design of the new stadium builds upon the heritage of the old to provide future generations of sports and music fans with a venue equipped for the twenty-first century. At almost four times the height of the original, covering twice the area, and with 90,000 seats, the new Wembley Stadium will be the largest all-covered football stadium in the world.

A key feature of the new stadium is its partly retractable roof. When retracted it will ensure that the turf gets sufficient daylight and ventilation to maintain a perfect playing surface, while in poor weather it can be closed within fifteen minutes to cover all seats. The roof is supported by a spectacular 133-metre-high arch that soars over the stadium, providing an iconic replacement for the old building's landmark twin towers. Dramatically illuminated at night, the arch will be visible from vantage points across London. Beneath this arch, stadium facilities are designed to maximise spectator comfort and enjoyment. The geometry of the seating bowl ensures that everyone has an unobstructed view from each of its three tiers; seats are wider than in the old stadium, with more leg-room; the upper tiers are accessed via escalators; and a new concourse wrapping around the building allows easy circulation and provides seated dining for over 10,000 spectators at any one time.

To create an intimate atmosphere during football and rugby games, the stadium has been designed with seats close to the pitch, yet it also has the potential to host track and field competitions, for which a running track and athletics arena can be installed when needed above the pitch on a rigid platform covering part of the lower tier. Acoustic studies have been undertaken to ensure that the new stadium will recreate the famous 'Wembley roar'.

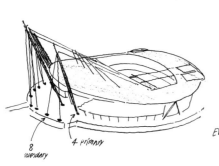

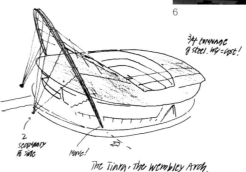

1

Reflective during the day, a symbol day & night.

3

glistening at night on the skyline, a jewel, a tiara!

4

5

1-4. Sketches by Norman Foster exploring the structural and symbolic role of the Wembley arch.

5. Fireworks to celebrate 'topping out'.

6. At night-time the stadium will be a glowing beacon on the skyline.

7, 8. The approach along Olympic Way, and the stadium as it will look on match days.

7

8

23

1

2

6

7

8

3

4

5

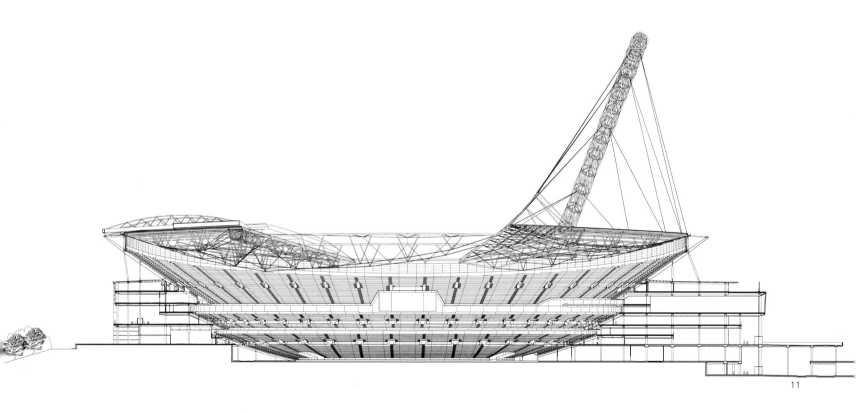

11

1-10. The Wembley arch gradually takes shape. This process took six weeks during the summer of 2004, using five turning struts that assisted in raising the 1,750 tonne, 133-metre-high arch into its final inclined position.

11. Cross-section through the stadium.

9

10

Boston Museum of Fine Arts
Boston, USA 1999–

Founded in 1870, the Museum of Fine Arts, Boston, is internationally recognised for the scope and quality of its collections. It stages an increasingly dynamic programme of exhibitions, lectures, films and educational events and is visited by more than one million people every year. However, in common with many such institutions that have grown incrementally over the years, the sheer scale of this audience places a great strain on the Museum's facilities. This masterplan presents a clear strategic framework within which the Museum's current accommodation will eventually be doubled to provide new galleries, a study centre, and temporary exhibition and education spaces. In the process, the visitor experience will be transformed.

Architecturally, the project echoes themes explored in the Reichstag and the Great Court at the British Museum, establishing a creative dialogue between old and new, and strengthening links with the local community by making the building more open and accessible. At the core of the scheme is the restoration of the symmetry and logic of the Museum's original Beaux-Arts plan, devised in 1907 by the American architect Guy Lowell. Following Lowell's intentions, the central axis of the main building on Huntington Avenue is reasserted with the reintroduction of the main entrance to the south and the reopening of the north entrance, which is currently closed to visitors. At the heart of this axis is a new information centre, from where all visitors will begin their tour of the galleries. A glazed structure – 'a crystal spine' – provides new accommodation and partly encloses the two grand courtyards at the centre of the Museum in a glass 'jewel box', creating valuable new space for visitor orientation, cafés, sculpture and special events.

The new buildings will be highly energy efficient; the courtyards will be naturally lit and the galleries and study centre will have state-of-the-art climate control, the gallery spaces configured to allow art to be displayed with a more obvious sense of clarity and light. Surrounding the Museum, extensive new landscaping is designed to strengthen links with the adjacent Back Bay Fens, originally laid out by Frederick Law Olmsted, architect of New York's Central Park. The landscape design follows the Olmsted tradition of winding paths and informal planting to draw the greenery of the Fens into the building, thus helping to erode distinctions between inside and outside.

3

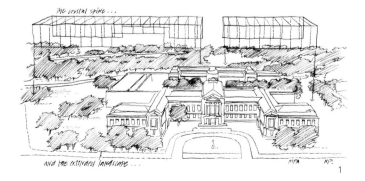

1

1. Sketch by Norman Foster explaining the concept of the new 'crystal spine'.

2. An aerial model view.

3. Visualisation of the completed building.

4, 5. Cross-section through the east courtyard, and (right) a visualisation looking through the glass walls of the same space.

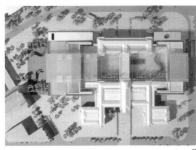

Elephant House
Copenhagen, Denmark 2002–

Set within a historic royal park, adjacent to the Frederiksberg Palace, Copenhagen Zoo is the largest cultural institution in Denmark, attracting over 1.2 million visitors a year. Among the Zoo's more than 3,000 animals, its group of Indian elephants is perhaps its most popular attraction. Replacing a structure dating from 1914, this new Elephant House seeks to restore the visual relationship between the zoo and the park and to provide these magnificent animals with a stimulating environment, with easily accessible spaces from which to enjoy them.

Research into the social patterns of elephants, together with a desire to bring a sense of light and openness to a building type traditionally characterised as closed, even fortified, provided powerful starting points. The tendency for bull elephants in the wild to roam away from the main herd suggested a plan form organised around two separate enclosures, which are dug into the site, both to minimise the building's impact in the landscape and to optimise its passive thermal performance. Covered with lightweight, glazed domes, these spaces maintain a strong visual connection with the sky and changing patterns of daylight. The elephants can congregate here, or out in the adjacent paddocks. Broad public viewing terraces run around the domes externally, while a ramped promenade leads down into an educational space, looking into the enclosures along the way. Barriers between the animals and visitors are discreet, and the paddock walls are concealed in an elongated pool of water so that the approaching visitor encounters the elephants as another 'surprise' in the Romantic landscape of the park.

Significantly, in terms of the elephants' well-being, the building sets new zoological standards. For example, the main herd enclosure will for the first time enable elephants in captivity to sleep together, as they would in the wild, while the floors are heated to keep them dry and thus maintain the health of the elephants' feet. Other key aspects of the design are the result of research into the elephants' natural habitat. The paddocks recreate a section of dry riverbed as found at the edge of the rainforest – a favourite haunt of Asian elephants. With mud holes, scattered pools of water and shading objects, it will be a place where the animals can play and interact freely.

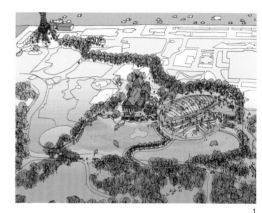

1

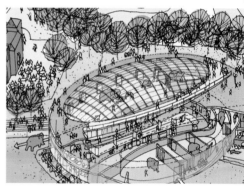

2

1. A rendering of the Elephant House showing its place within the context of Copenhagen Zoo.

2. A more detailed exploded axonometric view of the building's twin enclosures.

3. Concept sketches by Norman Foster exploring the double-domed structure.

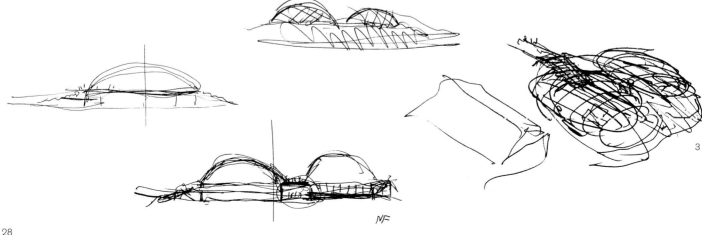

3

4

4, 5. Two views of the model.
The building is dug down
into the landscape and
a pedestrian artery runs
between the two enclosures.

5

Winspear Opera House

Dallas, USA 2002–

The Dallas Opera Company is internationally renowned for its dedication
to excellence and innovation and that commitment is evident in its plans
to build an opera house in the new Performing Arts District of Dallas.
Representing a radical rethinking of the traditional opera experience,
the design addresses the questions: 'What is the nature of the opera
house in the twenty-first century; and how can we create a building
that offers a model for the future?'

The design of the opera house follows on from the practice's
formulation of a masterplan for the Performing Arts District, which
will eventually contain buildings by other Pritzker Prize winners: Rem
Koolhaas, IM Pei and Renzo Piano. Designed to ensure accessibility and
legibility within a pedestrian-friendly environment, these new buildings
will relate to one another along the 'green spine' of Flora Street. The
Winspear Opera House faces the Grand Plaza and the Annette Strauss
Artist's Square performing space and will provide a focal point for
the entire district.

Organisationally, the Winspear reinvents the conventional typology
of the opera house, inverting its closed, hierarchical form to create a
transparent, publicly welcoming series of spaces, which wrap around the
rich red-stained drum of the 2,000-seat auditorium. The ambition is to
create a building that will not only be fully integrated with the cultural
life of Dallas, but will become a destination in its own right for the non-
opera-going public, with a restaurant, café and bookstore that will be
publicly accessible throughout the day. In elevation the building is
transparent,
its curved glass walls revealing views of the public concourse, upper-
level foyers and grand staircase. Entered beneath a broad overhanging
roof, which shades the outdoor spaces from the harsh Texan sun, the
transition from the Grand Plaza, through the foyer, into the auditorium
is designed to heighten the drama of attending a performance – in
effect, 'to take the theatre to the audience'.

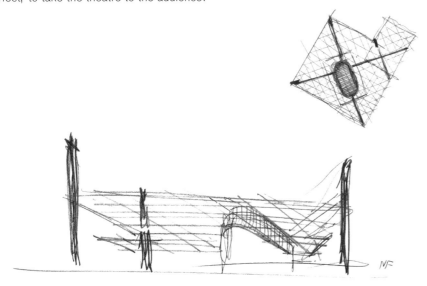

1

4

1. Concept sketches by Norman Foster exploring the form of the auditorium beneath the louvred canopy.

2. Night-time visualisation.

3, 4. Visualisations of the auditorium, looking across the stalls towards the box circle and upper tiers, and towards the proscenium.

2

3

Smithsonian Institution Courtyard
Washington DC, USA 2004–

The Smithsonian Institution occupies the former United States Patent Building, once described by the poet Walt Whitman as 'the noblest of Washington buildings'. Built between 1836 and 1867, the Patent Building is the finest example of Greek Revival architecture in the United States. Now designated as a National Historic Landmark, the building was rescued from impending demolition in 1958 by President Eisenhower, who transferred it to the Smithsonian Institution for use as the National Portrait Gallery and the Smithsonian American Art Museum. This scheme to enclose the building's grand central courtyard will transform the public's experience of the Smithsonian's galleries and provide the Institution with one of the largest event spaces in Washington.

The enclosed courtyard will form the centrepiece of the building's long-term renovation programme, which also includes a redesign of the galleries with contemporary interactive displays and the addition of a conservation laboratory, an auditorium, and 30 per cent more exhibition space. Visitors will be able to enter the surrounding galleries from the courtyard, and out of museum hours the space will be able to host a variety of social events, including concerts and public performances. Designed 'to do the most with the least', the fully glazed roof canopy develops structural and environmental themes first explored in the design of the Great Court at the British Museum, bathing the courtyard with natural light.

Structurally, the roof is composed of three interconnected vaults that flow into one another through softly curved valleys. The double-glazed panels are set within a diagrid of fins, which together form a rigid shell that needs to be supported by only eight columns. Visually, the roof is raised above the walls of the existing building, clearly articulating the new from the old. When it is seen illuminated at night from Pennsylvania Avenue, this canopy will float above the Patent Building, symbolising the cultural importance of the Smithsonian Institution and giving new life to a popular Washington landmark.

1. A sketch by Norman Foster showing the flowing glass canopy floating above the solid base of the old Smithsonian building.

2. Sketches by Norman Foster exploring the structural details of the new courtyard roof.

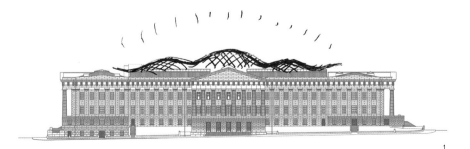

1

2

3

4

5

3. A cross-section through the Smithsonian showing the redesigned exhibition spaces that wrap around the courtyard.

4, 5. Renderings showing the courtyard and an aerial view of the space illuminated at night.

Supreme Court
Singapore 2000–

Singapore's new Supreme Court provides a major new judicial centre in response to the city's rapidly growing population and the limited courtroom facilities of the old Supreme Court building, alongside which it stands. Located within the Colonial District, on the north bank of the Singapore River, close to Padang Park, the building takes its cue from the scale of the neighbouring civic buildings, offering a modern re-interpretation of their colonial vernacular to convey an image of dignity, transparency and openness.

The new building houses twelve civil courts, eight criminal courts and three appeal courts, together with facilities for the Singapore Academy of Law, and is organised to reflect the hierarchies of the judicial system. Formally, it is articulated as a series of identifiable blocks, cut through with public arcades and passageways, which help to knit the building into the surrounding city fabric. The civil courts are located within a sequence of blocks on the lower floors, with the criminal courts above. The court of appeal, Singapore's highest court, is symbolically raised above the other courtrooms. It occupies a disc-like form at the top of the building – a contemporary iteration of the old courthouse's Classical dome – which, like the cupola of the Reichstag, incorporates a public viewing platform that offers a dramatic panorama across the city. The blocks containing the courts are punctuated by a broad central atrium, which forms the processional circulation route through the building, and brings daylight down through all the public spaces. Flanking the courts is a series of administrative blocks, which step back at ground level to create a sheltered public arcade along the street front.

The building is designed for long-term flexibility, including future changes in the size and configuration of the courtrooms and advances in electronic information systems. It employs a palette of high-quality materials including glazed stone – a laminate of glass and stone – which appears solid, but by day allows light to filter through it, and by night emits a warm glow. The building incorporates a range of passive climate-control devices, including shading to the east and west facades to protect the office spaces from direct sunlight. The roofs of the office blocks are planted with trees to form a continuous blanket of greenery, creating a public promenade shaded from the sun.

3. Visualisation, looking up at the elevated disc of the appeal court.

4, 5. Design studies by Norman Foster, exploring the external form of the appeal courts.

6. Cross-section through the courthouse and the central circulation route up through the civil, criminal and appeal courts.

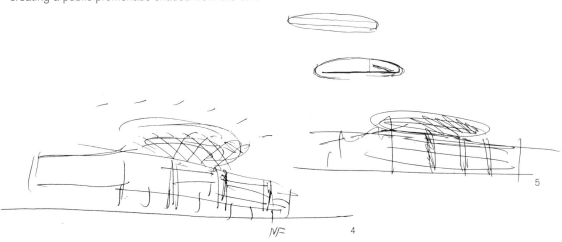

5

4

1. Model view, looking down into the appeal courts.

2. An aerial view of the new courthouse under construction. The building mediates between the scale of the low-rise Colonial District and the high-rise developments on the far side of the Singapore River.

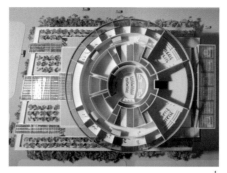

1

2

3

6

Yacht Club de Monaco
Monaco 2002–

In 2002 the government of Monaco commissioned the practice to design a yacht club as the symbolic centrepiece of the city's remodelled harbour front. The new building celebrates Monaco's spectacular coastline and its rich nautical heritage, creating a series of deck-like viewing terraces that step up along the harbour to offer unrivalled views out to yacht races at sea or inland over the course of the renowned Formula 1 Grand Prix circuit. Located on an area of reclaimed land alongside two newly refurbished jetties, the development extends the city's existing marina eastwards and can accommodate a range of craft, from small children's sailing boats to 100-metre super yachts.

Accessed either from the pedestrian promenade running along the quay, or by car from the roadside, the club is entered via a full-height glazed atrium that frames views out over the harbour. A spiral staircase leads up to the more exclusive areas of the club. On the first floor are a clubroom, bar and restaurant, which open out on to a broad terrace. Above the restaurant is a ballroom, and one floor higher is an apartment for the club secretary together with a series of 'cabins' for visiting guests. All these spaces are air-conditioned, using a low-energy, sea-cooled refrigeration system. The elevations facing the water are fully glazed to allow uninterrupted views, but incorporate adjustable louvres to provide shading from the sun.

Along with the yacht club, the scheme also introduces shops and other public amenities at quay level that will make the harbour a lively and animated place to be. The lower floors of the building contain a rowing club and sailing school, which have full-height sliding doors that encourage activities to spread out on to the quayside. Designed largely for children, the school provides classrooms, workshops and lofts for the small Pico and Laser boats. Inland there is a new landscaped embankment park on the roof of the sailing school. Bounded on one side by the club's restaurant terrace and leading on the other side to a new Maritime Museum, it complements the few green public spaces in this densely populated city and forms a new link in the pedestrian route between the quayside and Casino Square.

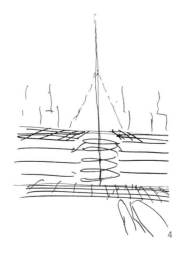

4

5

1, 2. Perspective renderings of the club showing the tiered sequence of terraces from the harbour side and road side.

3. Night-time visualisation of the yacht club looking north across Prince Albert Harbour towards Casino Square.

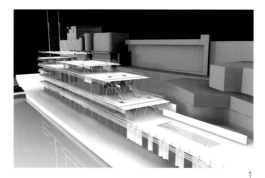

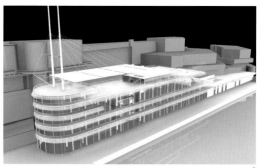

1

2

3

4-8. A series of concept sketches by Norman Foster exploring the building's central spiral staircase, its sectional relationship to the water and the city, and the configuration of its terraces.

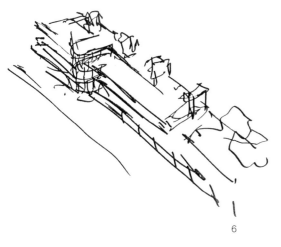

6

7

8

West Kowloon Cultural District
Hong Kong 2001–

Hong Kong's commercial and business-driven cultural legacy has generated a rich creative energy, but never a permanent home for the arts. Won as the result of an international competition, this masterplan for the West Kowloon Cultural District provides Hong Kong with an unprecedented collection of arts, performance, and leisure venues. Built entirely on a section of previously reclaimed land on the West Kowloon waterfront immediately opposite Hong Kong Island, the project will consolidate Hong Kong's reputation as a cultural destination while providing an iconic architectural image for the city.

The new district is conceived as a 'pleasure garden', integrating a series of arts, performance and leisure venues within an extensive urban park, set beneath a dramatic, all-enveloping canopy. Part open, part opaque, and with a variety of shading devices, the canopy will create a comfortable environment, protecting visitors from the extremes of the weather, and generating its own microclimate with cooling winds in the heat of the summer. Beneath it, a modern art museum, a major performance venue, and an assortment of theatres and concert halls congregate around the district's western end, while cinemas, restaurants, shops and leisure facilities extend east along the spine and the harbour-side. Each of these areas is accessed by a people-mover system, which is integrated with the city's existing transport networks, and elevated above park level, so that visitors can look out over Victoria Harbour and Hong Kong's skyline as they travel through the park.

The canopy suggests a rolling landscape, inspired by the natural topography of the Hong Kong peninsula. Beneath it, over 70 per cent of the site is given over to parkland, the informal planting of mature trees creating the impression of a wooded environment lying at the harbour's edge. A water amphitheatre forms the focus of the district's western edge, while trees and grassy banks cascade down along the southern waterfront. The permeable roof, natural environmental controls and network of gardens and social spaces, champion the objective to create characterful, enjoyable public spaces and a rich, all-encompassing cultural experience to redefine the very nature of the urban cultural quarter.

1. Sketched rendering looking along the waterfront and the pleasure garden.

2, 3. Night-time visualisation (above) and the new district seen from across Kowloon Harbour (below).

4. An aerial model view, showing the fluid form of the all-embracing roof.

1

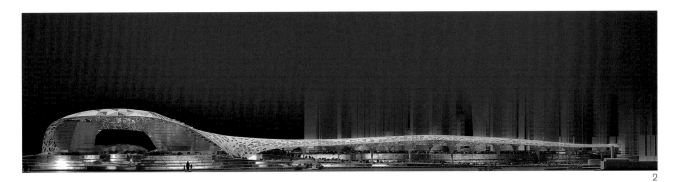

2

3

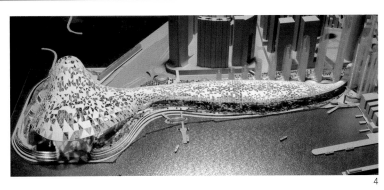

4

Palace of Peace
Astana, Kazakhstan 2004–

In September 2003, Kazakhstan – the largest of the former Soviet Republics – hosted the inaugural Congress of Leaders of World and Traditional Religions in the new capital, Astana. Spurred by its success, the President of Kazakhstan decided to make it a triennial event. Following an international competition, the practice was commissioned to design a permanent venue for the Congress – the Palace of Peace. The building is conceived as a global centre for religious understanding, the renunciation of violence and the promotion of faith and human equality.

In addition to representing all the world's religious faiths, the Palace houses a 1,500-seat opera house, educational facilities and a national centre for Kazakhstan's various ethnic and geographical groups. This programmatic diversity is unified within the pure form of a pyramid, 62 metres high with a 62 x 62-metre base. Clad in stone, with glazed inserts that allude to the various internal functions, the pyramid has an apex of stained glass by the artist Brian Clarke. Spatially, it is organised around a soaring central atrium, which is animated with subtle cast light patterns. The assembly chamber is elevated at the peak of the pyramid, supported on four inclined pillars – the 'hands of peace'. Lifts take delegates to a garden-like reception space from where they ascend to the chamber via a winding ramp. A broad glass lens set in the floor of the atrium casts light down into the auditorium of the opera house and creates a sense of vertical continuity from the lowest level of the building to the very top.

The Astanian climate posed a significant challenge, with an annual range from 40 °C in summer to -40 °C in winter. The construction schedule is extraordinarily rapid – the Palace has to be completed in time for the Meeting of the Second Congress in 2006. This led the design team to develop a structural solution that utilises prefabricated components, which can be manufactured off site during the winter months and erected during the summer. The entire process, from briefing to completion, is scheduled to take just twenty-one months.

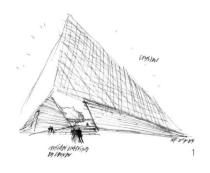

1

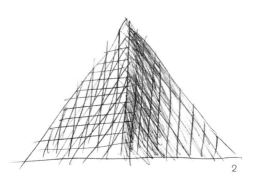

2

5

1, 2. Concept sketches by Norman Foster.

3. Aerial view of the Astana masterplan, looking along the ceremonial axis.

4. Site plan: the Palace of Peace faces the presidential palace across the Ishim River.

5. Cross-section through the atrium. The assembly chamber sits at the apex of the building, supported on four inclined pillars – the 'hands of peace'.

Milan Fiera Masterplan
Milan, Italy 2004

In 2004, the Milan Fiera held an international competition for architectural proposals to develop its existing site, which has proved too limited to host large-scale exhibitions. The Foster studio collaborated with Frank Gehry, Rafael Moneo and Cino Zucchi on the design of a scheme that sets new standards for urban living in the twenty-first century. A high-density development with a wide range of mixed uses, the defining feature of the plan is a new type of living-park – or 'greenfrastructure' – with architectural and landscape components that are enmeshed with the ecology of the city. It creates a new urban quarter where occupants can live, work, go to school, dine in a restaurant or visit the cinema, all in close proximity. If implemented, it would be the most advanced sustainable development in the world.

The scheme is woven into the existing urban fabric through a number of strands: the reinstatement of historical axial views across the site; the integration and rationalisation of transport systems; the promotion of on-site residential, commercial and educational activities; and the design of buildings that are sympathetic to the historical built vocabulary. The forms of the buildings themselves are designed to reinforce the environmental strategy, guiding wind movement, directing solar heating, providing passive cooling and shading, and controlling water flows.

Combining shaded, densely planted zones with open lawns, and laced through with streams and pools, the park is envisaged as the venue for a wide variety of recreational activities, from open-air concerts to ball games. Tree-shaded avenues structure and give scale to the gardens and stretch out to connect with Milan's existing park system. At the heart of the site, at the edge of a new lake, is an elongated piazza. Here, a cluster of tall buildings marks the new development on the city skyline. Working within the development guidelines, it is the concentrated footprint of these towers that allows a remarkable 80 per cent of the 25-hectare site to be used as green space. Leading from the piazza is a new entrance arcade for the remaining Fiera facilities, a space that promises as rich an urban experience as Milan's famous Galleria Vittorio Emanuele.

1

2

1. Sketch by Norman Foster exploring the scheme's landscape strategy, with park areas rising topographically as they converge towards the centre of the site.

2. View across the masterplan model looking towards the central residential tower and hotel.

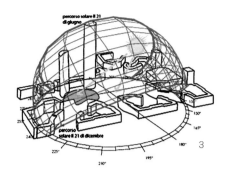

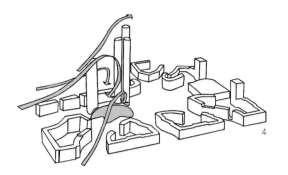

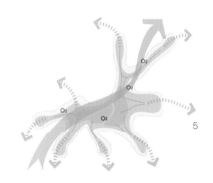

6

7

3-5. Extracts from a series of environmental studies, indicating how the Milan Fiera would respond to the path of the sun, wind direction, and its landscape strategy.

6, 7. Model of the proposal showing the entire Milan Fiera site, and (below) a detail of one of the new residential blocks.

126 Phillip Street
Sydney, Australia 1996–

Since the design of the Hongkong and Shanghai Bank, the practice has continued to redefine the nature of the office tower and to explore how it can respond to the context and the spirit of the city in which it stands. This new thirty-one-storey building, located on a prominent site close to the harbour, explores new strategies for flexible, column-free office space and creates a new 'urban room' in Sydney's dense central business district.

The building's unusual design and distinctive profile were guided by a number of factors, including the narrow site, the need for large open floor-plates, and exacting planning regulations that protected the amount of sunlight falling on two nearby public spaces. The orientation of the building exploits a number of environmental factors and maximises views over the harbour. Daylight is drawn into the office levels and down through the building via an atrium, which runs the full height of the tower between the core and the office floors, and is interlaced by a series of bridges that connect the offices to the vertical circulation routes. Movement through the building is clarified and celebrated, the atrium and lobbies being both physically and psychologically removed from the workplace. The main structural core is offset to the lower, western edge of the site and consists of two aluminium-clad concrete towers, which provide the main stiffening elements and act as solar buffers. To permit greater flexibility in planning office layouts, curtain walling on the three glazed facades has been turned 'inside out' with mullions and transoms placed externally.

At ground level, the private world of the tower meets the public realm of the city in a four-storey covered plaza – the 'assembly'. This soaring, light-filled space functions as a busy public square. A prelude to the office lobbies, it also contains shops, cafés and a crèche. The central water feature that runs the length of the space can be controlled to enable all kinds of activities, including fashion shows and parties to take place there at any time of day.

5

1-4. Early design sketches by Norman Foster exploring the tower's distinctive stepped profile.

5. Model view of the top of the tower, which is stepped to avoid overshadowing Sydney's Martin Place below.

6, 7. Construction photographs of the tower as seen from Chifley Square and Domain Park (right).

8. Visualised night-time view, seen from Sydney's botanical gardens.

4

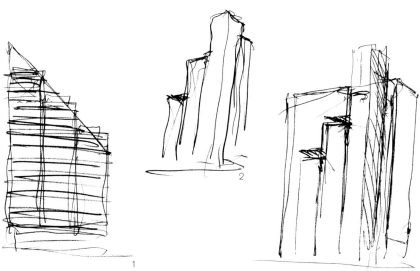

1

2

3

6

7

8

Hearst Headquarters
New York, USA 2001 –

The Hearst Headquarters revives a dream from the 1920s, when William Randolph Hearst envisaged Columbus Circle as a vibrant new quarter for media and entertainment companies in Manhattan. Hearst commissioned a six-storey Art Deco block on Eighth Avenue to house his publishing empire. When it was completed in 1928 he anticipated that the building would eventually form the base for a landmark tower, though no scheme was ever advanced. Echoing an approach developed in the Reichstag and the Great Court at the British Museum, the challenge in designing such a tower at some seventy years remove was to establish a creative dialogue between old and new.

The new forty-two-storey tower provides almost one million square feet of office space. It rises above the old building, linked on the outside by a transparent skirt of glazing that floods the spaces below with natural light and encourages an impression of the tower floating weightlessly above the base. The main spatial event is a lobby that occupies the entire floor-plate and rises up through six floors. Like a bustling town square, this dramatic space provides access to all parts of the building. It incorporates the main lift lobby, the Hearst cafeteria and auditorium and mezzanine levels for meetings and special functions. Structurally, the tower has a triangulated form – a highly efficient solution that uses 20 per cent less steel than a conventionally framed structure. With its corners peeled back between the diagonals it has the effect of emphasising the tower's vertical proportions and creating a distinctive faceted silhouette.

The new building is also distinctive in environmental terms. It is constructed using 80 per cent recycled steel and designed to consume 25 per cent less energy than its conventional neighbours. As a result, it will be the first new office building in the city to be given a gold rating under the US Green Buildings Council's Leadership in Energy and Environmental Design Program (LEED). Hearst places a high value on the concept of a healthy workplace – a factor that it believes will become increasingly important to its staff in the future. Indeed, the company's experience with the green building process may herald the more widespread construction of environmentally sensitive buildings in the city.

1. Visualisation of the building's third-floor lobby – a new 'town square' in Manhattan. Naturally lit during the day, the space is accessed from street level via escalators that rise up alongside a cascading water feature.

2, 3. Concept sketches by Norman Foster exploring the building's triangulated structure.

4, 5. Construction photographs, looking east out over Central Park (above), and seen from street level (below).

Right: Visualisation looking up at the building from the corner of 56th Street and Eighth Avenue.

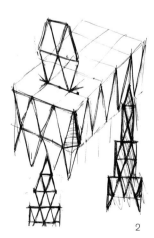

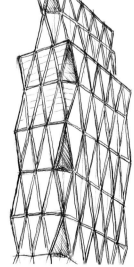

1

2

3

Repsol Headquarters

Madrid, Spain 2002–

This new headquarters building for Repsol – the Spanish oil and gas company – continues investigations into the sustainable workplace that can be traced through a family of recent office towers, most notably for Swiss Re and Commerzbank. With this new headquarters, Repsol – for whom the practice also designed new service stations and roadside identity – will be able for the first time to consolidate its 3,600-strong team in one location in Madrid in a building that communicates the company's core values.

The thirty-four-storey building is located on the site of the former Real Madrid training grounds, where the city council has assigned sites for four new towers by international architects. It marks a curve in the wide boulevard of the Paseo de la Castellana – the 'backbone' of Madrid – and is carefully positioned to maximise the exceptional qualities of its site. Compositionally, the building can be thought of as a tall arch, the services and circulation cores framing the open office floors. At ground level, a 22-metre glazed atrium provides the transition from the street, and accommodates a 'floating' glass-walled auditorium set into a mezzanine. At the top of the building, the void space beneath the uppermost section of the 'portal' frame is designed to house wind turbines capable of providing a significant proportion of the building's power supply. This is an innovation that both signals Repsol's commitment to environmental sustainability, and indicates its progressive investigations into potential alternative energy sources.

Although the building is conceived as a corporate headquarters, it also has the flexibility to be partly sublet, enabling Repsol to expand or contract its accommodation easily in the future as required. This degree of flexibility results in part from pushing the service cores to the edges of the plan – a strategy first used in the design of the Hongkong Bank – to create uninterrupted 1200-square-metre floor-plates. Vertical circulation routes occupy minimal space as a result of an intelligent lift system that requires fewer lift cars than conventional systems. The cores are strategically positioned so as to block west/east direct sunlight, a move that has the added benefit of framing spectacular views of the hills of Sierra de Guadarrama to the north and the centre of Madrid to the south.

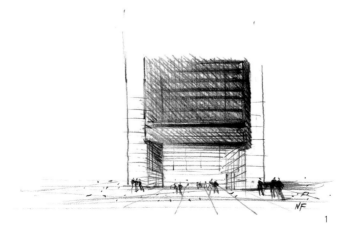

1

2

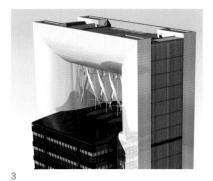

3

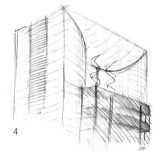

4

1. Sketch by Norman Foster.

2. Axonometric drawing showing the three blocks of office floors and the glazed panoramic lift wall.

3, 4. Vertical wind turbines at the top of the tower will supply a proportion of the building's energy needs.

5. Looking north along Paseo de la Castellana.

5

Dresden Station

Dresden, Germany 1996–

Dresden's main railway terminus, completed in 1898 to a design by Giese and Weidner, is one of the largest in Germany and one of the most impressive late-nineteenth-century railway stations anywhere in Europe. Linking Dresden with Berlin and Prague, the railway played a significant role in the city's industrial and economic growth in the first half of the twentieth century. During the Second World War, however, Dresden's station was severely damaged in Allied bombing raids. War-time destruction was compounded in the post-war period by poor maintenance, so that the building finally reached a state where remedial conservation was required.

Faced with this crumbling structure, the practice was commissioned to undertake the renovation and expansion of the station as part of a wider masterplan to revive the surrounding area. The station redevelopment removes various additions and alterations made to the building over the last hundred years in order to restore the integrity of the original design. Circulation within and through the station has been rationalised and the design allows for the future expansion of the station by extending the barrel-vaulted roofs over the outer platforms by 200 metres to provide cover for the new high-speed trains, which are almost twice the length of the old platforms. The central tracks have also been pulled back in order to create a large open space at the heart of the building, which can be used as a market place, or for cultural events.

The first element of this redevelopment to be carried out is the reconstruction of the 30,000-square-metre roof, a task made more urgent by the degraded and unsafe state of the old steelwork. Originally the roof was partially glazed, but after the war it was covered with timber, admitting no daylight. The entire structure is now being restored to its original condition and sheathed in a translucent skin of Teflon-coated glass fibre. This new roof will transmit 13 per cent of daylight and significantly reduce the station's reliance on artificial lighting. At night, light will reflect off the underside of the canopy, creating an even wash of illumination throughout the station, while from outside the whole structure will radiate an ethereal silvery glow.

1

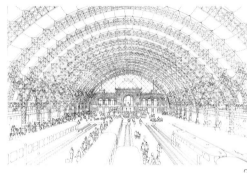

2

1. A computer-generated image of the translucent glass-fibre roof.

2. Perspective drawing by Helmut Jacoby, looking towards the main concourse.

3-5. Construction photographs showing completed sections of the new roof.

6. North elevation of the 450 metre-long station from Wiener Platz.

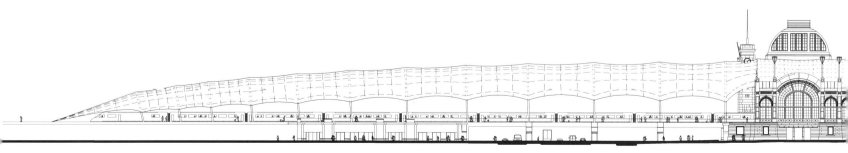

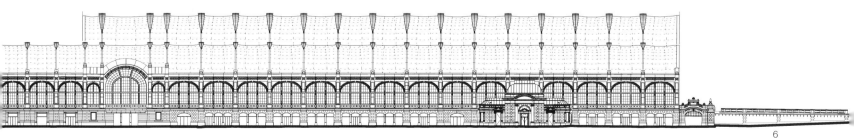

Florence High-Speed Railway Station
Florence, Italy 2003–

As part of the creation of a new high-speed rail network, the Italian Government has instituted a major programme of station restructuring, including the creation of many new stations. This competition-winning design for Florence Station provides a new facility that will connect with the city's existing Santa Maria Novella station via a new tramline. Driven by a deep respect for the architecture of this magnificent city and a quest for clarity of passenger movement, the scheme is both a celebration of the experience of entry into Florence and an attempt to reduce the complexities of modern travel.

The majority of the new Bologna-Florence high-speed line is in tunnels. Correspondingly, the platform level in the new station is located 25 metres below ground. The station chamber consists of a single volume, 454 metres long and 52 metres wide, built using cut-and-cover techniques similar to those deployed at Canary Wharf Station. Passengers move from platform to ground level via lifts or escalators. Between the platform level and the street are two levels of shops, while a terrace at street level offers a view over the tracks and trains arriving and departing. The composition is capped by an arching glazed roof, which evokes the great railway structures of the nineteenth century. Arriving in the station, the generous volume, with natural light flooding in from above, gives an immediate sense of space and light; one can see the sky and sense the air of the city.

The scheme is designed to ensure durability and ease of maintenance, to minimise energy consumption and reduce running costs. Natural light is a crucial part of this equation, so too is temperature control. The arching roof structure provides a system for effective temperature regulation by drawing warm air out through permanent vents. It also incorporates photovoltaic cells to generate power. The walls and floors are lined with a palette of rich materials familiar throughout the city – including a highly figured green and white marble – which will patinate gracefully over time. Sensitive to its historic location, but forward looking in its use of energy and other resources, the station offers a model for contemporary rail travel.

1-3. Visualisations of the station interior, showing the entry level, mezzanine level, and escalators down to the platforms.

4. Cutaway axonometric drawing of the station showing the three interior levels and the 450 metre-long barrel-vaulted roof.

Right: A cutaway perspective rendering of the approach into the station, looking across the central platform.

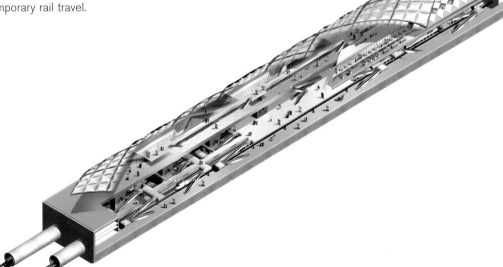

Beijing International Airport
Beijing, China 2003 –

Beijing's new international airport terminal will be the gateway to the city as it welcomes athletes and visitors from around the world to the twenty-ninth Olympiad in 2008. The world's largest and most advanced airport building – not only technologically, but also in terms of passenger experience, operational efficiency and sustainability – it will be welcoming and uplifting. A symbol of place, its soaring aerodynamic roof and dragon-like form will celebrate the thrill and poetry of flight and evoke traditional Chinese colours and symbols.

Located between the existing eastern runway and the future third runway, the terminal encloses a floor area of more than a million square metres and is designed to accommodate an estimated 43 million passengers per annum, rising to 55 million by 2015. Although conceived on an unprecedented scale, its design expands on the new airport paradigm created by Stansted and Chek Lap Kok. In that sense it represents the crest of a learning curve. Designed for maximum flexibility to cope with the unpredictable nature of the aviation industry, like its predecessors, it aims to resolve the complexities of modern air travel, combining spatial clarity with high service standards. Public transport connections are fully integrated, walking distances for passengers are short, with few level changes, and transfer times between flights are minimised. Like Chek Lap Kok, the terminal is open to views to the outside and planned under a single unifying roof canopy, whose linear skylights are both an aid to orientation and sources of daylight – the colour cast changing from red to yellow as passengers progress through the building.

The terminal building will be one of the world's most sustainable, incorporating a range of passive environmental design concepts, such as the south-east orientated skylights, which maximise heat gain from the early morning sun, and an integrated environment-control system that minimises energy consumption and carbon emissions. In construction terms, its design optimises the performance of materials selected on the basis of local availability, functionality, application of local skills, and low cost procurement. Remarkably, it will have been designed and built in just four years.

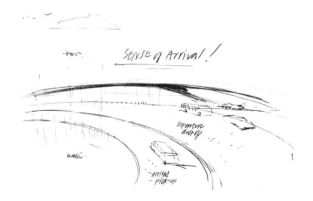

1, 2. Concept sketches by
Norman Foster exploring
the drama of road and rail
approaches.

3. The ground-breaking
ceremony in May 2004.

4. Site progress, July 2004.

3

4

5

6

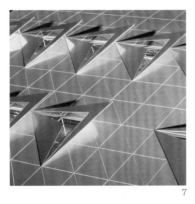

7

5. Model photograph
looking across the apron
and undulating roof line
of Terminal 3B.

6, 7. Model studies of the
airport's undulating roof,
which is punctured by
triangulated rooflights.

Overleaf: Visualisation of a
night-time approach to the
airport, looking north across
the ground transportation
centre and twin terminal
buildings.

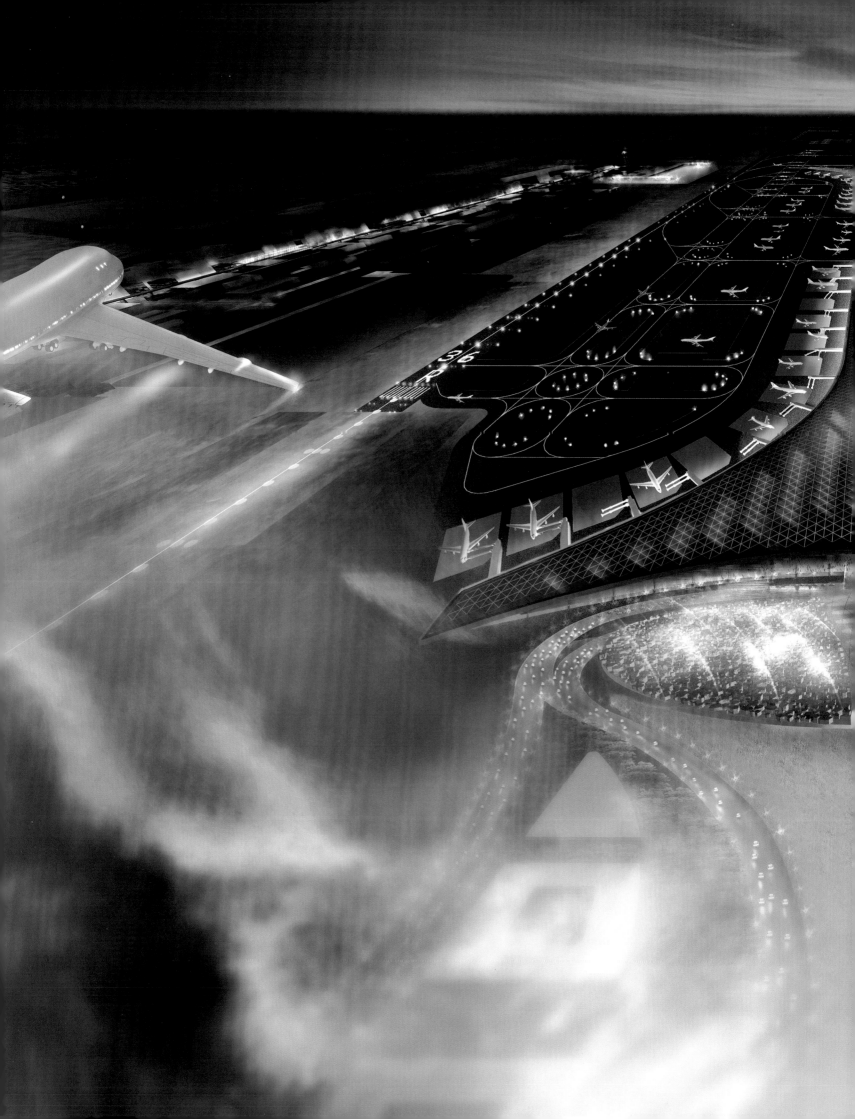

Projects

Stansted Airport
Stansted, England 1981–1991

Stansted Airport challenged all the accepted rules of airport terminal
design. It went back to the roots of modern air travel and literally stood
conventional wisdom on its head. The earliest airport buildings were very
simple: on one side there was a road and on the other a field where
aircraft landed into the wind. The progression from landside to airside
was a walk from your car through the terminal and out onto your plane,
which was always in view. Revealed through every aspect of its design,
Stansted was an attempt to recapture the clarity of those early airfields,
together with some of the lost romance of air travel.

From the traveller's point of view, movement through the completed
building is straightforward and direct – Stansted has none of the level
changes and subsequent orientation problems that are typical to most
airports. Passengers proceed in a fluid movement from the set-down
point through to the check-in area, passport control and departure
lounges, where they can see the planes. From there, an automated
transit system takes them to satellite buildings to board their aircraft.
This degree of clarity was achieved by turning the building 'upside down',
banishing the heavy environmental service installations usually found at
roof level to an undercroft that runs beneath the entire concourse floor.
This subterranean level also contains baggage handling and was able
to accommodate a mainline railway station, which was integrated into
the building late in the design process.

All service distribution systems are contained within the 'trunks' of the
structural 'trees' that rise up from the undercroft through the concourse
floor. These trees support a lightweight roof that is freed simply to keep
out rain and let in light. Entirely daylit on all but the most overcast of
days, the constantly changing play of light gives the concourse a poetic
dimension and also has significant energy and economic advantages,
leading to running costs half those of any other British terminal. Energy
efficient, environmentally discreet within its rural setting, technologically
advanced yet incredibly simple to use and experience, Stansted has
become a model for airport planners and designers around the world.

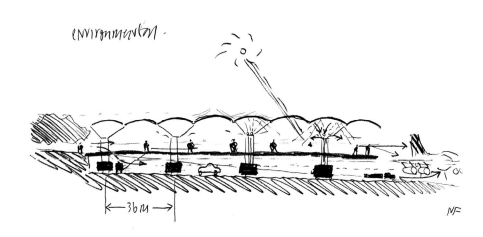

Previous pages, left:
Norman Foster's sketch of
the environmental concept:
a lightweight roof, freed
from services, allows natural
light to flood the concourse.
Right: The passenger set-
down point.

1. Norman Foster's sketch
shows the simplicity of
passenger flow through
the airport on a single level.

2. From the landside of the
terminal, aeroplanes landing
and taxiing across the
runway are clearly visible.

3. Shops and concession
stands are integrated
within flexible, free-standing
enclosures.

4. View across the baggage
hall; the main concourse
is naturally lit on all but
the most overcast of days.

5

6

7

8

5, 6. Approaches to the
terminal from the car
park and bus station.

7. The terminal's roof
extends by one structural
bay to form a canopy
over the set-down point.

8. The train station housed
in the building's undercroft
provides a direct link
to central London.

9. A cross-section from
airside to landside.
Passenger movement
through the terminal
building is clear and direct.
Baggage handling and
services are contained
within an undercroft
beneath the concourse.

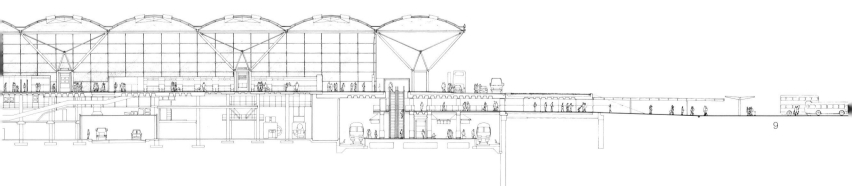

9

Hong Kong International Airport, Chek Lap Kok
Hong Kong 1992–1998

Lying at the hub of a global region reaching across Asia and Australasia, Chek Lap Kok is one of the world's largest airports. Completed in 1998 as Hong Kong's sole air terminal, by 2040 it will handle eighty million passengers per annum – the same number as London's Heathrow and New York's JFK airports combined. Among the most ambitious construction projects of modern times, the land on which the airport stands was once a mountainous island. In a major reclamation programme, its 100 metre peak was reduced to 7 metres above sea level and the island was expanded to four times its original area – equal to the size of the Kowloon peninsula.

The terminal building extends a concept pioneered by the practice at Stansted Airport – a model since adopted by airport planners worldwide. It is characterised by a lightweight roof, free of service installations; natural lighting; and the integration beneath the main concourse of baggage handling, environmental services and transportation. With its uncluttered spaces, bathed in light, it forms a spectacular gateway to the city. Equally important to the clarity of the space is the accentuation of natural orientation points both within the building and beyond: departing passengers are aware of the land and the water, and can see the aircraft. Similarly, the airport's vaulted roof provides a constant point of reference, whether you are arriving or departing. The direction of the vaults remains constant throughout the building, regardless of the divergent directions that the building's wings take, so that the roof itself becomes an aid to navigation. Departing passengers pass through the East Hall, the largest single airport retail space in the world; if an airport on this scale can be thought of as a city in microcosm, then this is its market square.

People reach the airport from Hong Kong via either mainland road or rail links, which cross two new bridges and a causeway to Lantau to the south, those arriving by train alighting at the Ground Transportation Centre at the eastern end of the terminal. The entire journey between city and airport can be completed in a remarkable twenty minutes.

Previous pages, left: Sketch by Norman Foster illustrating the airport's undulating roof. Right: View of the passenger set-down area, with Lantau Island in the background.

1. Cross-section through the airport's East Hall with an elevation of the twin, vaulted wings behind.

2. An aerial view of the terminal building, with its distinctive Y-shaped plan.

3. Norman Foster's concept sketch defining the directional roof vaulting.

4. View of the 'meeters and greeters' area in the arrivals hall.

The roof is developed out of one simple vault module
The height and width varies according to needs
The structure orders and lights the spaces.

The grain and angle of the structure
provides instant orientation
Both inside the building and also from the outside.

5

6

7

5, 6. Views of the check-in area at the eastern end of the terminal and the double-height arrivals atrium.

7. Detail of the daylight reflectors than run along the underside of the concourse roof.

Overleaf: Looking out from the check-in area towards the aircraft and the backdrop of Lantau Island.

HACTL Superterminal, Chek Lap Kok
Hong Kong 1992–1998

The Hong Kong Air Cargo Terminal (HACTL) Superterminal at Hong Kong International Airport is the largest and most technologically advanced single cargo terminal in the world. Designed to reinforce Hong Kong's status as a major centre for international commerce and communications in South-East Asia, it consists of two buildings: the Express Centre, a two-storey express cargo and courier facility, and the Cargo Terminal, a seven-storey cargo-handling facility. Together, these two buildings have the capacity to handle an astonishing 2.5 million tonnes of cargo annually – more than two-and-a-half times the capacity of the nearest rival at Heathrow Airport.

The Express Centre provides express cargo and courier operators with their own sorting facilities and can process 200,000 tonnes of cargo a year. Specialist facilities allow the Centre to handle anything from livestock to precious items, including diamonds, cash and gold bullion. The Cargo Terminal is a building on a vast scale. Like the Chek Lap Kok airport terminal, its vital statistics are record-breaking: 200 metres wide by 290 metres long, it has two container storage racking systems, each 250 metres long and 45 metres high, and two bulk storage racking systems – the largest fully automated, combined racking system ever built. The container racking lines the perimeter of the building, visible from the runway through fully glazed walls, while the bulk storage racking systems are located in a concrete enclosure at the heart of the building, where cargo can be stored for up to two months. Accommodation at each end of the building includes HACTL and airline offices, and a customer service hall.

While the building sets new standards in terms of capacity and performance, it also breaks new ground socially, providing an unprecedented level of amenities for members of staff and their families. In that sense, it continues a drive to civilise the workplace that has concerned the practice from its earliest days. In addition to a restaurant capable of serving 600 people at one sitting, HACTL employees have access to a swimming pool, a sports centre with squash, badminton and tennis courts, and they can relax on the largest roof garden in the world. Together, these amenities give the building an extraordinary social focus.

1

2

1. An aerial view of the Superterminal with Lantau Island in the background.

2. The staff swimming pool on the roof of the building.

3. A cross-section through the express centre and cargo terminal.

Right: Looking along the 'nave' of the Cargo Terminal, which is lined with containerised storage racking.

3

Metro System

Bilbao, Spain 1988–1995 and 1997–2004

———

The Bilbao Metro serves the city's one million inhabitants and was designed and constructed in two phases to create a pair of interconnecting lines along the banks of the River Nervion. A metro system is an excellent demonstration of how the built environment influences the quality of our daily lives. The building of tunnels for trains is usually seen in isolation from the provision of spaces for people – even though they are part of a continuous experience for the traveller, starting and ending at street level. The Bilbao Metro is unusual in that it was conceived as a totality: architectural, engineering and construction skills were integrated within a shared vision.

The great majority of subway systems today are uniformly difficult to negotiate, relying on elaborate signage systems to tell you where to go. In Bilbao, in contrast, the architecture itself is legible. Routes in and out, via escalators or glass lifts, lead directly via tunnels to cavernous stations, which are large enough to accommodate lightweight stainless steel mezzanines and staircases above the trains. The experience of moving through a single grand volume is dramatic, and the concept offers flexibility for future change. The curved forms of these spaces are expressive of the enormous forces they are designed to withstand, while their construction reflects Bilbao's strong tradition of technology. Most of the elements were made locally and Spanish engineers who had pioneered mobile gantries for the aerospace industry exploited this technology to erect the prefabricated concrete panels that line the station caverns.

The curved glassy structures – or 'Fosteritos' – that announce the inner-city Line 1 stations at street level are as unique to Bilbao as the Art Nouveau Metro entrances are to Paris, their shape evocative of inclined movement and generated by the profile of the tunnels themselves. The canopies admit natural light by day, and are illuminated at night, forming welcoming beacons in the streetscape. On Line 2, where deep-cut stations made it impossible to use escalators, banks of large-capacity lifts are grouped in threes to create iconic and easily recognisable entrance points.

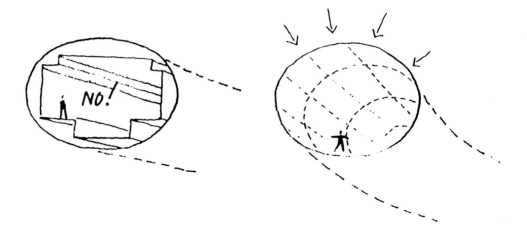

1   2   3

Previous pages, left:
Concept sketches by
Norman Foster arguing for
the direct expression of
structure in the stations.
Right: Passengers enter
and exit through the Metro's
distinctive glass canopies
– known popularly in
Bilbao as 'Fosteritos'.

1-4. 'Fosteritos' in the
streetscape.

5. Axonometric drawing
of a typical station showing
the direct route from
platform to street.

6-8. The sequence from
the station mezzanine, via
escalators up towards the
light of the street. Routes
are simple and clearly
defined; the need for
signage is minimised.

9. Looking along the cavern
of Abando station – a typical
subterranean Line 1 station.
The pre-cast concrete shell
expresses the form of the
tunnel and contrasts with
the lighter filigree of steel
stairs and mezzanines.

4

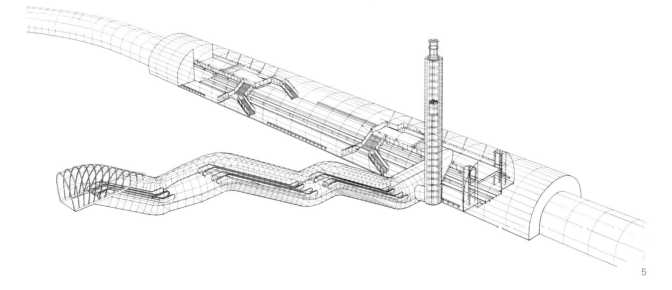

5

6   7   8

9

10   11

10. Some of the Line 1 stations, such as Sarriko, seen here, are located closer to ground level and were constructed using cut-and-cover techniques.

11. Similarly, Ansio station on Line 2, lies close to street level. Daylight floods down on to the platforms.

Canary Wharf Underground Station
London, England 1991–1998

The Jubilee Line extension represents one of the greatest acts of British architectural patronage of recent years, comprising eleven new stations by as many architects. The practice's station at Canary Wharf is by far the largest of these – when the development of the area is complete, it will be used by more people at peak times than Oxford Circus, currently London's busiest Underground destination.

The station is built within the hollow of the former West India Dock using cut-and-cover construction techniques, and at 300 metres in length is as long as Canary Wharf Tower is tall. At ground level, the entire roof of the station is laid out as a landscaped park, creating Canary Wharf's principal public recreation space; the only visible station elements are the swelling glass canopies that cover its three entrances and draw daylight deep into the station concourse. By concentrating natural light dramatically at these points, orientation is enhanced, minimising the need for directional signage. Twenty banks of escalators transport passengers in and out of the station, while administrative offices, kiosks and other amenities are sited along the flanks of the ticket hall, leaving the main concourse free and creating a sense of clarity and calm.

Due to the high volume of station traffic, the guiding principles in the building's design were durability and ease of maintenance. The result is a simple palette of hard-wearing materials: fair-faced concrete, stainless steel and glass. This robust aesthetic is most pronounced at platform level where the concrete diaphragm tunnel walls are left exposed. In contrast to the simplicity of its materials, the station introduces many complex security and technological innovations: glazed lifts enhance passenger comfort and deter vandalism; access to the tracks is blocked by platform-edge screens, which open in alignment with the doors of the trains. Servicing is also enhanced: cabling runs beneath platforms or behind walls, with access via maintenance gangways, allowing the station, consistent with its dramatic, almost theatrical atmosphere, to be maintained entirely from behind the scenes.

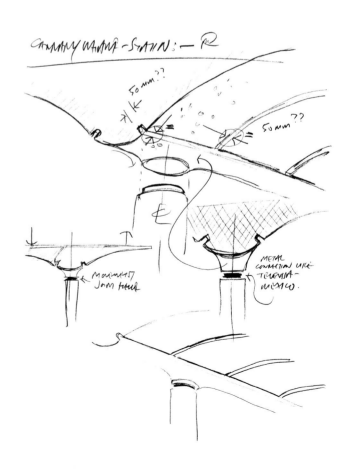

1

2

3

Previous pages, left: Design
sketches by David Nelson
exploring the detailing of
the junction between the
columns and the concrete
roof vault. Right: Looking
up the bank of escalators
that lead to the western
entrance.

1-3. Seen from above or
from street level, the station
entrance canopies convey
a sense of transparency
and lightness.

4. Escalators rise
dramatically from the
concourse towards the
light. The glazed canopies
concentrate natural light
at the exit points, thereby
aiding orientation within
the station.

4

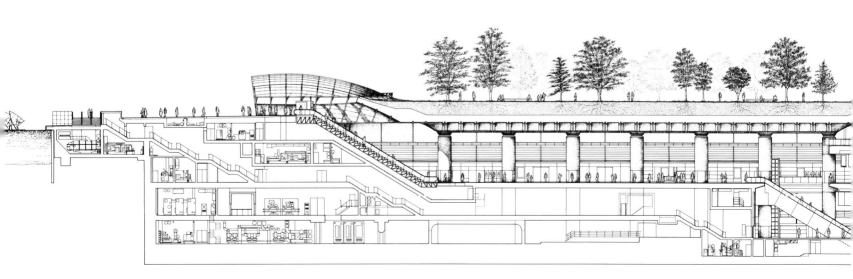

5

6

5. The station interior relies on a simple palette of hard-wearing materials: fair-faced concrete, stainless steel and glass.

6. The station's robust aesthetic is most pronounced at platform level where the concrete diaphragm tunnel walls are left exposed.

7. The station concourse during the early evening rush hour.

8. A long section through the station. At 300 metres in length, it is as long as Canary Wharf Tower is tall. Twenty banks of escalators move passengers in and out of the station.

7

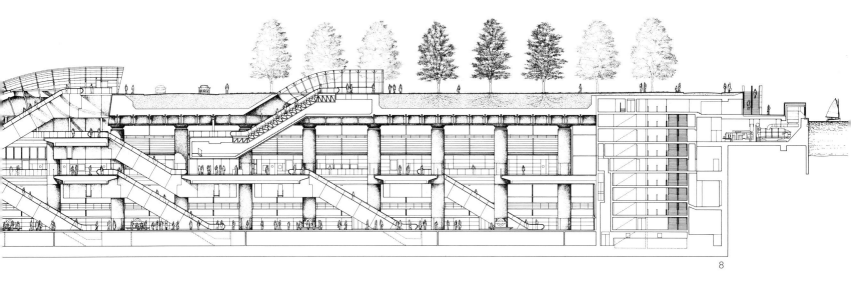

8

Expo Station

Singapore 1997–2001

Railway stations, like airports, are often the first buildings that people experience when arriving in a city and they therefore have an important symbolic role as urban gateways. Singapore's Expo Station is the first Mass Rapid Transport station that visitors to the city encounter when travelling along the new Changi Airport Line. Built to serve the new Singapore Expo Centre, its design is both a celebration of arrival and a response to one of the warmest climates in the world.

The station is announced externally by two highly sculptural roof elements, which overlap to dynamic visual effect and appear to hover weightlessly above the heavy concrete base. A 40 metre-diameter disc, clad in stainless steel, shelters the ticket hall and marks the station entrance, while a 130 metre-long, blade-like form, sheathed in titanium, covers the platforms, its reflective soffit constantly animated with the reflections of passengers and passing trains. The station is used by very large numbers of people at peak times and so creating clear sight-lines and a strong sense of orientation were fundamental to its design. At ground level, the concourse is open, with views on one side to the street, and on the other side to a lush tropical garden created between the station and the Expo Centre. The elevated platforms are reached from the concourse and ticket office at street level by lift or escalators. Enclosure is kept to a minimum and passengers can look up through a long cut in the floor structure to glimpse the trains coming and going overhead.

Environmentally, the station's open form has other benefits, encouraging a cooling flow of air through the building. The choice of roof materials also has an environmental significance. Internally, the polished metal surface reflects daylight down through the building, minimising the need for artificial lighting, while externally, the cladding deflects the sun's rays, thus helping to create a microclimate on the platforms that is refreshingly up to four degrees cooler than the outside temperature.

1, 2. Two views of the station at street level. A stainless-steel disc marks the entrance and ticket hall, while a titanium-clad, blade-like form roofs the platforms.

3. Long-section through the station showing the distinctive profiles of the two different roof forms.

Right: View along the platform; reflective panels in the roof canopy direct daylight down through the station.

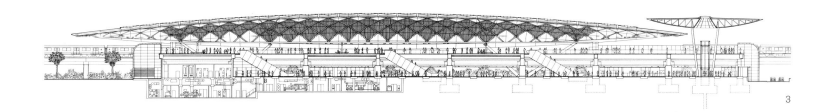

Renault Distribution Centre
Swindon, England 1980–1982

The Renault Centre has been described as the practice's most 'playful' structure. However, its development owes much to earlier, perhaps more reticent schemes for clients such as Reliance Controls and Fred Olsen, which delivered inexpensive, flexible buildings to tight schedules. The Centre was commissioned as the French car manufacturer's main UK distribution facility. In addition to warehousing, it includes a showroom, training school, workshops, offices and a staff restaurant. The notion that 'good design pays' has almost become a cliché, but in this case it is quantifiable: on the strength of the design, supportive local planners increased their site development limit from 50 to 67 per cent, allowing a floor area of 25,000 square metres. This is housed within a single enclosure supported by brightly coloured tubular masts and arched steel beams, forming a striking silhouette within its surrounding landscape.

The structural system that repeats itself to form this external outline is based around a 24 by 24 metre bay – a much larger than usual planning module developed so as to maximise the planning flexibility of the internal spaces. This expansive horizontal span is combined with an internal clear height of 7.5 metres, allowing the Centre to accommodate a range of uses from industrial warehouse racking to its subdivision into office floors. Enveloped by a continuous PVC membrane roof, pierced by glass panels at each mast, the building is also stepped at one end, narrowing to a single, open bay that forms a porte-cochère alongside a double-height 'gallery'. Primarily a showroom – as signified by suspended car body shells – the gallery was used by Renault as a popular venue for arts and social events, encouraging wider community involvement in the building.

As much as its internal spaces, however, it is the building's almost festive 'Renault-yellow' exoskeleton that gives the Centre such an identifiable character. Significantly, this created such a memorable image that the building, alone among the company's facilities, did not need to carry the Renault logo. In fact it was so closely associated with the brand that for many years Renault used it as a backdrop in its UK advertising campaigns.

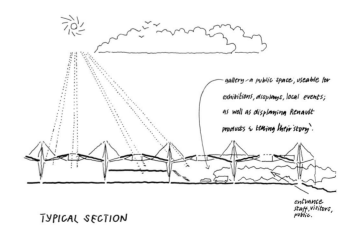

gallery – a public space, useable for exhibitions, displays, local events; as well as displaying Renault products & telling their story'.

entrance staff, visitors, public.

TYPICAL SECTION

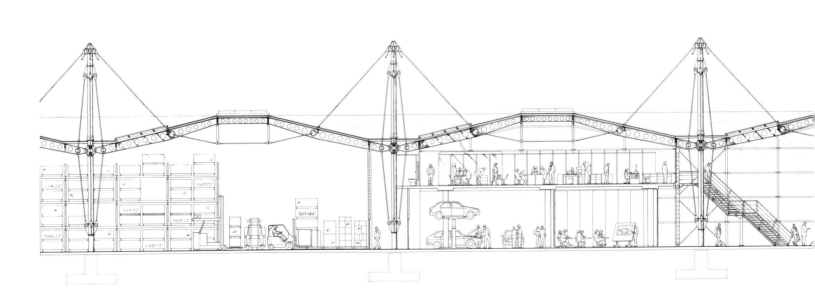

1

Previous pages, left:
Sketch by Norman Foster
highlighting the social
potential of the showroom
and the importance of
toplight. Right: The gallery/
showroom complete with
suspended car body shells.

1. The building seen from
the east; the 'Renault
yellow' exoskeleton has
a festive air and has been
described as the practice's
most playful structure.

2. Cross-section through
the southern end of the
building; the roof structure
extends by one bay to
form a porte-cochère.

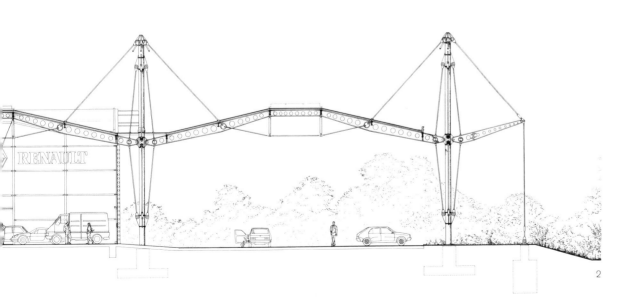

2

Willis Faber & Dumas Headquarters

Ipswich, England 1971–1975

The country headquarters for the insurance company Willis Faber & Dumas challenged accepted thinking about the office building while simultaneously maintaining a sense of continuity within the context of its urban setting. The unprecedented use of escalators in a three-storey structure, the central atrium, and the social dimension offered by its swimming pool, rooftop garden and restaurant, were all conceived in a spirit of democratising the workplace and engendering a sense of community. Outside, in contrast, the building reinforces rather than confronts the urban grain, with its free-form plan and low-rise construction responding to the scale of surrounding buildings, while its curved façade maintains a relationship to the medieval street pattern.

Floors are planned on a 14-metre-square structural grid, flexible enough to respond to the ad hoc acquisition of the site and to allow for a number of early plan configurations. A necklace of perimeter columns enables the building to flow to the edges of its site like a pancake in a pan. The sheath-like glass curtain wall, which encloses and defines this edge, was developed with the glazing manufacturer Pilkington. Pushing the limits of technology, the mullion-free solar-tinted-glass curtain wall is suspended from a continuous clamping strip at roof level. Corner patch fittings connect the panes, while internal glass fins provide wind bracing. By day, the glass reflects an eclectic collage of Ipswich's old buildings; by night it dissolves dramatically to reveal the building within.

Conceived before the oil crises of the mid-1970s and heated by natural gas, Willis Faber was a pioneering example of energy-conscious design. Its deep plan and the insulating quilt of its turfed roof ensure good overall thermal performance. Recognising these innovations, over the years it has attracted as many awards for energy efficiency as it has for its architecture. It also pioneered the use of raised office floors, anticipating the revolution in information technology. When Willis Faber introduced extensive computerisation, it was able to do so with minimal disruption. Paradoxically, although designed for flexibility, the building has since been given Grade 1 listed status: an honour that means it cannot be changed.

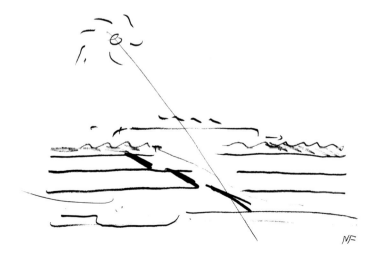

1

2

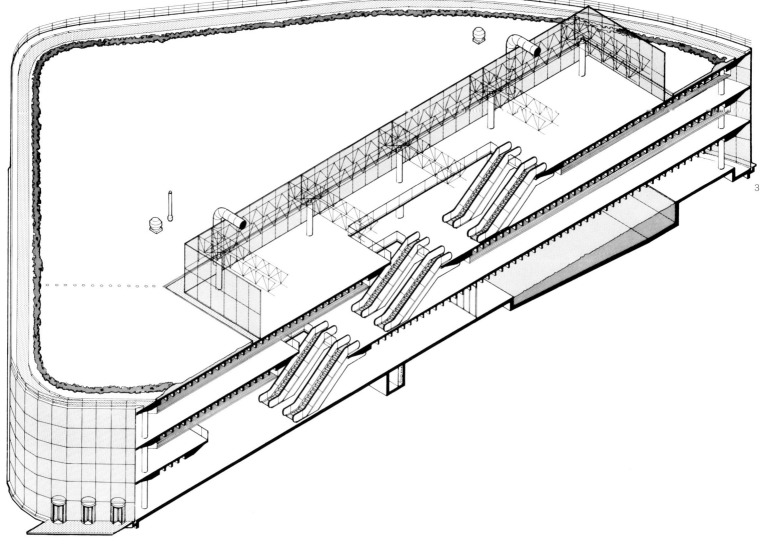

3

4

5

6   7

8

9

10

Previous pages, left: Sketch by Norman Foster capturing the diagrammatic simplicity of the building. Escalators move up towards the sunlight and the green space of the roof. Right: Night view, showing how the facade dissolves to reveal the inner workings of the building.

1. The roof garden – the first of the practice's 'gardens in the sky'.

2. The staff restaurant at garden level.

3. A cutaway axonometric showing the twin escalators rising up from the entrance foyer to the roof.

4, 5. Two images of the ground floor swimming pool (now decked over) with its water level flush with the floor.

6, 7. Two photographs, taken twenty years apart – in 1975 and 1995 respectively – show how the building has adapted easily to dramatic changes in information technology.

8. Looking across the upper floor towards the staff restaurant.

9. Athough it has a very deep plan, the heart of the building is bathed in daylight.

10. Early concept sketch by Norman Foster.

Electricité de France Regional Headquarters
Bordeaux, France 1992–1996

When the leading French utility company, Electricité de France (EDF), commissioned a new regional headquarters, it aimed to bring together managerial and technical staff previously scattered over a number of locations around Bordeaux. Appropriately, as an energy provider, it was also persuaded to embrace the efficient use of electricity for all its energy needs. The resulting building both exemplifies the practice's long-standing philosophy of encouraging social integration and amenity in the workplace and makes a compelling case for adopting more sustainable development strategies.

The building has a thermally efficient building envelope that capitalises on a tradition of excellence in concrete construction in France. In this respect, it draws on the lessons of earlier French projects, notably the Lycée Albert Camus in Fréjus, which employs passive climate control techniques dating back to traditional Arabic architecture. Like the Fréjus Lycée, the EDF building's reinforced-concrete frame and ceiling vaults – designed for good acoustic performance – have a high thermal mass, which helps to maintain constant internal temperatures. Natural ventilation and daylight are exploited as much as possible, both to reduce energy consumption and to create enjoyable working conditions. In the summer, high-level vents open automatically to cool the building fabric overnight. Daytime cooling is provided by chilled floors, which can alternatively be heated in the winter. The windows incorporate mirrors, or 'light shelves', to reflect light into the office interiors, while cedar louvres prevent solar gain. Following the strategy of relying on 'geometries, not mechanisms', the louvres are fixed and aligned to respond to very different light conditions on the east and west facades. Additionally, the building reuses its own waste energy, the heating and cooling system being run by an electric pump powered by the central exhaust stack.

A model for efficient energy management, the building is also rooted in the landscape traditions of the region. From the covered entrance plaza, which forms the visual focus of the scheme, the long entrance axis continues in an avenue of trees, the pleached limes and gravel recalling the scale and geometry of the nearby Château Raba as well as the great Place des Quinconces in the centre of Bordeaux.

1

1. Detail of the café terrace and the brise-soleil on the eastern facade.

2. Cross-section through the main body of the building.

Right: Looking through the building's shaded entrance court. The landscaping responds to the geometry and scale of the nearby Château Raba as well as the climate of Bordeaux.

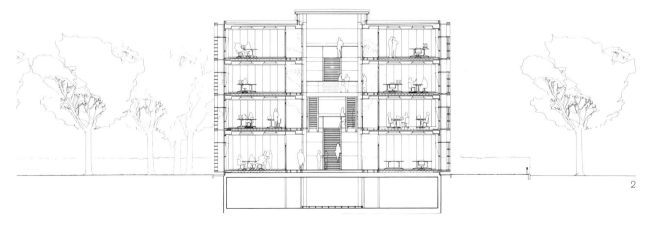

2

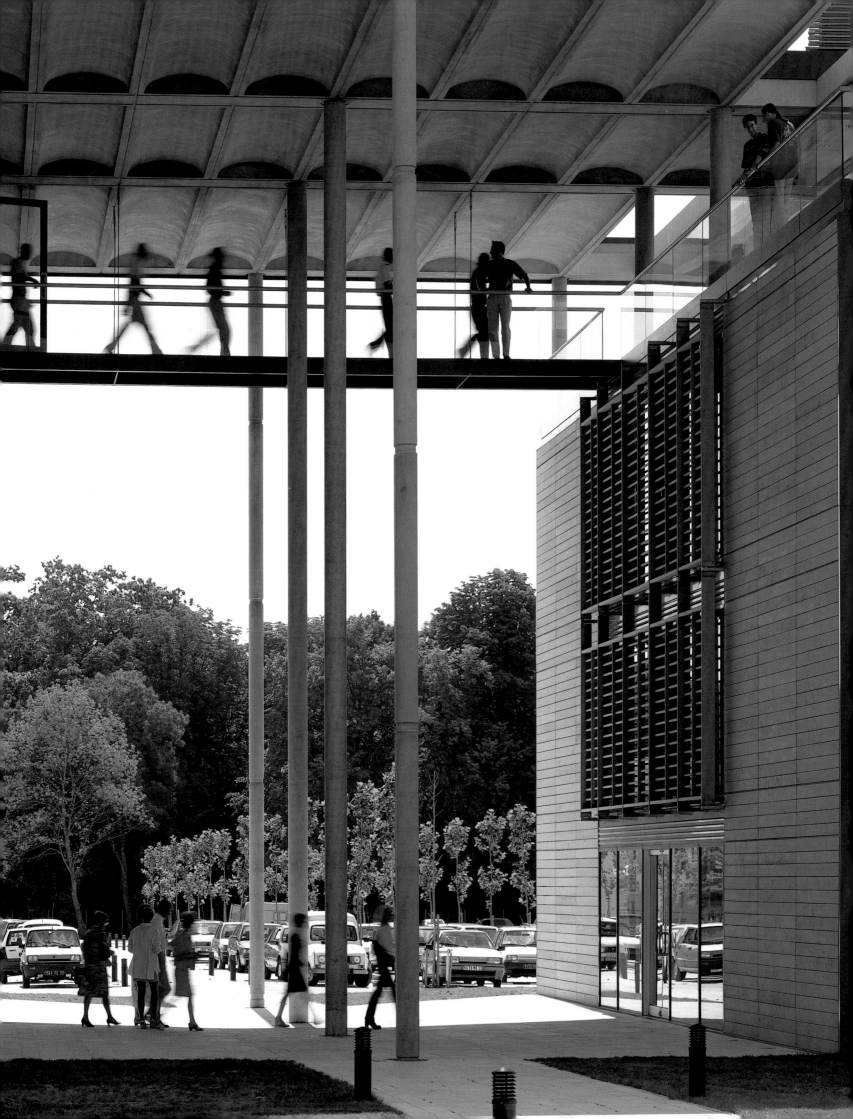

Tower Place

London, England 1992–2002

The low-rise, deep-plan, energy-conscious office building with flexible, full-access floors and improved circulation is a typology pioneered by the practice in the early 1970s with the design of the Willis Faber & Dumas Headquarters in Ipswich. Nearly thirty years after Willis Faber's completion, the practice is continuing to replace obsolete 1960s office towers with lower-rise structures for progressive developers. Although each is particular to its site, the design specifications are remarkably similar to those of Willis Faber. What was once avant-garde has entered the mainstream.

The City of London has traditionally been characterised by relatively small scale buildings laid out on an essentially medieval street plan. Situated within this context, these seven-storey offices in Tower Place, close to the Tower of London, replace an insensitive sixteen-storey office development that obstructed important view corridors between Greenwich and St Paul's Cathedral and between the Monument and the Tower. The new buildings help to restore the site's traditional urban grain, while reinstating historical views and creating a new public plaza with trees and water in front of All Hallows Church.

The development provides 42,000 square metres of office space in two blocks, broadly triangular in plan. Their stone and glass cladding system is designed to allow maximum daylight penetration, while blade-like aluminium louvres provide solar shading and add a shifting textural layer to the facades. Linking the two blocks is a glazed atrium – one of the largest such spaces in Europe. The engineering of the atrium's glass walls is highly advanced: rows of glass panels are hung like curtains from tension cables stretched between the two buildings. They terminate one storey above ground level, creating an open, naturally ventilated space that forms a covered extension of the piazza outside. This new space incorporates two designated City Walkways, inviting people to use it as a thoroughfare or as a sheltered place to meet friends and colleagues throughout the day.

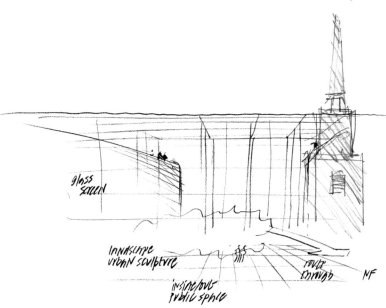

1   2

Previous pages, left:
Concept sketch by Norman
Foster. Right: Looking out
through the glazed wall of
the atrium towards All
Hallows Church.

1. Night-time view looking
west over Byward Street.

2. The spiralling access
ramps on the south side
of the building, illuminated
at night.

3. The atrium is conceived
as very much a part of the
public realm – a continuation
of the precinct in front
of All Hallows Church.

4. Cross-section through
the atrium; six floors of
offices sit above two floors
of parking for cars and
tourist buses.

5. View along the executive
floor of the east building.

6. Sol Lewitt's mural in the
lobby of the west building.

7, 8. The glass wall of the
atrium appears suspended
in space: the glass panels
are hung like curtains from
tension cables stretched
between the two buildings.

9. Detail of the limestone
cladding and aluminium
brise-soleil of the east
building.

3

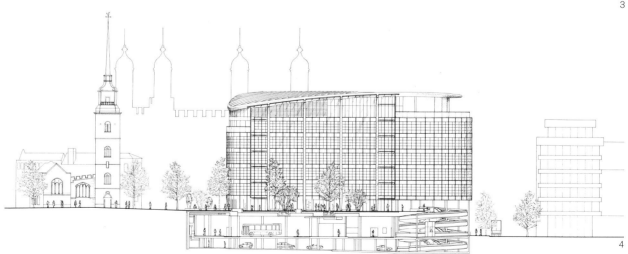

4

5

6

7

8

9

10 Gresham Street
London, England 1996–2003

The City of London and its environs are characterised by relatively low-rise buildings laid out on an essentially medieval street plan. Designing infill buildings in this context is a delicate balancing act between commercial requirements, the need for flexibility, and respect for the area's historical character and traditional materials. This new office development is located in a particularly sensitive area of the City, just south of the Guildhall, and close to two nineteenth-century livery halls, the Wax Chandlers Hall and Goldsmiths' Hall.

Eight storeys above ground, the building adopts the optimum template for new office development in the City: 18 metre deep, uninterrupted floor-plates line a wide central atrium, which extends below ground level to bring daylight down into the basement floors, dissolving conventional distinctions between ground and subterranean levels. Heightening this sense of light and space, the lifts and lobbies are all glazed so as to refract sunlight around the circulation spaces. Externally, the building responds to the City tradition of rich natural materials. The corner stair towers, which anchor the building visually, are clad in limestone, the stone flank walls wrapping into the building to provide a point of continuity between inside and outside. The ventilated, triple-glazed office facades, which incorporate wooden louvres to control solar gain and glare, are designed to maximise natural light levels, minimise energy consumption and ensure a high level of environmental comfort.

The development takes advantage of a site bounded almost entirely by streets, to create a stand-alone building, a comparatively rare achievement in the City. To the south, it is pulled back from the site boundary to create a more respectful relationship with the Wax Chandlers Hall. The resulting passage between the two buildings opens out into a small public court, used as a cut-through to the adjacent Gutter Lane or simply as somewhere to sit and have lunch. The new building, in this way, not only offers a light and flexible workspace but also reinforces the traditional pattern of streets and passageways that give the City its charm and character.

1

2

1. Looking across the timber louvres and atrium towards the glazed lift shaft.

2. Standing on the fifth floor beneath the clear glass ceiling of the atrium.

3. Cross-section through the atrium.

Right: Limestone-clad stair towers anchor the building on Gresham Street.

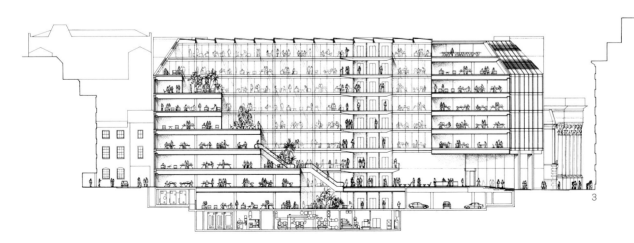

3

Electronic Arts European Headquarters
Chertsey, England 1997–2000

Through the design of a number of company headquarters and office buildings, beginning with Reliance Controls in 1966, the practice has consistently encouraged companies to adopt flexible, non-hierarchical working environments. In the design of its European Headquarters, the leading computer-game software development company Electronic Arts wholly embraced this philosophy. The headquarters sets new standards in this fast-moving industry, providing high-quality workspace, a state-of-the-art media centre for presentations, and an extensive range of on-site facilities.

Bound to the north by an eighteenth-century lake, the building comprises a group of three-storey office blocks arranged as 'fingers' projecting into the landscape. These fingers are linked by a sweeping glass wall that encloses a street-like atrium. As an animated showcase for Electronic Arts' work and the social focus of the campus, this atrium provides primary circulation at ground level and forms an environmental buffer between the offices and the landscape beyond. Electronic Arts' staff takes pride in working as a family with common values. In keeping with this ethos, a huge range of facilities is provided, including games arcades, a gym and sports pitch, a library, a bar and a 140-seat restaurant. With this wealth of leisure options, staff members have joked that the experience is like 'homing from work'.

In tandem with these programmatic elements, the building also satisfies a number of complex technological criteria. In offices equipped with large amounts of hardware, cooling and ventilation are the chief environmental concerns. As a result, the building employs a low-energy environmental strategy and a range of new-technology building systems. Comfortable conditions are maintained by combining displacement ventilation with natural cooling from the high thermal mass of the building's exposed structure. When supplementary ventilation and cooling are required, the building management system can simply open the windows or, on the very hottest days, switch on the air-conditioning. Heat gain is minimised by extensive use of brise-soleil as part of the low-energy facade design, so that the building is comfortable and controllable whatever the season.

1   2   3   4

Previous pages, left: Sketch by Norman Foster imagining the building's curved lakeside facade. Right: A view of the triple-height internal 'street' that runs along the lakeside.

1-5. Details of the interior, from informal games, meeting, and eating areas, through to the top-floor design studio, and first-floor marketing offices.

6. Looking out through the glazing of one of the building's three 'fingers' of offices.

7. Detail of the main staircase.

8. Night view, looking towards the main entrance.

9. The building as seen across the lake.

10. A cross-section through the atrium, from the car-park entrance on the left, through studio spaces, the main staircase and 'street', to the lakeside terrace on the right.

8

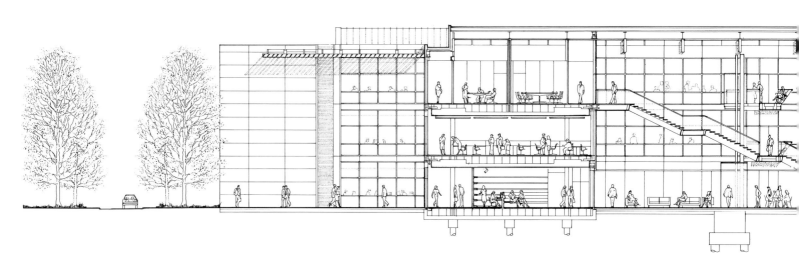

5

6

7

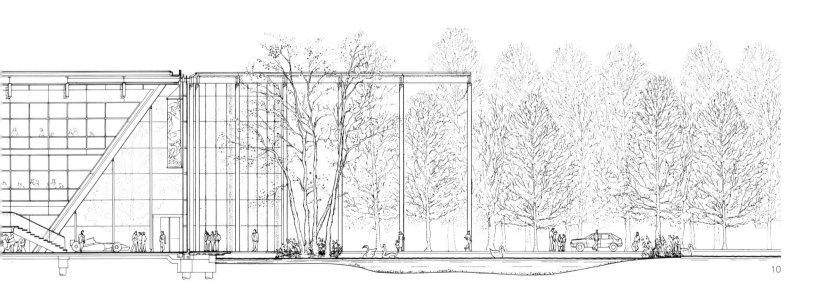
9

10

McLaren Technology Centre
Woking, England 1998–2004

The McLaren Group is a collection of high-tech companies involved in the design and development of Formula One cars, high-performance road cars, electronic systems and composite materials. Since McLaren began competing in Formula 1 in 1966, it has established a global reputation as one of the most successful teams in the history of the sport. The McLaren Technology Centre provides a headquarters for the majority of the group's staff. It includes design studios, laboratories and testing and production facilities for Formula 1 and road cars, including the Mercedes-Benz SLR McLaren.

Viewed on plan, the building is roughly semi-circular, the circle being completed by a formal lake, which forms an integral part of the building's cooling system. The principal lakeside facade is a continuous curved glass wall, developed in part using McLaren's own technology, and shaded by a cantilevered roof. Internally, the building is organised around double-height linear 'streets,' which form circulation routes and articulate 'fingers' of flexible accommodation. These house production and storage areas on the lower levels, with toplit design studios, offices and meeting rooms above. Directly behind the facade a circulation 'boulevard' leads to areas for hospitality and to the staff restaurant, both of which look out across the landscape.

A Visitor Centre is located in a separate building at the entrance to the complex. It houses educational facilities, a temporary exhibition space and presentation theatre and is linked to the main centre by a subterranean building. This two-storey structure is buried underground – like the rest of the Technology Centre it is designed to make a minimal intervention in the landscape – and is visible only by its circular rooflight.

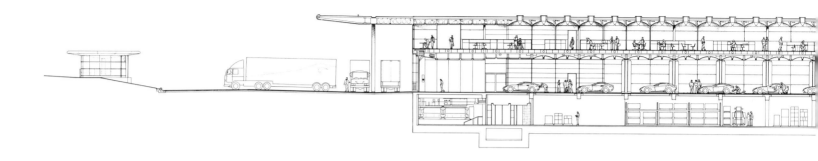

Previous pages, left: Sketch
study by Norman Foster.
Right: View of the double-
height internal 'boulevard'
looking south along the
curving lake front.

1. Cross-section through the
car assembly line and lake.

2. Looking along the main
boulevard with a line of
McLaren Formula 1 cars.

3. The Mercedes-Benz SLR
McLaren assembly line.

4. Looking down from
one of the reception
areas into the boulevard.

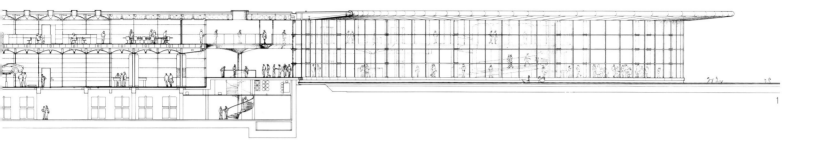

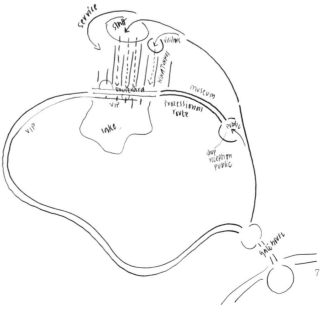

5. The lakeside frontage illuminated at night.

6. Double-height linear 'streets' form circulation routes and articulate the 'fingers' of flexible office/ workshop accommodation.

7. Sketch by Norman Foster, indicating how VIPs, staff, service vehicles and visitors take different routes through the site.

Lycée Albert Camus
Fréjus, France 1991–1993

The Lycée Albert Camus is located in the rapidly expanding town of Fréjus on the Côte d'Azur, and as part of the French lycée polyvalent system it offers a semi-vocational education to young people in their last three years of schooling. Like the more recent City Academies, the school's design challenges the heaviness of the established educational building standard with a flexible and open structure.

Developed in response to its site and to a low-energy concept for the Mediterranean climate, the school's linear plan was designed to keep active building services to a minimum. Interestingly, in paring down these services, the most effective ecological diagram was seen to correspond to the most obvious social diagram, with a linear 'street' forming the heart of the school both as a natural air movement system and a central circulation space. Bisected by an entrance hall, the street, at this point, forms a kind of 'village square', with its own café and casual seating, acting as a focal point for the students. Fresh air is pulled through the street, while the layering of the roof, with a light metal shield protecting the concrete vaults from the sun, also encourages a cooling flow of air – a technique found in traditional Arabic architecture. Further enhancing the natural ecology of the building, a solar chimney effect allows warm air to rise through ventilation louvres, whilst brise-soleil along the southern elevation provide a broad band of dappled shade.

The structure of the school is configured to contain two floors of classrooms alongside double-height reception spaces, and is oriented to separate a public entrance on the north side from a more private, shaded southern edge. Throughout, materials were chosen in response to the climate and to exploit local construction expertise, notably the exposed concrete frame, which comprises simple repetitive elements and continues the French tradition of high-quality in-situ concrete. Its high thermal mass allows this structure to act as a 'heat sink', slowing the rate of temperature change within the building and enabling it to be cooled naturally without mechanical refrigeration.

1

2

3

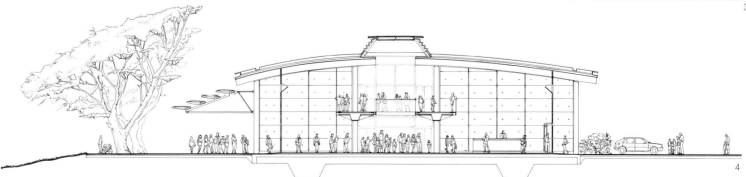

4

1-3. A sequence through
the school's interior showing
the central 'street', a typical
barrel-vaulted classroom,
and the double-height
entrance space and café.

4. A cross-section through
the entrance hall and
central street.

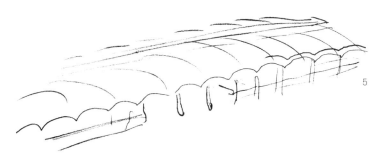

5

6

5. Concept sketch by
Norman Foster showing
the repeating pattern of
the school's vaulted roof.

6. Looking along the
school's southern facade,
shaded by brise-soleil
and cypress trees.

Academies

Bexley and Brent, England 2001–2004

The concept of a visionary, light-filled school that would be democratic and flexible, without corridors or institutional barriers, can be traced to the practice's proposals for Newport School in 1967. Newport anticipated trends that today form the basis of the Academies Programme, a radical new enterprise funded jointly by the DfES and private sponsors. The Academies – each focusing on a specialist subject – offer a new kind of secondary school experience, one that promotes a broad range of opportunities for pupils and encourages community participation. The practice's first two Academies, in Bexley and Brent, reflect a common operational structure but respond to very different sites and requirements.

Bexley Business Academy, which places an emphasis on business, art and technology, was the first new Academy to be completed in the UK. It replaces a failing school in a poor part of London and the effect has been dramatic: attendance levels and academic standards have soared. An open-plan, compact design, the school is based around three courtyard spaces that reflect its specialisms and are linked to teaching spaces on different levels. These spaces are divided by flexible partitions that allow for either large or more intimate seminars, and among the school's state-of-the-art facilities is a mini stock exchange with large plasma screens, which gives students a taste of City trading.

The emphasis in the Capital City Academy in Brent is on sport and the school plays a leading role in outreach sports development in the area. The building has a curving linear form, with bands of teaching spaces arranged on either side of a central 'street'. With ramps along its length that respond to changes of level on the site, this space provides a social hub and contains informal research and study areas. Teaching spaces have glazed walls that create visual links between different departments, and can be reconfigured as needs evolve. Like the Bexley Academy, the school offers an inspirational environment for children and teaching staff, and a new focus for the whole community.

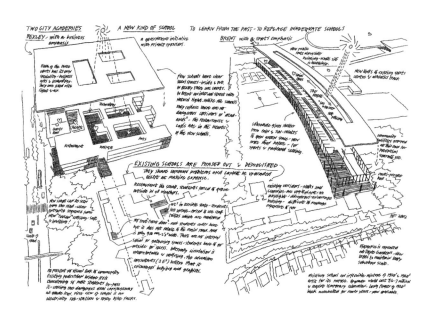

Previous pages, left: Sketch
by Norman Foster illustrating
two different architectural
strategies: the courtyard
scheme for Bexley, and the
'street' scheme for Brent.
Right: looking into the triple-
height business court of
the Bexley Academy.

1. Wall display at Bexley.

2. Approaching the school's
main entrance.

3. Cross-section through
one of the three atria.

4. Looking across the
business court through
the glass walls of the classrooms in the east wing.

1

2

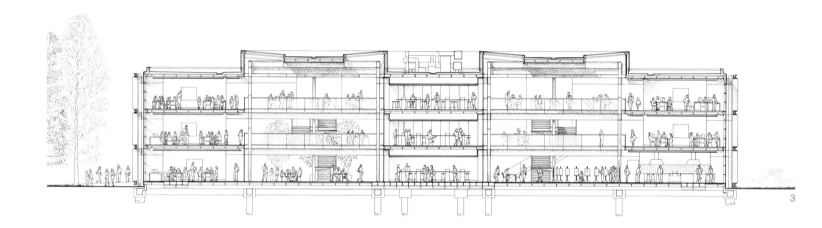

3

4

5

6

7

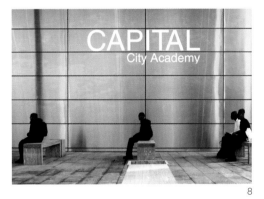

8

9

10

5. The entrance canopy
of the Capital City Academy
in Brent.

6. The school's gymnasium.

7. The central curving 'street'
is toplit and crossed by a
series of bridges linking the
two banks of classrooms.

8, 9. Stone benches create
gathering points in the
school's covered forecourt.

10. A curving colonnade
lines the building's west
elevation.

University of Cambridge, Faculty of Law
Cambridge, England 1990–1995

Cambridge University has the largest law school in Britain, with 800 undergraduates and 200 postgraduate students. Combining its own sense of tradition with a forward-looking commitment to change, the Faculty of Law required a new building that would provide state-of-the-art facilities for teaching and research, comprising the Squire Law Library, five auditoria, seminar rooms, common rooms and administrative offices.

Located at the heart of the University's Sidgwick site, the focus of humanities education at Cambridge, the new building is surrounded by lawns and mature trees. This low density, green garden context is the essence of Cambridge. The challenge was to preserve this natural setting and to minimise the building's apparent size. The response was to create a rectangular plan cut on the diagonal to follow the geometry of James Stirling's neighbouring History Faculty and pedestrian routes across the site. The building has a relatively small footprint, yet provides 8,500 square metres of accommodation without exceeding four storeys. This was achieved by burying the auditoria below ground, while the curving glass of the north facade helps the building to recede visually.

The Faculty of Law building has also set new standards for energy efficiency on the Cambridge campus, deploying a number of passive and active strategies. Natural lighting is used to dramatic effect, especially in the library, which occupies the upper three terraced floors and enjoys uninterrupted views of the gardens, while the full-height atrium that forms the focus of the building draws daylight into the lower levels. The building's partially buried structure and exposed concrete frame combine to give it high thermal mass, making it slow to respond to outside temperature changes. Together with high insulation values, this allows the use of mechanically assisted natural ventilation throughout – only the lecture theatres require seasonal cooling. A lighting management system reduces energy consumption, while heat recovery coils, linked to the air extract, reclaim waste heat. Interestingly, the building's environmental performance was put to the test during its first summer, one of the hottest on record. Happily, it performed extremely well.

1

2

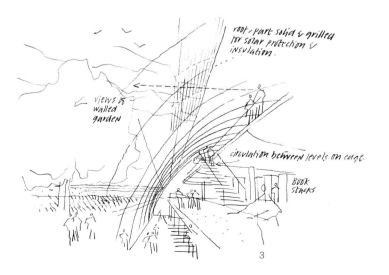

3

1. Staircases cascade down through the triple-height atrium space.

2. The library occupies four terraced floors and has uninterrupted views over the gardens.

3. Sketch by Norman Foster exploring movement and views through the library.

4

5

4. An aerial view of the building highlights its place within the garden setting of the Sidgwick site.

5. Night-time view of the curving north facade, which is designed to minimise the building's impact in the landscape.

6. Cross-section through the auditorium and terraced library floors.

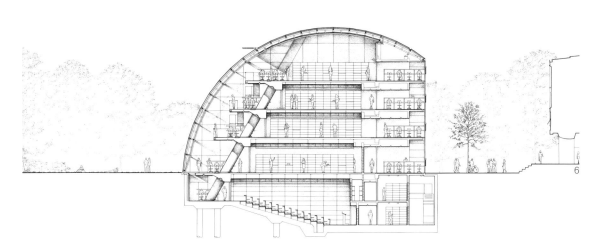

6

Imperial College Buildings
London, England 1994–2004

Imperial College of Science, Technology and Medicine is an independent constituent part of the University of London. Located in London's scientific and cultural heartland in South Kensington, it occupies a campus whose large-scale redevelopment after the Second World War left a legacy of poorly coordinated building stock and impoverished public spaces. In response, the practice was asked to formulate a masterplan for the campus's long-term renewal. The masterplan identifies key sites for redevelopment, including environmental improvements and, to date, four new buildings have been completed: the Sir Alexander Fleming Building, the Flowers Multi-Disciplinary Research Building, the Faculty Building, and the Tanaka Business School.

The Sir Alexander Fleming Building represents a major advance in medical research facilities. Designed for long-term flexibility in response to rapid changes in microbiological research, it also encourages social and intellectual interaction to an unprecedented degree. A central five-level research forum structures internal circulation and allows researchers to interact across disciplines and age groups. Laboratories are wrapped around the forum, as are undergraduate teaching spaces, administration and a café. Fully glazed at its northern end, the forum overlooks the Queen's Lawn and Queen's Tower, one of the last vestiges of the original Edwardian campus. The smaller Flowers Building is similarly designed for long-term flexibility, although its laboratories have more specialised maintenance requirements that require services installations to be exposed for ease of access.

The Faculty Building brings together all the College's administrative staff in a building that is designed to facilitate communication. It forms a new edge to Dalby Court and its vivid blue cladding is in direct contrast to the utilitarian architecture of the 1960s buildings that surround it. Located strategically between Dalby Court and Exhibition Road, the Tanaka Business School spans between newly built elements and the refurbished historic Royal School of Mines to create a unified street facade for the College. Circular lecture theatres, based on the interactive Harvard Business School model, are contained within a distinctive six-storey-high drum. Clad in stainless steel, the drum stands at the heart of an atrium space that also serves as a new 'entrance hall' for the campus and provides exhibition space to showcase the College's achievements in the fields of science, technology and medicine.

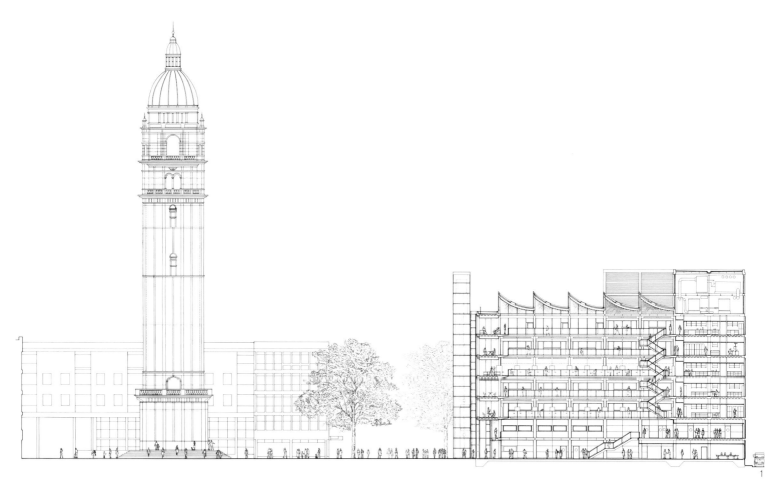

1

Previous pages, left: Sketch by Norman Foster. Right: The five floors of the research forum in the Sir Alexander Fleming Building.

1. Cross-section through the Sir Alexander Fleming Building, with the Queen's Tower to the north.

2. View of the upper floors and curving roof profile of the research forum.

3, 4. Day- and night-time images of the building's glass facade.

5, 6. Exterior and interior of the Faculty Building.

7, 8. The main circulation stair and facade of the Flowers Building.

9. The Tanaka Business School as seen from Exhibition Road.

10. Detail of the six-storey drum containing the Business School's circular lecture theatres.

11, 12. Staircase detail and café space in the atrium of the Business School.

2

3   4

5

6

7

8

9

10

11

12

Center for Clinical Science Research, Stanford University

Stanford, USA 1995–2000

Stanford University has long been recognised as a centre for clinical excellence. The new Center for Clinical Science Research (CCSR) provides the School of Medicine with state-of-the-art modular laboratory and office space for its ongoing programme of research into cancer and other diseases. Its design responds to emerging trends for interdisciplinary biomedical research, encouraging intercommunication and providing flexible, light-filled working spaces in which research teams can expand and contract with ease.

The brief called for close proximity between laboratories, core support areas and offices. Two symmetrical wings frame a central courtyard, connected at roof level by a screen of louvres. Shading the courtyard from direct sunlight, the louvres create a comfortable environment for social interaction, and this space has become both the social heart of the building and a key route through the university campus. Offices overlook the courtyard through bay windows, and a bamboo screen at ground level offsets the open and social working environment with a degree of privacy for office occupants. Environmental systems take advantage of Palo Alto's climate, which is among the most benign in the United States. The offices are naturally ventilated for most of the year, with mechanical assistance only on extremely hot days, and the laboratory and office spaces are predominantly naturally lit. Seismic performance was a key concern: the campus lies close to the San Andreas Fault and the laboratories contain highly sensitive equipment. In response, the building employs a concrete shear-wall structural system and bridges spanning the courtyard rely on friction pendulum bearings to allow for seismic movement between the wings.

Over the years Stanford University has pioneered new approaches to clinical and scientific research. Most recently it has spearheaded an international sea change that embraces an interdisciplinary approach. The CCSR established the first wave of change at Stanford, which was consolidated by the more radical Clark Center. Together, these two buildings have had a significant impact on the architecture of research facilities around the world. Not only have they set new technical standards, they represent an exciting new research environment in which interaction between disciplines and individuals is encouraged as an essential part of daily life.

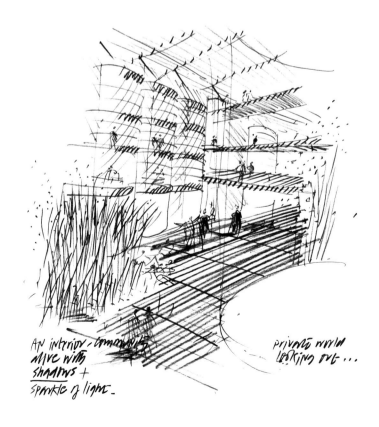

An interior, common space with shadows + sparkle of light.

private world looking out...

1

2

Previous pages, left: Design sketch by Norman Foster. Right: Looking into the central courtyard – a space animated by the play of light.

1. Looking up at the glazed roof of the courtyard.

2. Shadow patterns on the courtyard floor.

3. The building seen through the trees of the Stanford campus, with the Santa Cruz mountains in the distance.

4-7. A series of interior views of the conference room, laboratory modules, and the interconnecting bridges, linking laboratory spaces to the central courtyard.

8. View into the café area of the central courtyard – the social hub of the building.

9. Cross-section through the building showing the close connection between laboratory, office and support spaces.

3

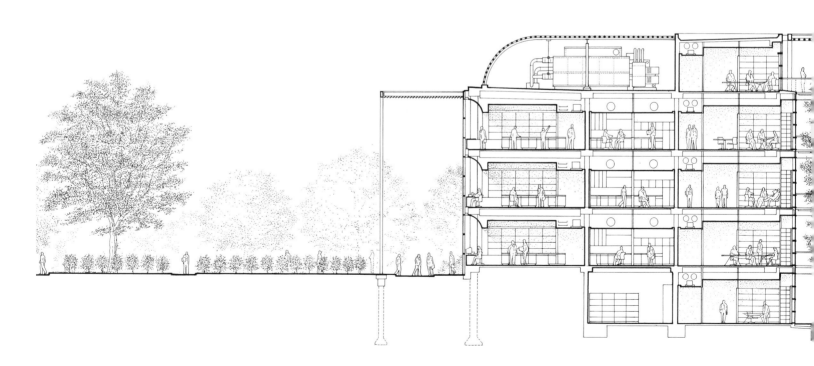

4   5   6   7

8

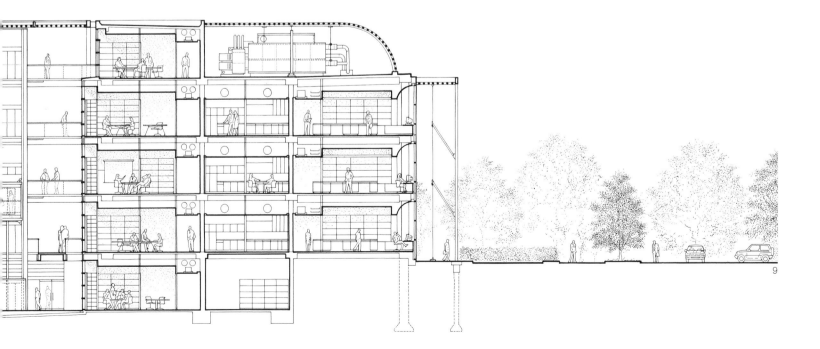

9

James H Clark Center, Stanford University

Stanford, USA 1999–2003

The Clark Center continues the practice's investigations into the physical nature of the research environment, which began at Stanford University with the Center for Clinical Science Research (CCSR). The CCSR reflected changes that were beginning to take root in research methodology at the time and was designed to facilitate an inter-disciplinary approach and promote interaction between scientists. The Clark Center takes this formula a stage further, driven by the pioneering Bio-X programme, which has remodelled the landscape of science and technological research at Stanford.

Providing laboratory, office and social spaces for 700 academics from the Schools of Humanities and Sciences, Engineering and Medicine, the Clark Center is strategically located at the heart of the campus, between the core science and engineering buildings and the medical centre. It acts as a social magnet for the University, encouraging students, lecturers and researchers from diverse disciplines to mix. In striking contrast to the traditional laboratory facility with its closed rooms and corridors, the Clark Center is open and flexible: external balconies replace internal corridors and laboratory layouts can be reconfigured at will. All benches and desks are on wheels and can be moved to allow ad hoc team formation that can respond easily to fast-evolving research needs. This versatility is further enabled by workstations that plug into an overhead unistrut system of exposed services and flexible connections.

Externally, the three-storey building takes the form of three wings of laboratories, clad in rust-red painted steel and limestone to echo the tiled roofs and stone facades of Stanford's architectural vernacular, that frame an open courtyard overlooked by balconies. A forum at the heart of the courtyard is used for exhibitions, concerts and other events, while a restaurant on the ground floor of the south wing offers a new social focus for the entire campus with tables spilling out into the courtyard. A coffee bar on the third floor is located to encourage people to pass by the laboratory spaces, further distinguishing the building as a place in which social encounters and impromptu conversations are regarded as integral to scientific endeavour.

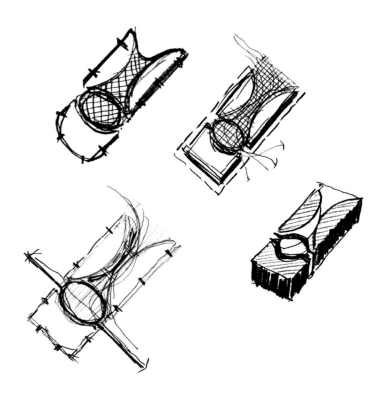

1

2

3

Previous pages, left: Design sketches by David Nelson. Right: Looking down the central courtyard; balconies and inter-connecting bridges replace internal corridors.

1-4. A series of interior views of the laboratory modules: any bench and desk configuration can be plugged into the flexible overhead services.

5. A cross-section through the courtyard, showing the two wings of laboratory space and the subterranean low-vibration physics laboratory.

6. The entrance to the building lies on a main pedestrian route through the campus.

7. Looking up at the bridges that link the two wings.

8, 9. A view across the building's central forum, as seen during the opening ceremony in October 2003, and (below) the forum space on a typical term-time day.

4

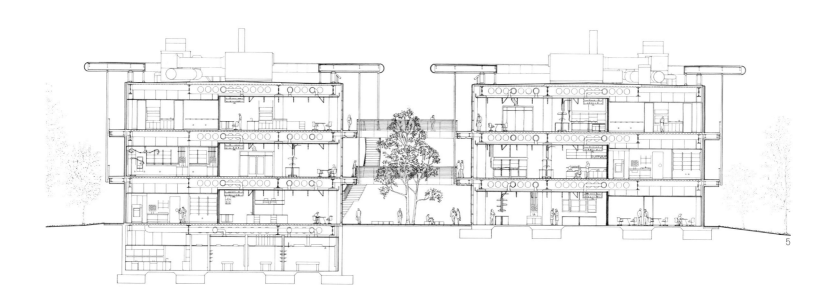

5

6

7

8

Petronas University of Technology
Malaysia 1998–2004

The Petronas University of Technology was founded in 1997 at the
invitation of the Malaysian Government, and is the region's largest
academic centre for the study of civil, mechanical, chemical and electrical
engineering. Fully funded by the Malaysian oil company Petronas, it aims
to blend the best academic training with hands-on industrial experience
to produce a new generation of graduates who can contribute to
Malaysia's industrial development.

Located within the beautiful and dramatic landscape at Seri
Iskandar, 300 kilometres north of Kuala Lumpur, the 450 hectare site
is characterised by steep hills and lakes formed by flooded disused tin
mines. The design responds to the physical landscape of the site and to
the weather patterns particular to this part of the world. While it can be
intensely hot in the sun, in the monsoon season the skies open every
afternoon to bring torrential rain, creating a cycle in which the ground is
alternately scorched and soaked. To allow students to move around the
campus while shaded from the sun or protected from heavy downpours,
soaring crescent-form roofs protect the pedestrian routes that wind
around the edge of the site. Held aloft by slender columns, these
canopies intersect to encircle a central landscaped park. Where possible,
the jungle forming the park has been left in a natural state, although
some marshy land has been activated to form a natural water installation.

Arranged around the edge of the park are buildings for teaching and
research, contained in four-storey blocks that tuck beneath the edges of
the canopies. Cafés and other communal student facilities are located at
the canopy intersections, which also correspond to the entrances to the
housing blocks. Marking the main entrance to the University is the drum-
like form of the resource centre. Containing a library and multi-purpose
theatre, it will be the chief social hub of the campus. Future expansion
will see the completion of a sports stadium and a mosque – amenities
that will be shared with the residents of a new town planned adjacent
to the University.

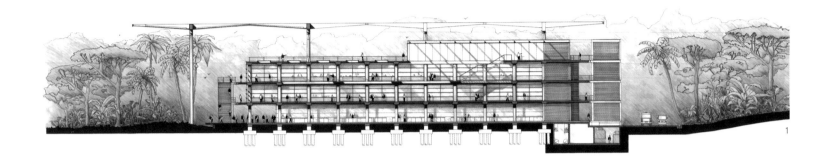

Previous pages, left:
Concept sketch by Norman
Foster illustrating the idea of
a flowing roof canopy. Right:
Looking across the park
towards a section of one of
the campus' crescent roofs.

1, 2. A section and elevation
(right) through one of the
academic departments
showing the clear separation
between roof canopy and
building blocks below.

3. An aerial view of the
completed campus.

4-6. Views in and around
one of the sun protected
'pocket' spaces at the
intersection of the roof
canopies.

7. Interior view from within
the chancellor complex
looking across the public
plaza from the library
to the convocation hall.

8, 9. Laboratory spaces
inside the academic block.

10. The interior of the
main campus library.

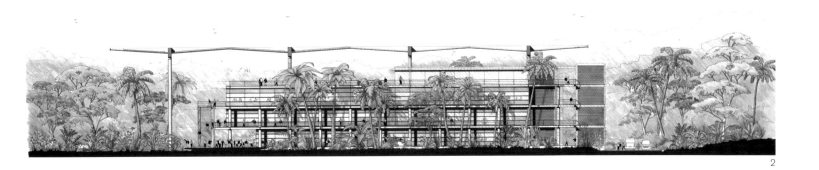

2

7

8

9

10

Sainsbury Centre for Visual Arts
Norwich, England 1974–1978 and 1988–1991

With the donation in 1973 of their collection of ethnographic and twentieth-century art to the University of East Anglia, together with an endowment for a new building, Sir Robert and Lady Sainsbury sought to establish the Sainsbury Centre for Visual Arts as an academic and social focus within the university campus. The Sainsburys shared a belief that the study of art should be an open, pleasurable experience, one not bound by the traditional enclosure of object and viewer. As a result the Sainsbury Centre is much more than a conventional gallery, where the emphasis is on art in isolation. Instead, it integrates a number of related activities within a single, light-filled space.

The building itself brought a new level of refinement to the practice's early explorations into lightweight, flexible structures. Structural and service elements are contained within the double-layer walls and roof. Within this shell is a free-flowing sequence of spaces that incorporates a conservatory reception area, coffee bar, exhibition areas, the Faculty of Fine Art, senior common rooms and a restaurant. Full-height windows at either end of the structure allow the surrounding landscape to form a backdrop to the exhibition and dining areas, while aluminium louvres, linked to light sensors, line the interior to provide an infinitely flexible system for the control of natural and artificial light. Large enough to display the Sainsburys' extraordinary collection, yet designed to be intimate and inviting, the main gallery space extends the spirit of the collection's originally domestic setting.

A new gift from the Sainsburys in 1988 allowed the building to be extended to provide space for the display of the reserve collection, together with curatorial and conservation facilities and a gallery for exhibitions and conferences, giving the Centre far greater flexibility in its programming. The new wing extends the building at basement level, exploiting the natural contours of the site to emerge naturally in the form of a glazed crescent incised into the grassy bank. In 2004 a further programme of improvements was initiated to provide additional display space, an internal link between the main and Crescent Wing galleries, improved shop, café and other visitor facilities, and a new education centre.

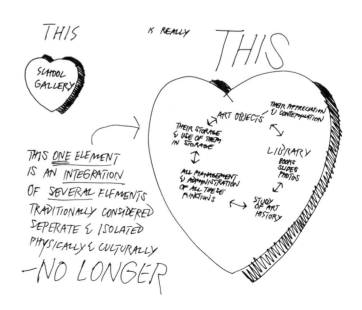

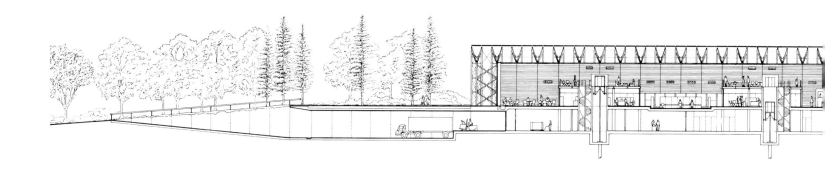

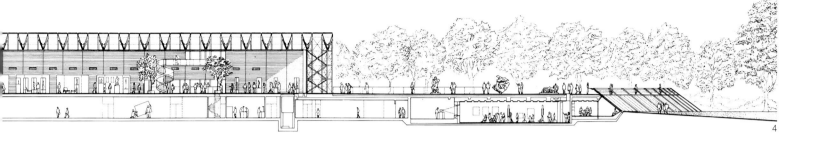

4

5   6   7

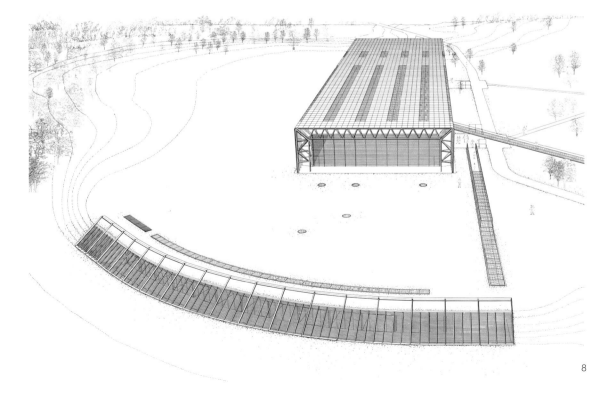

8

Previous pages, left:
Concept sketch by Norman
Foster highlighting the
advantages of a multi-
faceted but integrated arts
centre. Right: The Sainsbury
Centre at dusk, seen from
across the University's lake.

1. The glazed wall of the
restaurant at the western
end of the building.

2. The senior common
room at mezzanine level.

3. The open-plan gallery
space with purpose-
designed display cases
and screens.

4. A long-section through
the Sainsbury Centre and
Crescent Wing reveals
how the extension forms a
logical continuation of the
original undercroft level.

5, 6. Views of the new
Reserve Collection.

7. Looking along the
circulation zone and the
sweeping glass wall that
define the perimeter
of the Crescent Wing.

8. An aerial perspective of
the Sainsbury Centre and
Crescent Wing.

Overleaf. The Crescent Wing
with the Sainsbury Centre
behind, showing how the
extension is dug into the
natural slope of the site.

Carré d'Art
Nîmes, France 1984–1993

Médiathèques exist in most French towns and cities. Typically they embrace magazines, newspapers and books as well as music, video and cinema. Less common is the inclusion of a gallery for painting and sculpture. In Nîmes, the interaction within the same building of these two cultures – the visual arts and the world of information technology – held the promise of a richer totality. The urban context of Nîmes also acted as a powerful influence. The site faces the Maison Carrée, a perfectly preserved Roman temple. The challenge was to relate new to the old, but at the same time to create a building that represented its own age with integrity.

A singular modern building, yet one that references the courtyard and terraced vernacular of the region, the Carré d'Art is articulated as a nine-storey structure, half of which is sunk deep into the ground, keeping the building's profile low in sympathy with the scale of the surrounding buildings. The lower levels house archive storage and a cinema, while above, a roofed courtyard forms the heart of the building, exploiting the transparency and lightness of modern materials to allow natural light to permeate all floors. These upper levels are connected by a cascading staircase, linking the toplit galleries to the shaded roof-terrace café overlooking a new public square.

The creation of this urban space was an integral part of the project. Railings, advertising boards and parking spaces were removed and the square in front of the building was extended as a pedestrianised realm. The geometry of this piazza follows Nîmes' Roman grid in recreating tree-lined streets alongside the building and providing a new setting for the Maison Carrée. Lined with café tables and thronged with people, the new square has reinvigorated the social and cultural life of Nîmes. Together with these urban interventions, the Carré d'Art shows how a building project, backed by an enlightened political initiative, can not only encourage a dialogue between ancient and modern architectures but can also provide a powerful catalyst for reinvigorating the social and physical fabric of a city.

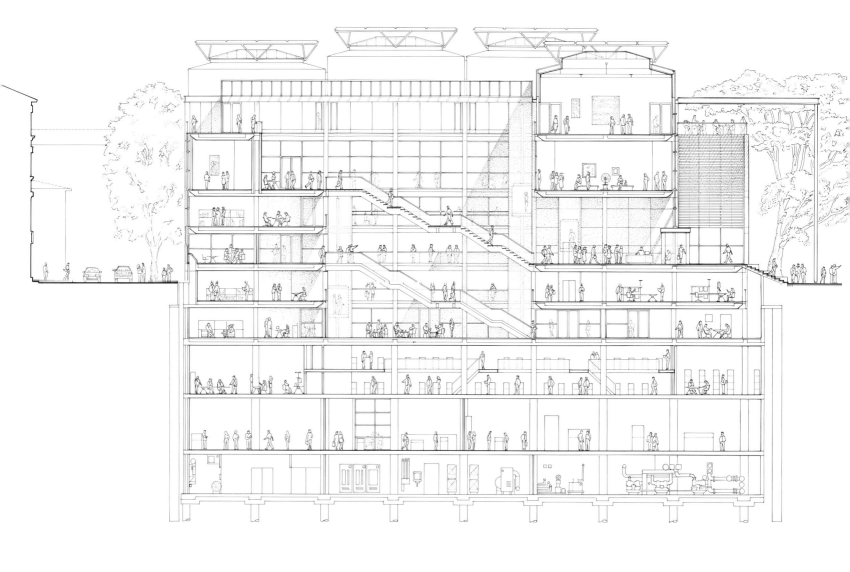

Previous pages, left: Sketch
by Norman Foster outlining
what would become the
defining view of the Carré
d'Art, from the steps of the
Roman Maison Carrée.
Right: Detail of the front
of the building.

1. Cross-section through
the building. In order to
respect the roof-line of the
surrounding city, five of the
building's floors are sunk
below ground and daylit
via the central atrium.

2. The revitalised urban
square in front of the Carré
d'Art, renamed Place de
la Maison Carrée.

2

3

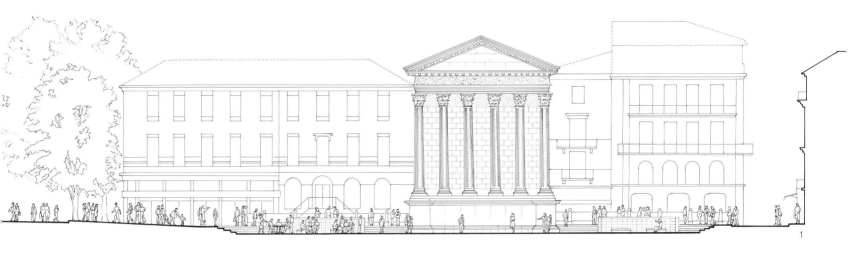

1

4

5

6

3. View out towards the Maison Carrée from the café terrace.

4. The triple-height volume of the adult library.

5. Rising six stories through the heart of the building, the atrium staircase links all the main public areas.

6. One of the galleries on the upper level.

Overleaf: The loggias of the old Maison Carrée and the new Carré d'Art face each other across the square.

Sackler Galleries, Royal Academy of Arts

London, England 1985–1991

The commission for the Sackler Galleries at the Royal Academy of Arts provided the practice with its first opportunity to work within a historical building. Although perceived by the visitor as a single entity, the Royal Academy actually consists of two buildings: the original Palladian house, converted by Lord Burlington in the eighteenth century, and a subsequent Victorian gallery behind, linked by a grand central staircase. The project brief required the replacement of the undistinguished nineteenth-century Diploma Galleries at the top of Burlington House and the improvement of access routes through the building.

The project demonstrates how contemporary interventions can enhance the old by relying on sensitive juxtaposition rather than historical pastiche. The key to unlocking the design solution was the rediscovery of the lightwell between Burlington House and the Victorian extension, into which a new lift and staircase were inserted. In the process, redundant historical accretions were peeled away, revealing the garden facade of Burlington House for the first time in over a century. Cleaned and repaired, this elevation contrasts strikingly with the Victorian structure and the free-standing new insertions. The new work is demonstrably of its own time, using modern materials for modern ends, but it also enables a rediscovery of the potential of Burlington House and the Victorian galleries, much of which had become inaccessible over time.

In addition to this historical reclamation, the Sackler Galleries achieved new environmental standards, allowing the Academy to meet the exacting criteria set by international exhibitions. These include a glazed reception area incorporating the parapet of the Victorian galleries. Sculpture from the Academy's permanent collection is displayed along this simultaneously modern and antique route, most notably Michelangelo's tondo of the Virgin and Child with the Infant St John, powerfully revealing a contrast between old and new. The Royal Academy was the first in a line of projects demonstrating a clear philosophy about contemporary interventions in historical structures, which continued with the Reichstag in Berlin and the Great Court at the British Museum.

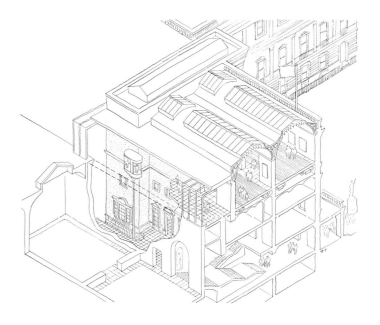

Previous pages, left: A cutaway drawing by Norman Foster of the final scheme. Right: View of the new glass lift with the newly revealed garden facade of Burlington House behind.

1-3. Details of the glass staircase that rises up to the Sackler Galleries.

4. A cross-section through the Sackler Galleries, taking in the Royal Academy's courtyard and entrance hall.

5-7. Studies of the sculpture promenade by artist Ben Johnson: Classical figures and busts are displayed on the existing parapet.

8. A view of the south gallery.

9. The main entrance to the galleries, along the sculpture promenade.

10. The galleries are naturally lit from above. Adjustable louvres are used to control lighting levels.

1

2

3

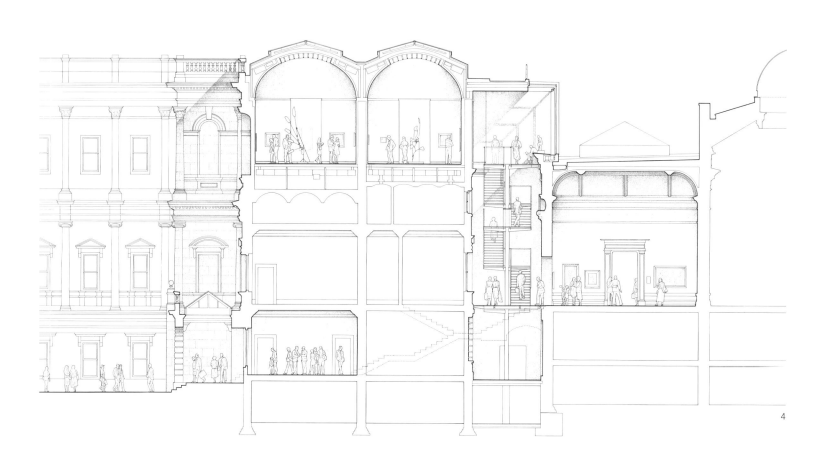

4

144

5

6

7

8

9

10

American Air Museum, Duxford
Duxford, England 1987–1997

Duxford airfield in Cambridgeshire was a Battle of Britain fighter station. Later, as one of a hundred US Airforce bases in Britain, it was the headquarters of the 78th Fighter Group. Now maintained by the Imperial War Museum, it has the finest collection of American aircraft outside the United States. Nineteen of its thirty-eight aircraft are airworthy and it attracts some 350,000 people to its summer air displays. The centrepiece of the collection is also the largest – a B-52D bomber.

The building to house this collection has three starting points. First, it commemorates the role of the American Air Force in the Second World War and the thousands of airmen who lost their lives. Second, it provides the optimum enclosure for the B-52 and twenty other aircraft dating from the First World War to the Gulf War. Third, and equally important, was a desire to exploit the activity of the runway and create a window onto that world. The building's drama comes from the single arc of the roof – engineered to support suspended aircraft – and the sweep of the glazed southern wall overlooking the runway. Entry is via a ramp, on axis and at 'nose' level with the B-52. Around and beyond is a panorama of aircraft of every scale. The structure is partly sunk into the ground and its form has been compared to 'blister hangars', which were designed to be invisible from the air. A continuous strip of glazing around the base of the vault washes the interior in daylight.

In 1998 the Museum won the RIBA Stirling Prize Building of the Year Award. The jury wrote: 'The success of this project lies in the resonance between the elegant engineered form of the building and the technically driven shapes of the aeroplanes. The building itself sustains the fascination of these objects.'

Previous pages, left: Norman Foster's concept sketch emphasises the B-52 as generator of the building's section. Right: Looking through the glazed end wall out on to the runway.

1. Lining the curving approach to the entrance is a sequence of etched glass panels by the artist Renato Niemis, which forms a memorial to the American airmen killed during the Second World War. Each panel depicts in silhouette individual aircraft lost in action by the fighter and bomber groups.

2. The building's entrance, a discreet doorway that gives little indication of the space beyond.

3. The airfield seen on one of Duxford's popular summer air-display days.

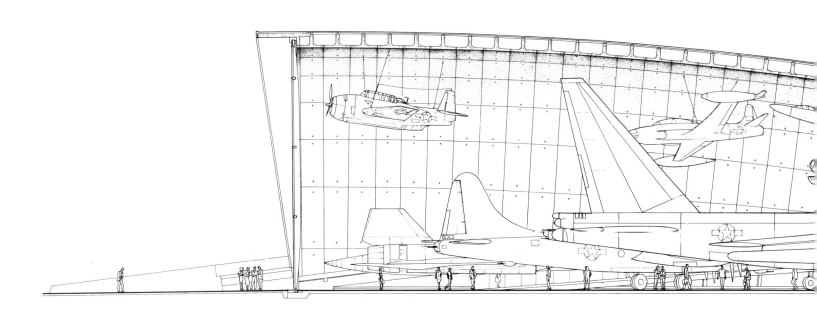

4

5

6

4. Visitors to the museum find themselves nose to nose – quite literally – with the aircraft on display.

5. The panorama of the runway as seen through the museum's full-height glass end wall.

6. Looking along the ramp that curves around the perimeter of the building.

7, 8. The museum has the largest collection of USAAF aircraft outside the United States, spanning a historical spectrum from the First World War to the first Gulf War. Many of the aircraft are still airworthy.

9. Cross-section through the building; visitors enter at a raised level, corresponding with the cockpit of the B-52.

7

8

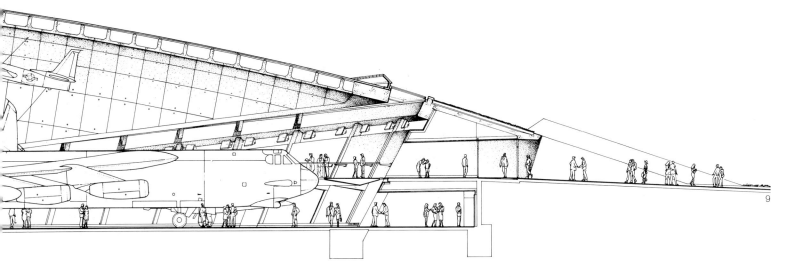

9

Musée de Préhistoire des Gorges du Verdon

Quinson, France 1992–2001

This museum, located in the medieval village of Quinson in Haute Provence, preserves and illustrates the rich traces of Stone Age life uncovered within the exceptional archeological site of the nearby Gorges du Verdon. The architecture of Quinson is characterised by traditional stone buildings and drystone walls and the new building responds to this context by combining modern construction techniques with local materials used in their simplest, most expressive form.

The museum is one of a family of Foster buildings that are partially buried or cut into their sites in order to reduce their apparent scale. Here, the sloping ground was used to advantage, allowing the museum to be 'folded' into the landscape in section. The 'dug-in' edge of the lenticular plan – a form reminiscent of a *calisson*, a Provençal delicacy – is defined by a long drystone retaining wall. This wall continues the line of an existing village wall and flows into the building to guide visitors into the double-height foyer, a space that is designed to be cool and refreshing on a hot summer's day – reminiscent of a wine cellar, or one of the caves that the museum celebrates.

The building is multi-functional, including areas for academic study alongside a reference library and research laboratories. On the ground level, accessed from the foyer, a children's teaching area reinforces the building's social and educational programme, while its auditorium, capable of seating 100 people for lectures, can be used independently for village events. From the foyer, a curved ramp leads up to the first floor to begin the circular route around the museum display. Ambient light levels within the galleries are kept to a minimum and light is focused on the objects rather than the space. The centrepiece of the exhibition is a reconstruction of one of the caves in the Gorges du Verdon, which are inaccessible to the public. This is supplemented by dioramas showing hunting and other scenes from Stone Age life.

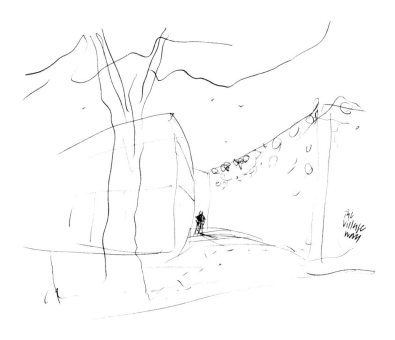

Previous pages, left: Norman Foster's sketch study shows how an existing village drystone wall is continued and folded into the museum, forming the link between old and new. Right: An aerial view of the museum looking south over the Gorges du Verdon.

1. The village of Quinson is characterised by traditional stone buildings and drystone walls.

2. The in-situ concrete facade uses an aggregate matched to the colour of the local stone.

3. A detail of the entrance with its oversailing canopy.

4. Norman Foster's sketches explore the detailing of the 'prow' of the museum's concrete facade.

5. From the entrance hall, a ramp arcs up to the first floor to begin the route through the exhibition.

6, 7. In the display areas ambient light levels are kept to a minimum; light is focused on the objects rather than the space.

8. Visitors line the ramp leading up to the exhibition spaces.

9. A cross-section through the entrance hall, first floor exhibition spaces, and the museum's centrepiece – a reconstructed cave from the Gorges du Verdon.

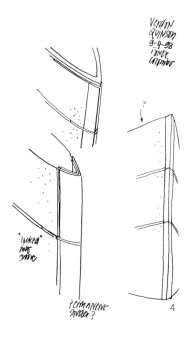

6

7

8

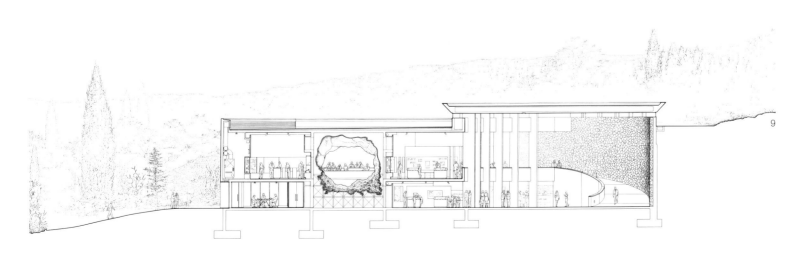

9

Addition to Joslyn Art Museum

Omaha, Nebraska, USA 1992–1994

The museum or cultural centre has the power to become a very strong social focus in the community. In extending the Joslyn Art Museum and addressing its external spaces so that they could work for outdoor events, this project aimed not only to bring the old building and its environment back to life, but also to create something that was more than the sum of its parts.

Completed in 1931, the Joslyn is one of the finest Art Deco buildings in America. The brief for a new wing called for over 5,000 square metres of gallery and workshop space, together with the limited refurbishment of the existing building. The Joslyn is unusual among North America's arts venues in combining art and music in one complex, with a 1,200 seat concert hall flanked on each side by two narrow floors of art galleries. Analysis showed that the main entrance, with its Classical portico reached by a majestic, if forbidding, flight of stone steps, was being underused as most visitors entered the building by a side door next to the car-park. The challenge was to re-emphasise the public front of the Museum and design a new wing that did not detract from the clarity of the original concept.

Clad in matching pink Etowah Fleuri marble from the Georgian quarry that supplied the original building, the new wing adopts a solid, unarticulated form with similar proportions to the existing Museum. Linking the new and old wings, and set back from both, a glass atrium forms a new social space, providing restaurant facilities and a secondary public entrance. On the main level of the new wing are temporary exhibition galleries, lit from above by indirect, controlled daylight. The floor below comprises storage vaults, workshops, cloakrooms, a kitchen and a restaurant servery. At the front of the Museum, the original access road and car-park were reinstated to reinforce the principal axis and encourage use of the original entrance. In front of the building there is space for an open-air amphitheatre – a venue for summer concerts – which would broaden the range of the Joslyn's activities and give it a yet stronger community attraction.

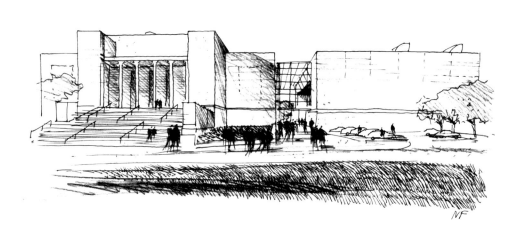

1

2

3

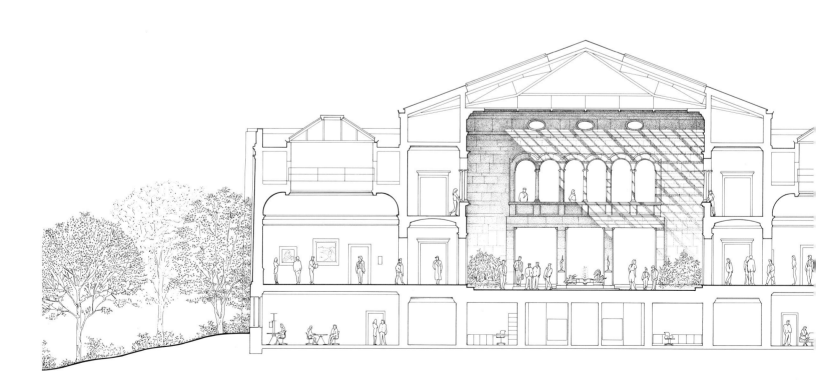

4

5

Previous Pages, left: Design sketch by Norman Foster. Right: Bright and welcoming during the day, the atrium link between the new and old buildings is illuminated at night, drawing people in.

1. A broad granite stair leads from the floor of the atrium to the bridge that spans between the new and the existing galleries.

2. The café, which occupies the western end of the atrium, is a popular venue for social functions outside museum hours.

3. The Joslyn Art Museum is one of America's finest Art Deco buildings. The new extension is designed to complement rather than compete with the original building.

4-6. The new galleries are configured not as rooms but as a sequence of inter-connecting spaces. Free-standing dividing walls run along the east-west axis, while thicker walls, which conceal storage for partitions and movable furniture, articulate the galleries in the north-south direction.

7. A north-south cross-section through the existing building and the new wing.

6

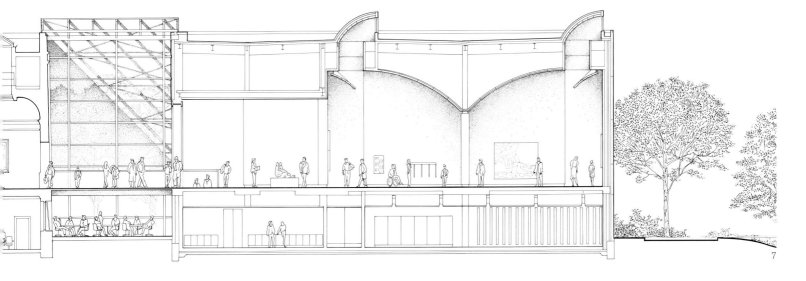

7

Great Glasshouse, National Botanic Garden of Wales
Llanarthne, Wales 1995–2000

The Great Glasshouse at the National Botanic Garden of Wales reinvents the glasshouse for the twenty-first century, offering a model for sustainable development. The largest single-span glasshouse in the world, it contains more than a thousand plant species – many of them endangered – and conserves specimens from Mediterranean climates around the world. Set in rolling hills overlooking the Tywi Valley in Carmarthenshire, the building forms the centrepiece of the 230-hectare park of the former Middleton Hall.

Elliptical in plan, the building swells from the ground like a glassy hillock, echoing the undulations of the surrounding landscape. The aluminium glazing system and its tubular-steel supporting structure are designed to minimise materials and maximise light transmission. The toroidal roof measures 99 by 55 metres, and rests on twenty-four arches, which spring from a concrete ring beam and rise to 15 metres at the apex of the dome. Because the roof curves in two directions, only the central arches rise perpendicular to the base, the outer arches leaning inwards at progressively steep angles. The building's concrete substructure is banked to the north to provide protection from cold northerly winds and is concealed by a covering of turf so that the three entrances on the northern side appear to be cut discreetly into the hillside. Within this base are a public concourse, a café, educational spaces and service installations.

To optimise energy usage, conditions inside and outside are monitored by a computer-controlled system. This adjusts the supply of heat and opens glazing panels in the roof to achieve desired levels of temperature, humidity and air movement. The principal heat source is a biomass boiler, located in the park's Energy Centre, which burns timber trimmings. This method is remarkably clean when compared with fossil fuels, and because the plants absorb as much carbon dioxide during their lifetime as they release during combustion, the carbon dioxide cycle is broadly neutral. Rainwater collected from the roof supplies 'grey water' for irrigation and flushing lavatories, and lavatory waste is treated in reed beds before being released into a watercourse.

Previous pages, left: Norman Foster's sketch, showing how the Glasshouse nestles in the landscape. Right: Looking up through the Glasshouse's overarching toroidal glass roof.

1. A long-section through the Glasshouse; its gently curving form echoes the undulating profile of the Carmarthenshire hills.

2-4. The glass roof allows maximum light to reach the plants but overheating is avoided through the use of computer-controlled panels in the glazing, which open automatically to ventilate the building.

5, 6. The Glasshouse in the landscape.

2

3

4

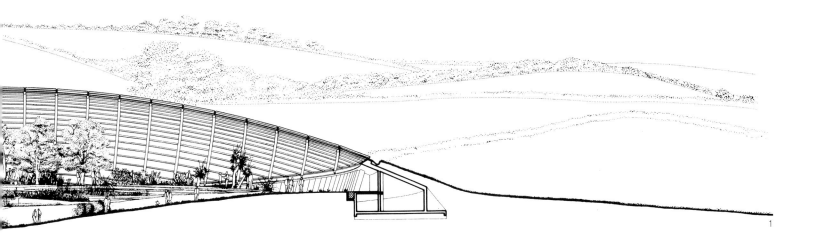

1

5

6

The Great Court at the British Museum
London, England 1994–2000

Before the advent of the Great Court, the courtyard at the centre of
the British Museum was one of London's long-lost spaces. Originally
an open garden, soon after its completion in the mid-nineteenth
century it was filled by the round Reading Room and its associated
bookstacks. Without this space the Museum was like a city without
a park. This project is about its reinvention.

In terms of visitor numbers – over five million annually – the British
Museum is as popular as the Louvre in Paris or the Metropolitan
Museum of Art in New York. However, in the absence of a centralised
circulation system this popularity caused a critical level of congestion
throughout the building and created a frustrating experience for the
visitor. The departure of the British Library to St Pancras provided
the opportunity to clear away the bookstacks and to recapture the
courtyard to give the building a new public focus. The Great Court
is entered from the Museum's principal level, and connects all the
surrounding galleries. Within the space – the largest enclosed public
space in Europe – there are information points, a bookshop and a café.
At its heart is the magnificent space of the restored Reading Room,
now an information centre and library of world cultures, which for the
first time in its history is open to all. Broad staircases encircle the
Reading Room and lead to a gallery for temporary exhibitions with a
restaurant above. Below the level of the Court are the new Sainsbury
African Galleries, an education centre, and facilities for schoolchildren.

The glazed canopy that makes all this possible is a fusion of state-
of-the-art engineering and economy of form. Its unique geometry is
designed to span the irregular gap between the drum of the Reading
Room and the courtyard facades, and forms both the primary structure
and the framing for the glazing, which is designed to maximise daylight
and reduce solar gain. As a cultural square, the Court also resonates
beyond the confines of the Museum, forming a new link in the
pedestrian route from the British Library to Covent Garden and the
river. To complement this civic artery, the Museum's forecourt has
been freed from cars and restored to form a new public space. Like
the Great Court it is open to the public from first thing in the morning
to early evening, creating a major amenity for London.

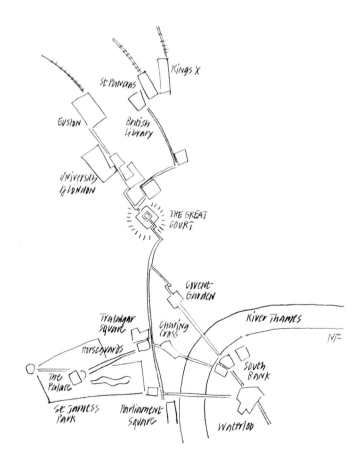

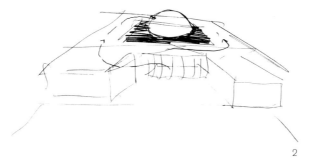

Previous pages, left: Sketch by Norman Foster highlighting the pivotal position occupied by the Great Court on the pedestrian route between Bloomsbury, the South Bank and Westminster. Right: Looking up at the newly clad drum of the Reading Room.

1. The restaurant terrace, with its fabric awning.

2. Early design sketch by Norman Foster.

3. Although it is covered, the Great Court retains the feel of an outside space.

4-6. An urban experience in microcosm, the Great Court encourages exploration and recreation in equal measure.

7. The new Sainsbury African Galleries, located below the Great Court

8. The restored Reading Room plays a central role as the main information centre within the Museum, housing the Paul Hamlyn Library.

9. A cross-section along the north-south axis of the Museum, from the forecourt and front hall, through the Great Court to the north entrance.

Overleaf: Looking into the Great Court from the Museum's front hall.

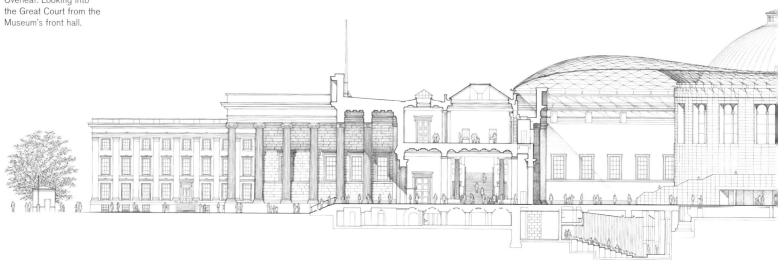

4

5

6

7

8

9

The Sage Gateshead
Gateshead, England 1997–2004

Opened in December 2004, the Sage is a regional music centre of international standing, with an expected half million visitors each year. Designed after extensive consultation with audiences and musicians, the Sage fills a 'gap on the map' for music venues in the North-East and has helped to consolidate Tyneside's position as an arts destination in its own right. The building is already a local landmark, forming the heart of an exciting project to regenerate the area's river frontage. It lies alongside the new pedestrian Baltic Millennium and the Tyne Bridge with its great arch, which is echoed in the shell-like form of the Sage's roof.

The Sage provides three auditoria and accommodation for the Regional Music School and also acts as a base for the Northern Sinfonia and Folkworks, which promotes folk, jazz and blues performances. The largest of the three main performance spaces is acoustically state-of-the-art and seats up to 1,650 people. The second hall caters for folk, jazz and chamber music, with an informal and flexible seating arrangement for up to 400 people. The third space is a large rehearsal hall for the Northern Sinfonia and also forms the focus of the Music School. The School is accessible to children, schools and people of all ages, and has raised the profile of the region as an innovative provider of musical education.

Each auditorium was conceived as a separate enclosure but the windswept nature of the site suggested a covered concourse along the waterfront to link them. As a result the entire complex is sheltered beneath a broad, enveloping roof that is 'shrink-wrapped' around the buildings beneath and extends over the concourse. Containing cafés, bars, shops, an information centre and the box office, the concourse is a major public space. It acts as a foyer for the auditoria and as a common room for the Music School, which is located beneath it. Back-of-house hospitality areas have been kept to a minimum to encourage performers to interact with students during the day and to mix with their audiences in the concourse bars in the evenings. With its informal atmosphere and unrivalled views out across the Tyne, this is one of the city's great social spaces.

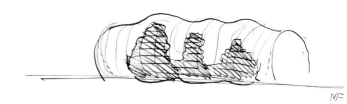

Previous pages, left:
Concept sketches by
Norman Foster exploring
the form of the roof over
the Sage's three auditoria.
Right: Night-time view,
looking across the Tyne.

1. The central stage
of Hall Two.

2. The rehearsal space
in the Northern Rock
Foundation Hall.

3. Children practising in the
Children's Education Centre.

4. The main stage of the
largest of the auditoria, Hall
One, as seen from the first
tier of seating.

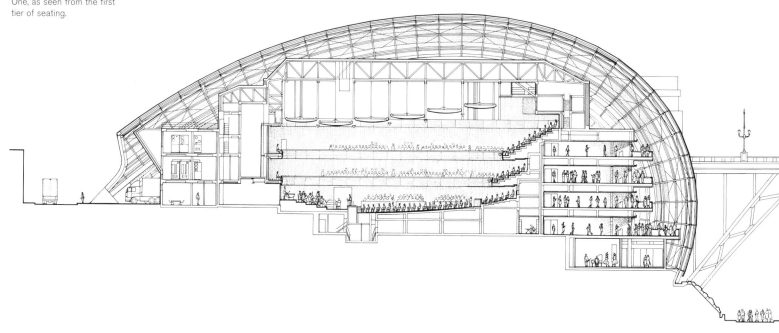

5

6

5-7. The foyers wrap around the auditoria and enjoy spectacular views out across the Tyne.

8. Cross-section through Hall One looking towards the Tyne Bridge.

Overleaf: The silvery form of the Sage seen across the roofscape of nineteenth-century Newcastle.

7

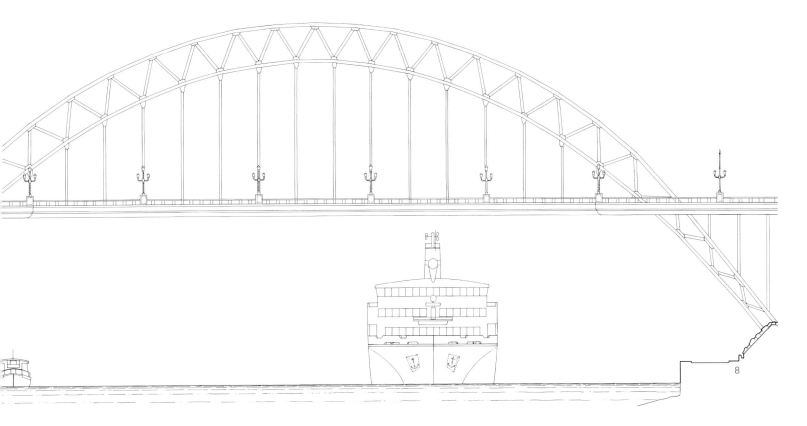

8

BBC Radio Centre

London, England 1982–1985

The BBC Radio Centre was the brainchild of the then chairman of the BBC, Lord Howard, who held an international competition in 1982, which the practice won. At the heart of the proposal was an attempt to remedy the perception of the BBC as an introverted organisation, seemingly at odds with its commitment to public service broadcasting. Working closely with BBC staff and management, the practice structured its proposal around a series of strategies designed to make the Corporation more publicly accessible in its new home.

Located opposite Broadcasting House and John Nash's All Souls' Church at the southern end of Portland Place, the context was highly challenging – both historically and in terms of urban design. The BBC also had stringent criteria: the building had to provide technical capacity to allow for every foreseeable broadcasting development; construction could not interfere with broadcasting activities; and the new building had to replace as many of the BBC's scattered London facilities as possible.

The design responded to three contextual problems: the relationship with Cavendish Square to the south-west, the need for a punctuation mark at the southern end of Portland Place, and the juxtaposition with Broadcasting House and All Souls' on the bend of the street. The resulting scheme stepped gradually upwards in keeping with neighbouring buildings. A low elevation faced Cavendish Square, while a cluster of glazed lift towers on the north-east elevation formed a climax to Portland Place. A seven-storey glass wall opposite All Souls' marked the main entrance and the glazed atrium that bisected the building diagonally. Lined with shops and cafés and placed on an axis with All Souls', the atrium formed the public heart of the building. Radio facilities were placed on either side of the atrium and below it in three subterranean storeys of sound studios and auditoria. In 1985, following the appointment of a new chairman with a different vision for the BBC, the site was sold and the scheme abandoned, just as it was to be submitted for planning permission.

THERE IS NO LANGHAM PLACE - NASH HAD A GARDEN HERE -

COMPARE THE AGRESSION OF THIS CORNER WITH THE 'INVITATION' OF ALL SOULS !

NOTE HOW THE LEVEL CHANGE LIFTS YOU ABOVE THE TRAFFIC - VISUALLY BUT ALSO SMELLS - A BETTER PROSPECT THAN PAVEMENT LEVEL.

NF

NOTE HOW THE PERISTYLE IS INVITING - A PUBLIC SPACE - A SYMPATHETIC GESTURE - PEOPLE SIT ON THE STEPS EVEN IN THE COLDEST WEATHER !

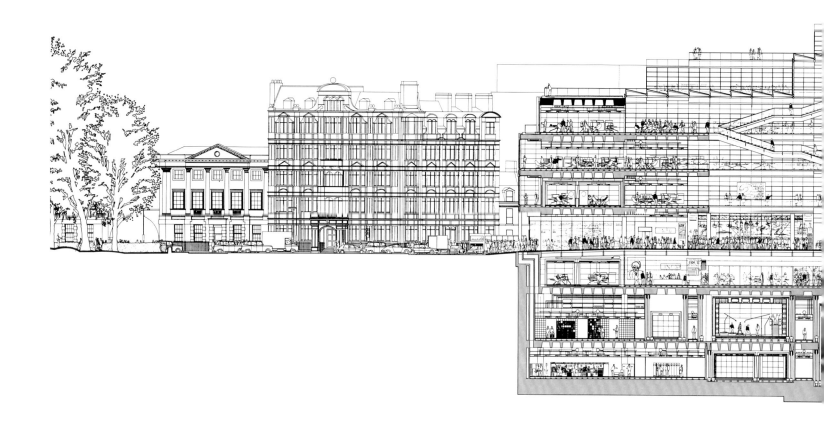

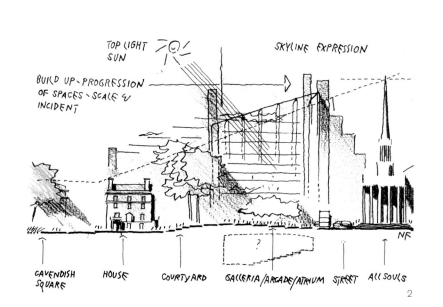

TOP LIGHT SUN

SKYLINE EXPRESSION

BUILD UP-PROGRESSION
OF SPACES-SCALE &
INCIDENT

?

NF

CAVENDISH
SQUARE   HOUSE   COURTYARD   GALLERIA/ARCADE/ATRIUM   STREET   ALL SOULS

2

3

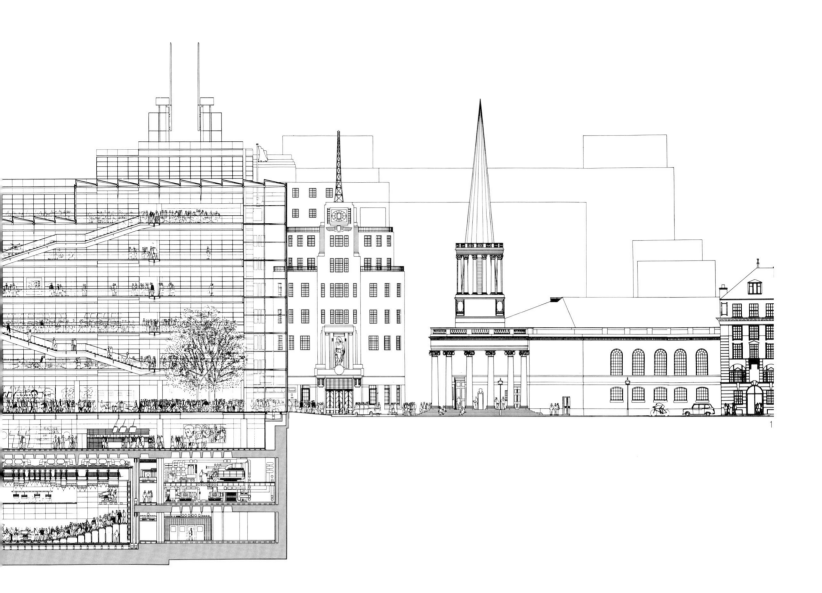

Previous pages, left: Sketch by Norman Foster exploring the urban and social dynamic of Langham Place. Right: Visualisation looking from the peristyle of John Nash's All Souls' Church towards the public atrium.

1. A long-section through the atrium of the new building, from Cavendish Square on the left to All Souls' on the right.

2. Early design sketch by Norman Foster.

3-5. Views of the model showing the glazed atrium from above, looking out towards All Souls', and the building approached from Portland Place.

Congress Centre

Valencia, Spain 1993–1998

As communications technology makes it easier to work in isolation, paradoxically the demand for new kinds of places for face-to-face discussion continues to grow. Conferences and conventions are now an international industry, and congress centres are important assets for cities keen to compete in a world market. Valencia's Congress Centre is an example of this phenomenon. A leading European conference venue, it combines state-of-the-art facilities with an architectural celebration of this historic Mediterranean city.

The Congress Centre provides three auditoria, seating 250, 460 and 1,460 people respectively, with the smallest of these capable of being subdivided into two. In plan, the building forms a convex lens or 'eye', defined by two arcing facades of unequal length. The auditoria and the nine seminar rooms fan out from the tighter curve of the western edge, while the public areas – including the broad, linear foyer – run along the eastern facade. The Centre is oriented to respond to the climate and quality of light and shade, water and green spaces found in the city. The foyer looks out onto shady trees and gently curving asymmetrical pools. Fresh air is cooled as it passes over these pools and is drawn into the foyer, minimising the need for mechanical air conditioning. Similarly, reflected sunlight is balanced by shading from brise-soleil so that natural illumination in the foyer is even and finely veiled. Except in the auditoria, daylight is drawn deep into the plan, in some places entering gently, in others forming fine piercing rays.

Following principles rooted in the vernacular local architecture, the roof consists of two layers: an outer metal shield floats above a heavy concrete shell, encouraging a cooling flow of air in between, thus optimising the building's passive thermal performance. The roof sweeps through 180 metres in a single line, surging forward at its peak to create a canopy above the entrance, which provides shelter from the sun. Completed to a tight budget, the Centre combines local skills, materials and construction techniques with the minimum of imported systems. In this sense, as well as in its environmental stance, it is truly a Valencian building – rooted in tradition but forward looking.

1

2

3

1. The east elevation is shaded by translucent brise-soleil.

2. The foyer takes the form of a broad 'street', which runs the length of the building and provides access to all the principal spaces.

3. Looking down into the main auditorium, which seats 1,500 people.

4. This sketch by Norman Foster shows early ideas for the creation of a lofty canopy facing the Avenida de las Cortes.

Right: Toplit stairs lead from the foyer into the auditoria.

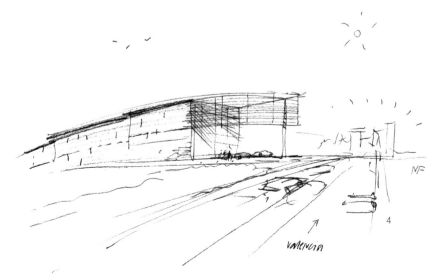

4

Her Majesty's Treasury
London, England 1996–2002

Most office buildings dating from the late-nineteenth and early-twentieth centuries are not naturally suited to modern working practices. Externally, however, they add an important sense of heritage to the architectural wealth of our cities and many can be restructured to fit contemporary needs. Her Majesty's Treasury is such a building. Situated between Parliament Square and Horse Guards Parade, it was completed in 1917 and is Grade II listed. In refurbishing and reorganising the building, the challenge was to transform a labyrinthine and frequently under-utilised set of spaces into an efficient, enjoyable place to work.

The existing building has a roughly symmetrical plan, with two halves linked by a drum-like courtyard. Each half of the building is punctuated by smaller courtyards and lightwells, which were hitherto unused. In an echo of the strategy deployed in the Great Court at the British Museum, some of the courtyards have been reclaimed and capped with translucent roofs to create five-storey-high spaces that now house a library, cafés, training rooms and a new entrance atrium. Other courtyards have been landscaped with planting and pools to form recreation spaces for staff, while the central circular courtyard, previously used for parking, has been emptied of cars and landscaped to form a new public space for London. Inside, more than 7 miles of partitions have been removed from the offices to create open-plan workspaces. This radical reorganisation has enabled the entire Treasury staff to be accommodated comfortably in the western half of the building, freeing the remainder for use by other government departments.

Significantly, the refurbished building also sets new environmental standards in Whitehall. In addition to opening up the offices, the lightwells help to ventilate the building naturally, forming thermal chimneys through which stale air from the office spaces is exhausted by vents at roof level. Fresh air is drawn into the building through the windows, which have also been upgraded to provide improved security. This natural ventilation cycle is assisted by 'windcatchers' mounted on the roof. Heating, lighting, IT and communication systems have been similarly modernised, so that the building combines a sense of history with a reinvigorated and contemporary working environment.

1

2

3

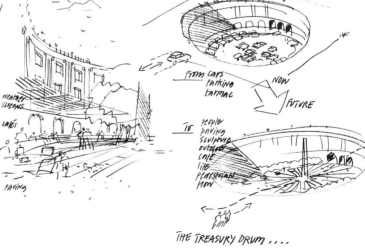

THE TREASURY DRUM ....

5

6

7

1, 2. The large courtyards within the Treasury building have been landscaped to provide a major new staff amenity.

3. An aerial view of the Treasury building, with Parliament Square in the foreground and St James's Park beyond.

4. Norman Foster's sketches describe the transformation of the central drum-shaped courtyard, which is to be reopened as a public route.

5-7. The smaller lightwells that punctuate the building have been roofed over to create a library, a café and a range of other facilities. The roofs are formed from clear polycarbonate 'pillows'.

8. Looking into the staff café, created during the first phase of the Treasury's redevelopment. The hanging banners are by Danish artist Per Arnoldi.

8

New German Parliament, Reichstag

Berlin, Germany 1992–1999

The Reichstag's transformation is rooted in four issues: the Bundestag's significance as a democratic forum, a commitment to public accessibility, a sensitivity to history, and a rigorous environmental agenda. As found, the building was mutilated by war and insensitive reconstruction; surviving nineteenth-century interiors were concealed beneath a plasterboard lining. Peeling away these layers revealed striking imprints of the past, including graffiti left by Russian soldiers. These scars are preserved and historical layers articulated; the Reichstag has become a 'living museum' of German history.

The reconstruction takes cues from the old Reichstag – the original *piano nobile* and courtyards have been reinstated – but in other respects it is a complete departure. Within its masonry shell it is transparent, opening up the interior to light and views and placing its activities on view. Public and politicians enter together through the reopened formal entrance. The public realm continues on the roof and in the cupola – a new Berlin landmark – where helical ramps lead to an observation platform, allowing the people to ascend above the heads of their political representatives in the chamber below.

The building's energy strategy is radical. It uses renewable bio-fuel – vegetable oil – which, when burned in a co-generator to produce electricity, is far cleaner than fossil fuels. The result is a 94 per cent reduction in carbon dioxide emissions. Surplus heat is stored as hot water in an aquifer deep below ground. The water can be pumped up to heat the building or to drive an absorption cooling plant to produce chilled water. This, too, can be similarly stored below ground. The Reichstag's modest energy requirements allow it to perform as a power station for the new government quarter. The Reichstag's cupola is also crucial to its lighting and ventilation strategies. At its core a 'light sculptor' reflects light into the chamber, with a moveable sun-shield blocking solar gain and glare. As night falls, this process is reversed. The cupola becomes a beacon, signalling the vigour of the German democratic process.

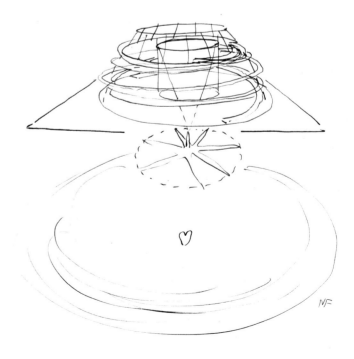

1

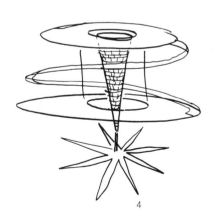

2

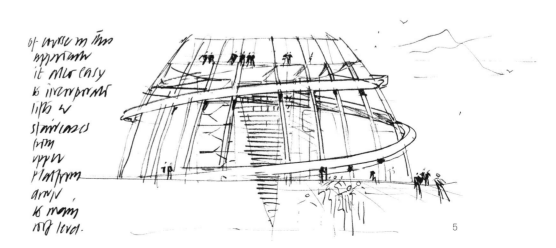

3

4

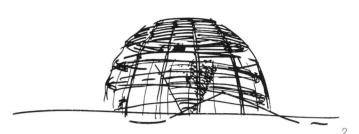

5

6

7

8

9

10

Previous pages, left: Concept sketch by Norman Foster. Right: Gerhard Richter's 'Flag' seen through the Reichstag's portico.

1. At night, the Reichstag's cupola becomes a beacon, visible across the city.

2. Design sketch of the cupola by Norman Foster.

3. The west front of the Reichstag.

4, 5. Early design studies by Norman Foster.

6, 7. The Reichstag has redefined notions of public space and in the process has become one of Berlin's leading visitor attractions.

8. The restaurant terrace.

9. Looking into the chamber towards the seat of the President of the Bundestag.

10. A suspended steel bridge in the north corridor.

11. North-south cross-section through the parliamentary chamber.

Overleaf: Inside the cupola.

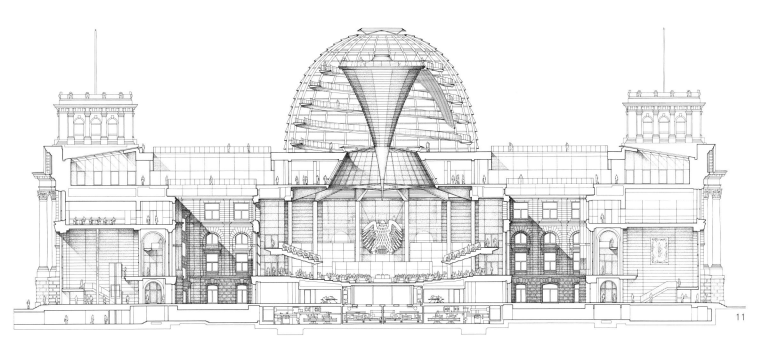

11

City Hall
London, England 1998–2002

City Hall houses the assembly chamber for the twenty-five elected members of the London Assembly and the offices of the mayor and staff of the Greater London Authority. Located on the south bank of the Thames, alongside the new More London development, it is one of the capital's most symbolically important new projects. Advancing themes explored earlier in the Reichstag, it expresses the transparency and accessibility of the democratic process and demonstrates the potential for a sustainable, virtually non-polluting public building.

Designed using advanced computer-modelling techniques, the building also represents a radical rethinking of architectural form. It has no front or back in conventional terms. Rather, its shape is derived from a geometrically modified sphere, a shape that achieves optimum energy performance by minimising the surface area exposed to direct sunlight. Analysis of sunlight patterns throughout the year produced a thermal map of the building's surface, which is expressed in its cladding. A range of active and passive shading devices is also employed: to the south the building leans back so that its floor-plates step inwards to provide shading for the naturally ventilated offices; and the building's cooling systems utilise ground water pumped up via boreholes from the water table. These energy-saving techniques mean that chillers are not needed and that for most of the year the building requires no additional heating. Overall, it uses only a quarter of the energy consumed by a typical air-conditioned office building.

The chamber faces north across the river to the Tower of London, its glass enclosure allowing Londoners to see the Assembly at work. Members of the public are also invited to share in the life of the building. At its base, opening on to a piazza is a café overlooking the river; and from the entrance foyer, gentle ramps allow visitors to move up through the building. A flexible public space on the top floor – 'London's Living Room' – can be used for exhibitions or functions, while its riverside terrace allows visitors to enjoy unparalleled views out across the city.

1

2

3

Previous pages, left: Early concept sketch by Norman Foster. Right: View from the entrance foyer looking directly up through the spiralling ramp that forms the main public route through the building.

1-3. Views from the ramp as it winds around the London Assembly chamber, the foyer, and atrium respectively.

4. Cross-section through the elevated Assembly room, office floors, and the top-floor reception space – London's Living Room.

5. Sketch by Norman Foster, exploring the building's relationship with the riverside embankment.

6. In this sketch, Norman Foster examines the profile of the glazed 'flask' at the front of the building, which holds the Assembly chamber and public circulation ramp.

7. The building seen at night from the Tower of London.

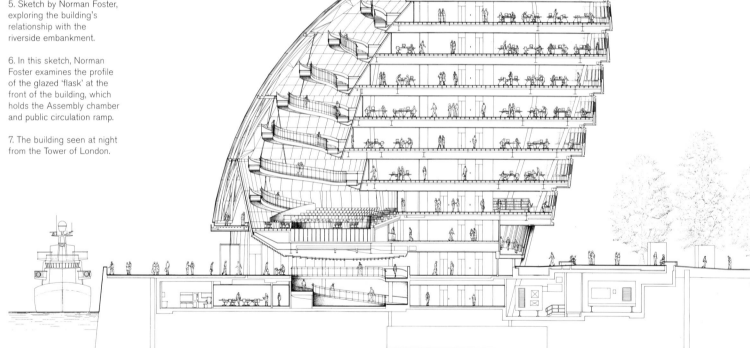
4

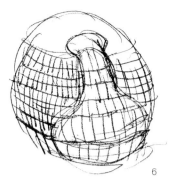

5

6

7

Microelectronic Park
Duisburg, Germany 1988–1996

Given the trend towards clean and quiet manufacturing industries, the potential exists to create new kinds of neighbourhoods, which integrate places to live, work and play. In 1988 a masterplan was established to integrate new technology companies – which are replacing the old heavy industries of the Ruhr heartland – within a residential district of Duisburg. The first of the practice's German projects to be realised, Duisburg brought with it new attitudes towards energy and ecology that would inform a range of schemes developed during the 1990s.

The masterplan creates a landscaped public park and three new buildings. The focal point of the development is the Telematic Centre. Circular in form, with offices arranged around a full-height atrium, it houses the management centre for the entire complex and provides space for small and medium-sized companies. The forum at the heart of the building provides a public space for exhibitions, conferences and musical performances, together with a restaurant and bar. The largest building on the site, the Microelectronic Centre provides multi-use flexible accommodation, such as laboratories, production areas, classrooms, offices and meeting rooms. Within an overall climatic envelope, three fingers of accommodation are articulated by two glazed atria, which create a sheltered buffer zone for exhibitions and cafés. A variety of passive cooling and shading devices are employed to minimise energy consumption.

The Business Promotion Centre takes this strategy a stage further. Its multi-layered outer skin is so thermally efficient that no heating is required, even in the coldest winter. In addition, the building generates and harvests its own energy, burning natural gas to produce electricity by means of a co-generator. The by-product of this process – heat that would normally be wasted – passes through an absorption cooling plant to produce chilled water. Instead of conventional air conditioning, dramatic temperature drops are achieved by distributing this water through miniaturised pipes embedded in the structure in a system similar to the fins on a car radiator. This is not only an ecologically responsible solution: in fact the developer makes a significant annual profit from energy management.

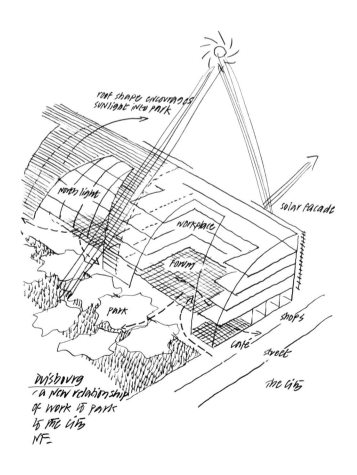

roof shape encourages sunlight into park

north light

solar facade

workplace

forum

park

shops

café

street

the city

Duisburg
– a new relationship
of work to park
to the city
NF–

1

2

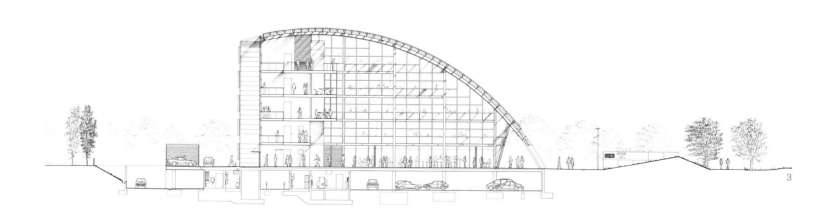

3

4

5

6

7

Previous pages, left: Concept sketch of the Microelectronic Centre by Norman Foster. Right: One of the atria in the Microelectronic Centre.

1. A masterplan model of the Microelectronic Park showing the integration of new technology companies and the creation of a new public garden within an established residential district.

2. Looking out across the park from the entrance to the Microelectronic Centre.

3. Cross-section through the Microelectronic Centre.

4, 5. The terraced upper level of the Business Promotion Centre.

6. Daylight floods into the Telematic Centre through its glazed full-height atrium.

7. The curving triple-glazed skin of the Business Promotion Centre.

8. Cross-section though the Telematic Centre.

9. Cross-section though the Business Promotion Centre.

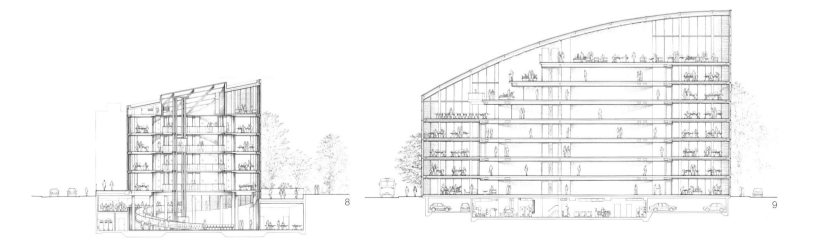

8

9

Inner Harbour Masterplan
Duisburg, Germany 1991–2003

Duisburg, in the heart of the Ruhr valley, is a city in the process of reinventing itself following the decline of its traditional heavy industries. In 1991 an international competition was held to establish a masterplan for the urban renewal of the Inner Harbour – the largest inland harbour in the world. It provided an opportunity to test, at a larger scale, ideas about mixed use and sustainability then being developed for the nearby Microelectronic Park.

The Inner Harbour occupies an 89-hectare site close to the city centre. The masterplan aims to draw the life of the city to the waterfront, combining new construction with the selective refurbishment of existing buildings to provide housing, offices and light-industrial uses together with a wide range of social and cultural amenities. A guiding principle was to create a flexible framework that would allow individual elements to be developed independently over time. New infrastructure and public amenities were put in place first to establish the harbour as an attractive place in which to live and work. A tree-lined promenade was created along the waterfront and new watercourses were excavated as armatures for new housing development. Arranged in five-storey terraces, the new housing blocks face on to the water or inland on to the streets where they enclose communal gardens. Future developments include the landmark Eurogate, situated on the harbour's northern bank. It will provide five levels of public facilities with terraces at the water's edge, together with parking for the entire harbour area. It incorporates a south-facing photovoltaic wall that will be able to supply the new building's energy needs or, with the advent of electric cars, recharge parked vehicles.

The practice's work in Duisburg demonstrates that, given the trend towards clean, quiet industries, the potential exists to reinvigorate declining urban areas and create sustainable communities for the future, which combine places to live, work and play. In place of the zoned and functionally segregated city of the twentieth century, it offers a new twenty-first century paradigm of mixed use in the inner city.

1

2

1. The Steiger Schwanentor – an embarkation point for Rhine pleasure cruises.

2. Many of the existing harbour buildings have been restored and put to new uses.

3. Sketches by Norman Foster, indicating how the city centre might be reconnected with the waterfront.

4. New 'canals' form armatures for residential development, by a variety of architects.

5, 6. A five-storey housing development by the Foster studio, which overlooks a secluded garden.

7. The masterplan offers a framework for development that will be implemented gradually over several years.

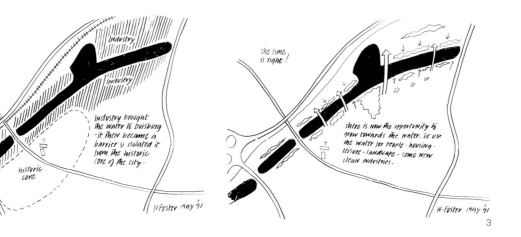

3

4

5

6

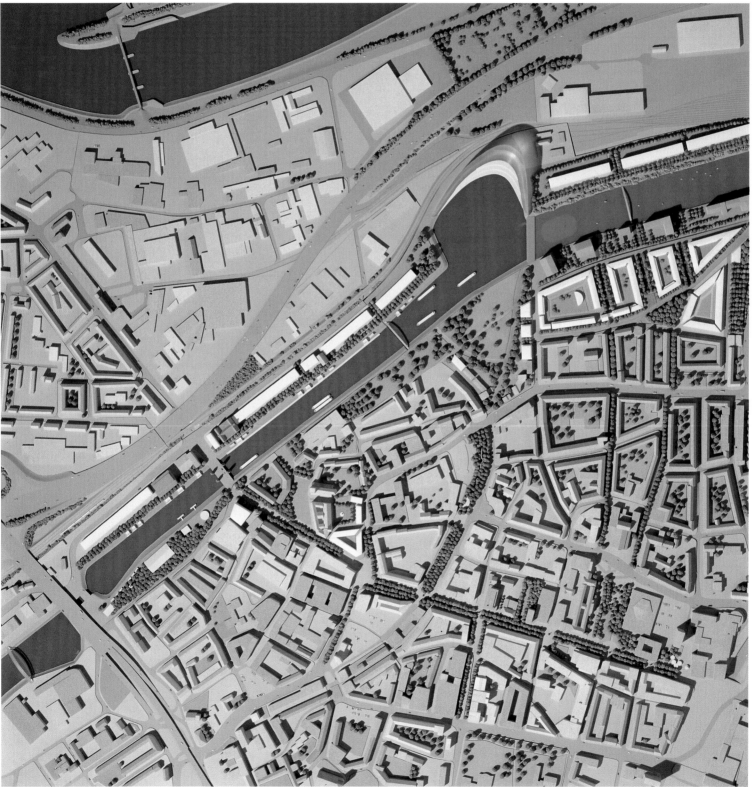
7

World Squares for All Masterplan
London, England 1996–2002

'World Squares for All' provides a detailed masterplan for the environmental improvement of Trafalgar Square, Parliament Square and Whitehall in Central London. It aims to improve pedestrian access and enjoyment of the area while enhancing the settings of its buildings, monuments and spaces. The masterplan area is familiar the world over. It contains a World Heritage Site – the Palace of Westminster and Westminster Abbey – and such national emblems as Nelson's Column and the Cenotaph. Yet as found by the masterplan team when this exercise began in 1996, the area was a largely unfriendly environment, dominated by motor vehicles, its squares reduced to traffic gyratories. There were few facilities for Londoners or the thousands of people who visit each year.

Cities such as Amsterdam, Barcelona and Paris have shown how the containment of traffic can contribute to the economic and cultural vitality of city centres. However, a project of this kind is a balancing act, which must promote genuinely integrated solutions. This holds true for any historical urban environment attempting to sustain contemporary activities. The first step, therefore, in formulating a strategy was to initiate an extensive programme of research. This involved major studies of traffic and pedestrian movement together with consultations with more than 180 public bodies and thousands of individuals. One of the tools utilised was a plan model of London developed by Space Syntax at University College, London, which demonstrated the potential for connectivity and pedestrian access. This research led to the development of two possible approaches, which were launched at a public exhibition in Whitehall in November 1997. The response was overwhelming support for change.

The first phase of the masterplan to be implemented focuses on Trafalgar Square. As part of a comprehensive programme of detailed improvements, the northern side of the square in front of the National Gallery has been closed to traffic and a broad pedestrian plaza created which connects via a broad flight of steps to the main body of the square. Although it is a discreet architectural intervention, its effect has been radical, transforming the experience of the square for the pedestrian and with none of the traffic chaos predicted by the critics.

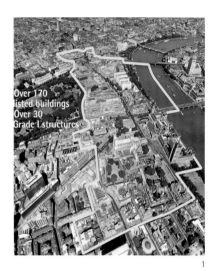

Over 170 listed buildings
Over 30 Grade I structures

1

1. An aerial view of the World Squares for All masterplan area, which runs from Trafalgar Square in the north through to Parliament Square and Great Peter Street in the south.

2. Norman Foster's sketch map of the same area, highlighting its landmarks and thoroughfares.

3, 4. The masterplan proposals followed a long period of research and public consultation, from a space-use analysis by Space Syntax to observational data collected in the field.

5, 6. Before and after views of Trafalgar Square, looking towards the National Gallery.

7, 8. Before and after images of Trafalgar Square looking towards St Martin-in-the-Fields. Instead of being isolated by traffic, the National Gallery and the square now form part of a unified spatial sequence.

9, 10. Parliament Square as it appears today, and a visualisation of how it might be transformed under the masterplan proposals. The southern side of the square, closest to Westminster Abbey, would be closed to traffic.

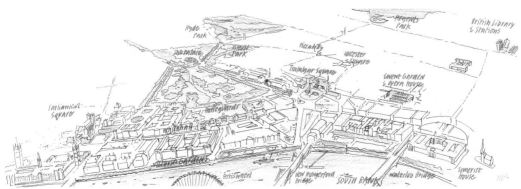

2

3

4

5

6

7

8

9

10

Trafalgar Square
London, England 2002–2003

The transformation of Trafalgar Square represents the first phase of the practice's 'World Squares for All' masterplan – the culmination of years of work to improve the urban environment in the heart of London. It is the result of a careful balancing act between the needs of traffic and pedestrians, the ceremonial and the everyday, the old and the new.

Trafalgar Square was laid out between 1840 and 1845 to the designs of Charles Barry. Dominated by Nelson's Column, the square is lined by fine buildings, including the Church of St Martin-in-the-Fields and South Africa House to the east, Canada House to the west, and the National Gallery and National Portrait Gallery to the north. Yet, despite its picture-postcard grandeur, by the mid-1990s the square had become choked by encircling traffic, the central area visited only by those willing to risk their own safety. There was an obvious need and support for change. Proposals were developed in the light of research that included consulting over 180 separate institutions and thousands of individuals. The most significant move was the closure of the north side of the Square to traffic and the creation of a broad new terrace, which forms an appropriate setting for the National Gallery and links it via a grand flight of steps to the great body of the square. Below the terrace, a new café with outdoor seating provides a much-needed visitor amenity.

Detailed improvements in the square and the adjacent streets include additional seating, improved lighting, consolidated traffic signage and a paving strategy that utilises visual and textural contrasts. The contemporary interventions continue the boldness of Barry's original design, using traditional materials – York stone, granite and bronze – in addition to salvaged granite bollards and slabs, which originally formed part of the north terrace retaining wall. Every aspect of the redesign improves universal access, including two new platform lifts and disabled lavatories. The cumulative effect has been to transform the life of the Square. A once forlorn and unfriendly urban environment has been restored as a truly civic space – one that can be enjoyed by Londoners and visitors alike.

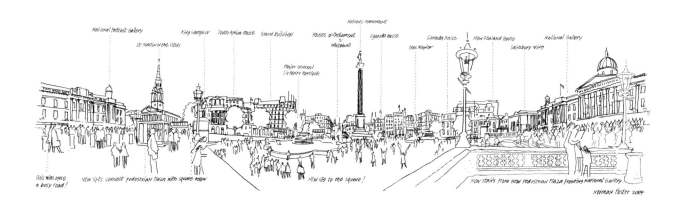

1

AS IT WAS BEFORE
PEDESTRIANS FORCED AROUND THE EDGE
ROADS TO ALL FOUR SIDES

2

3

4

5

Previous pages, left: Norman Foster's sketch of the transformed Trafalgar Square. Right: The newly completed square, opened up and immediately enlivened as a publicly accessible space.

1. Looking north towards the portico of the National Gallery. The broad flight of steps that now connects the square with the new terrace in front of the gallery has become a popular vantage point – a place to sit and enjoy the view.

2. Sketch by Norman Foster of the square as it was before – hemmed in on all four sides by traffic.

3-5. A series of mid-summer views of the new grand staircase leading down into the square.

6. Taken from the balcony of Canada House, on the western side of the square, this panorama shows how Trafalgar Square has been reinvented as a public space, freed from the traffic congestion that once made it inhospitable.

6

Millennium Bridge
London, England 1996–2000

The Millennium Bridge springs from a creative collaboration between architecture, art and engineering. Developed with sculptor Anthony Caro and engineers Arup, the commission resulted from an international competition. London's only dedicated pedestrian bridge and the first new Thames crossing since Tower Bridge in 1894, it links the City and St Paul's Cathedral to the north with the Globe Theatre and Tate Modern on Bankside. A key element in London's pedestrian infrastructure, it has created new routes into Southwark and encouraged new life on the embankment alongside St Paul's.

Structurally, the bridge pushes the boundaries of technology. Spanning 320 metres, it is a very shallow suspension bridge. Two Y-shaped armatures support eight cables that run along the sides of the 4-metre-wide deck, while steel transverse arms clamp onto the cables at 8-metre intervals to support the deck itself. This groundbreaking structure means that the cables never rise more than 2.3 metres above the deck, allowing pedestrians uninterrupted panoramic views up and down the river and preserving sight-lines from the surrounding buildings. As a result, the bridge has a uniquely thin profile, forming a slender arc across the water, and spanning the greatest possible distance with the minimum means. A thin ribbon of steel by day, it is illuminated to form a glowing blade of light at night.

The bridge opened in June 2000 and an astonishing 100,000 people crossed it during the first weekend. However, under this heavy traffic the bridge exhibited greater than expected lateral movement, and as a result it was temporarily closed. Extensive research and testing revealed that this movement was caused by synchronised pedestrian footfall – a phenomenon of which little was previously known in the engineering world. The solution was to fit dampers discreetly beneath the deck to mitigate movement. This proved highly successful and the research undertaken by the engineers has resulted in changes to the codes for bridge building worldwide.

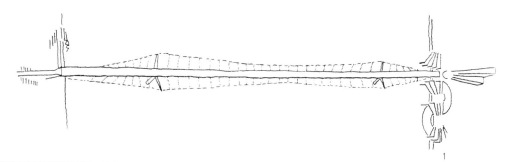

1

2

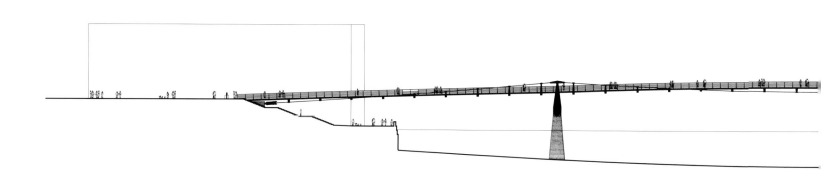

3

4

5

6

Previous pages, left: Norman Foster's early concept sketch for the bridge drew upon the importance of its axial relationship with St Paul's Cathedral. Right: Looking north across the bridge towards St Paul's and the distant towers of the Barbican.

1. In this plan study of the bridge by Norman Foster, the design of the southern end of the bridge is still being explored.

2-6. As the only dedicated pedestrian crossing on this section of the Thames, the Millennium Bridge is thronged with people throughout the day. Not only has it brought increasing numbers of visitors to St Paul's Cathedral and Tate Modern, it has transformed the economic fortunes of Bankside and a wider swathe of Southwark.

7. An elevation of the bridge running from north (left) to south. A very shallow suspension structure, it spans 320 metres from bank to bank.

Overleaf. The bridge's low-slung cables and arms allow pedestrians to enjoy uninterrupted views in either direction.

7

Millau Viaduct

Gorges du Tarn, France 1993–2004

Bridges are often considered to belong to the realm of the engineer rather than that of the architect. But the architecture of infrastructure has a powerful impact on the environment and the Millau Viaduct, designed in close collaboration with structural engineers, illustrates how the architect can play an integral role in the design of bridges. It follows the Millennium Bridge over the River Thames in expressing a fascination with the relationships between function, technology and aesthetics in a graceful structural form.

Located in southern France, the bridge connects the motorway networks of France and Spain, opening up a direct route from Paris to Barcelona. The bridge crosses the River Tarn, which runs through a spectacular gorge between two high plateaux. Interestingly, alternative readings of the topography suggested two possible structural approaches: to celebrate the act of crossing the river or to articulate the challenge of spanning the 2.5 kilometres from one plateau to the other in the most economical manner. Although historically the river was the geological generator of the landscape, it is very narrow at this point, and so it was the second reading that suggested the most appropriate structural solution.

A cable-stayed, masted structure, the bridge is delicate and transparent and has the optimum span between columns. Each of its sections spans 350 metres and its columns range in height from 75 metres to 235 metres (equivalent to the height of the Eiffel Tower), with the masts rising a further 90 metres above the road deck. To accommodate the expansion and contraction of the concrete deck, each column splits into two thinner, more flexible columns below the roadway, forming an A-frame above deck level. The tapered form of the columns both expresses their structural loads and minimises their profile in elevation. The bridge not only has a dramatic silhouette, but crucially, it also makes the minimum intervention in the landscape.

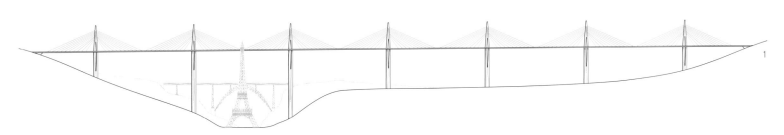

2

3

Previous pages, left:
Concept sketches by
Norman Foster arguing
for a visually light structure,
and emphasising how the
viaduct should be thought of
as spanning the whole valley
rather than simply the river.
Right: View looking west
downstream along the Tarn
and up towards the highest
of the viaduct's seven masts.

1. Scale comparison,
showing the Eiffel Tower
and Eiffel's Viaduc de
Garabit – two structural
engineering icons of the
nineteenth century – in
relation to the road deck,
which at its highest point
is 235 metres above
ground level.

2. The road deck hovers
dramatically above the
cloud line in the Tarn valley.

3. A detail of the viaduct's
aerodynamic edge screen.

4. A dramatic aerial view
of the viaduct. The wide
angle lens used in this
shot makes the structure
looked curved, though in
reality it crosses the Tarn
Gorge in a straight line to
establish a direct motorway
connection between
Paris and Barcelona.

4

Wind Turbine Generator
1993

Modern installations for non-polluting energy production have a dual responsibility to the environment, which can be measured both in terms of their ecology – how efficiently they perform – and in terms of their visual impact upon the landscape. This new generation of wind turbines, developed with the German power company Enercon, addresses both these issues, harmonising the practice's long-standing interest in developing sustainable forms of energy generation with its broader commitment to exemplary design.

The clarity of the turbine's design developed through a singular approach to its three principal components, with rotor spinner, ring generator and tower all formed through natural paraboloid geometries. Allied to this formal consistency, the turbine's engineering is both innovative and highly efficient since the generator is driven directly by its 32 metre long rotor blades, avoiding the need for a gearbox. Maintenance problems and noise pollution usually associated with turbine gearboxes are therefore avoided. Instead, kinetic energy from the wind is converted directly into regulated electrical current – a far more efficient solution. With an individual power rating of up to 2 megawatts, the resulting turbine can generate enough clean, renewable energy to supply 1,600 homes.

The turbine's blades are constructed from lightweight glass fibre and epoxy composite – like the wings of a sailplane – while the tower is formed from prefabricated steel units that are light enough to be easily transported and rapidly assembled. Variable rotor speed and blade-pitch adjustment ensure that power yield is maximised, while upturned 'winglets' at the blade tips – inspired by precedents in the aerospace industry – reduce aerodynamic noise and allow the turbine to perform efficiently at lower rotor speeds, a factor that helps to create a visually calming effect. The tapering of the 100 metre tower improves the transition of dynamic loads to ground level and also means that the turbine occupies less ground area than conventional turbines of equivalent power output. Taken together, these features enhance the turbine's integration within the landscape, whether that is in land-based wind farms or in offshore installations.

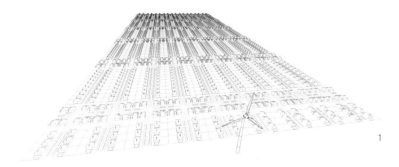

1

5

2   3   4

1. A single turbine can supply clean, renewable energy to 1,600 homes.

2, 3. A typical turbine being assembled in the Enercon workshops in Germany.

4. Looking into a nearly completed turbine nacelle.

5. A visualisation of an off-shore installation – the most environmentally friendly way of siting wind turbines.

Motor Yacht *Izanami*

1991–1993

The design of most sea-going vessels – from floating 'gin palaces' to cross-Channel ferries – tends to split responsibilities, with a naval architect working on the exterior and hull, while the superstructure and interior are completed by a designer. The results are often top-heavy, with interiors that are the reverse of shipshape. In contrast, the development of this 58.5-metre private yacht saw architects and engineers working closely together – just as they would on the design of a building. Inspired by naval vessels, in which functional efficiency takes precedence over styling, *Izanami* is as sleek and fast as a patrol boat, but with open decks and interiors suggestive of a traditional sailing yacht.

The hull is the largest to be built in aluminium to date, with hull and superstructure together forming a semi-monocoque construction of welded skin, frames and longitudinal stiffeners. The form of the superstructure represents a radical departure from tradition. It is articulated as three elements – suggesting the head, thorax and abdomen of an insect – which define the owner's cabin, the crew's quarters and the wheelhouse respectively. The structure is formed from large plates, some of which rise through the full two levels. Most of these apparently flat panels were, in fact, rolled to create a slight convex curve. This not only increased their rigidity, but also – like entasis on a Classical entablature – helped to avoid the concave appearance sometimes encountered when flat planes meet at an angle. Picture windows in these planes allow generous views from the main cabin and upper-deck spaces, and the interiors focus on high-quality craftsmanship and appropriate materials, with equally comfortable accommodation provided for passengers and crew.

Izanami has transatlantic and worldwide cruising capabilities and is built to German Lloyd's certification and ABS standards. It is powered by two MTU diesel engines rated at 4,800 horsepower and has a design speed of 30 knots, although 34 knots was achieved during sea trials. That is equivalent to the speed of sleek transatlantic liners of the past, and almost twice that possible using a conventional displacement hull of the same size. In Norman Foster's phrase, *Izanami* is 'a Ferrari of the water'.

1

2

1-2. Two views of the owner's suite – looking in from the main deck, and a corner of the saloon.

3. Starboard elevation showing *Izanami*'s full 58.5 metre length.

Right: *Izanami* photographed during sea trials in the North Sea. The vessel is immediately distinguished by its planar wheelhouse and sleek, almost military appearance.

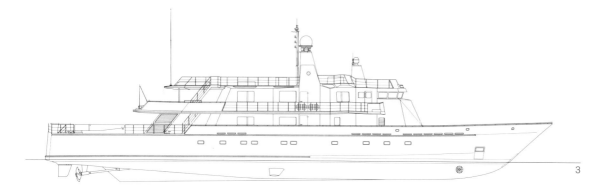

3

Repsol Service Stations

Spain 1997

When the Spanish oil and gas company Repsol commissioned the practice to design a new service station system, the challenge was to update the company's distinctive roadside identity while delivering a highly flexible solution capable of adaptation to suit the more than 200 sites planned around Spain.

The result is a modular canopy system in the Repsol signature colours of red, white and orange. Clusters of these structures form overlapping 'umbrellas' sheltering each station forecourt. The canopy head is an inverted pyramid, its crisp edges balanced by the less emphatic lines of the cladding. The umbrellas vary in number, height and in the degree of overlap between them, according to the size and specifics of each site. The associated shop unit, car wash, petrol pumps and signage elements all belong to a related family of pure, box-like forms. Together, this 'kit of parts' provides the maximum flexibility in planning and can respond to virtually any site configuration. All these lightweight elements are factory made and easily transported and installed on site, providing cost benefits while ensuring consistently high quality standards and rapid delivery.

The canopies are arranged according to a predetermined sequence, which ensures that a red one is always the tallest. This brightly coloured combination creates a strong three-dimensional image. Even from the air, Repsol's identity is clearly announced. On the road, the stations are identifiable from a distance and are vivid and inviting when approached.

1

3

2

1. Norman Foster's sketch study explores the visual impact of the new service station system from the perspective of a passing motorist.

2, 3. Details of a typical station forecourt seen at night. The 'umbrellas' are finished in Repsol's signature colours of red, orange and white.

Furniture

From its earliest days the practice has designed furniture systems and fixtures in order to give greater cohesion to particular building projects. Often proprietary products have been neither suitable nor flexible enough for a defined need, and so new designs have been developed. The Tabula system is typical of this approach. Originally developed for use in the Carré d'Art in Nîmes to suit many different purposes, including library tables, benches and display cases, it is now marketed by Tecno. The structure comprises two aluminium extrusions, one for the legs and one for the top. The inherent flexibility of Tabula means that tables or benches of almost any dimensions can be produced; and because the top is not structural, any surface material can be specified.

The design of furniture has also developed as a discrete activity within the Foster studio and products are designed for major manufacturers, unrelated to specific building commissions. A recent example, the Foster 500 series armchair, produced by Walter Knoll, is a system based on a dimensional module that can be configured to create a variety of spatial arrangements. Another, the A900 range of seating for Thonet, was developed in response to the need for a family of chairs that could be used throughout a building, in both interior and exterior spaces. The solution is based on a 'kit-of-parts' approach whereby a small number of components can create a large number of products: the frame in this case comprises only three aluminium extrusions and two castings, but generates nine chair types.

A similar approach, of marrying a high degree of flexibility with tight manufacturing discipline, informed the design of the Kite! chair, which was originally commissioned by Tecno to accompany the Nomos range of desks. The office environment has moved towards greater informality in working patterns and more flexibility for personal expression, and Kite! reflects these changes. Like a kite, it comprises an efficiently engineered frame over which soft fabrics can be stretched. By specifying different combinations of upholstery and paint colours for the frame and seat back, the mood and appearance of the chair can be changed dramatically.

1

2

3

4

5

6

7. Kite! is a flexible seating system, designed to complement the Nomos table and desk, and can be specified in a wide range of finishes and colours.

8. This early sketch by Norman Foster highlights the associations that gave the chair its name.

7

1. The Tabula Bench as used in the Carré d'Art.

2. The Tabula Table in Cacharel's rue Tronchet menswear shop.

3. The Foster 500 series armchair was developed for Walter Knoll.

4. A plastic-seated chair from the A900 range of chairs for Thonet.

5, 6. Airline seating system for Vitra.

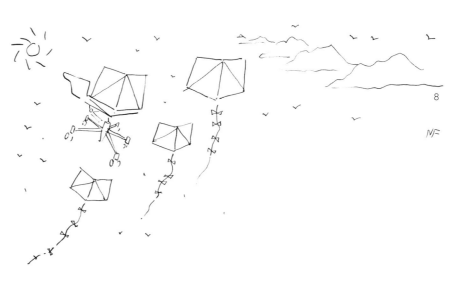

8

KITE!

221

Nomos Table and Desking System

1985–1987

Office furniture, like the office itself, must be adaptable to changing patterns of work. The Nomos concept is rooted in an earlier foray into furniture design. In 1981, when the practice expanded into a new studio, no existing furniture system could provide tables that were adjustable for meetings, drafting or display. The outcome was a custom-designed table, made in a small production run by a sympathetic workshop (modified versions of which were used in the reception areas, offices and restaurant of the Renault Distribution Centre in Swindon). The Italian furniture manufacturer Tecno subsequently commissioned the practice to develop the design, requiring a system that could optimise floor space, accommodate cabling, and be easily reconfigured. Launched in 1987, the Nomos range has been in production ever since.

The concept of Nomos (a Greek word meaning 'fair distribution') is based on the relationship between the users and the space they occupy. At the heart of the design is a flexible kit of precision-engineered components that can be combined to create miniature working environments for individuals or groups. The starting point is the spine, to which are added legs, feet, supports, work surfaces and superstructures, while a vertebra-like conduit carries cabling. Characterised by its splayed feet – an undercarriage more evocative of motion than the legs of a traditional table – some critics have suggested references to the lunar landing module, or to the grasshopper with its slim body and gangly legs. Utilising this highly stable frame, the system can accommodate shelves, storage, screens, lighting and signage – an assembly governed by the ergonomics of the human body, seated or standing.

In 1999 Tecno commissioned a new table to mark the millennium. The rectangular and circular-topped versions are established favourites, but in the quest for another classic shape, smooth curves were investigated to encourage better eye contact across the table's length, making it feel more friendly. Heightening this more informal approach, the primary frame is also expressed in a vivid palette – red, yellow or blue – with other elements in bright chrome, while a more classical option has a chrome frame with the secondary elements in black.

1

2

222

1. Norman Foster's concept sketch for Nomos, conceived as a flexible office desking system.

2. The Nomos desking system and Kite! chair used together.

3-6. Like a bicycle, the Nomos table's frame can be specified in a variety of colour options.

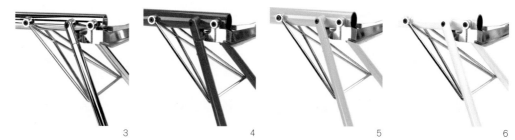

3   4   5   6

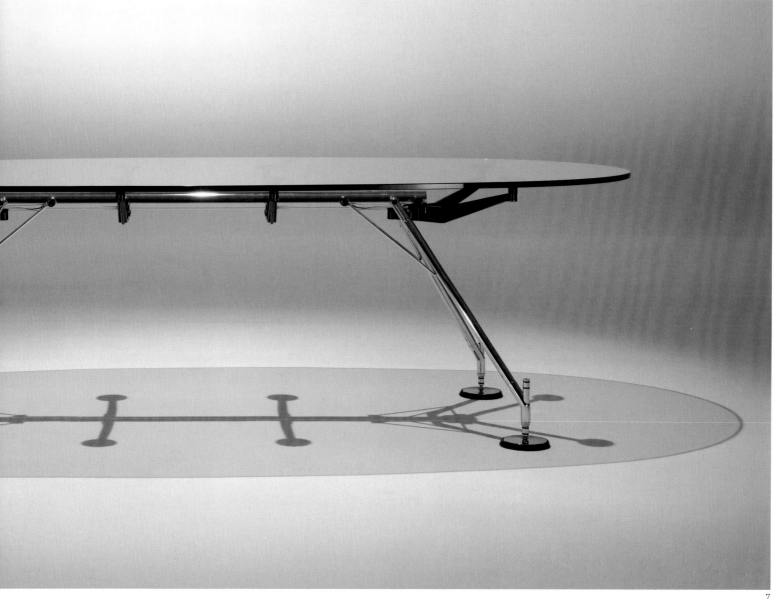

7

7. Commissioned to celebrate the Millennium, the Nomos 2000 table has a distinctive oval top, which encourages better eye contact across its length and makes it ideal for use as a dining or boardroom table.

8. A plan view of the assembled Nomos table frame.

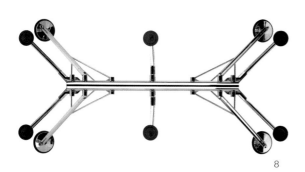

8

223

Product Design

The smallest details of daily life, from the shape of a door handle to the finish of a breakfast tray, are often taken for granted, but it is with these small elements that we have the most direct contact. These objects are like architecture in miniature: they must be functional but also pleasing to use, possessing good ergonomic, aesthetic and tactile qualities. The practice has an established team of industrial designers, working on items ranging from tableware to electronic goods, both for specific building projects and for manufacture.

Bathroom suites normally consist only of 'ceramic' items, requiring people to match taps, accessories and other elements as best they can. The practice has a holistic approach to the design of interiors and believes this separation to be artificial. It has collaborated with two German companies – Duravit and Hoesch – to design a bathroom suite with a complementary range of sanitaryware, furniture, taps and accessories, which provides cohesive interiors for domestic and commercial bathrooms. Similarly, in the design of the Library Storage System for Acerbis, a key criterion was the ability to integrate a multitude of accessories, including computer shelves and CD and video racks, together with drawers and sliding doors for the domestic market.

At a smaller scale, the NF 95 Door Handle for the Italian manufacturer Fusital was partly inspired by the bird-shaped form of a medieval door handle in Magdeburg Cathedral, and also by the design of penknives, in which blades and mechanism are sandwiched between grips in a variety of materials. The handle consists of a metal plate held between grips contoured to the shape of the hand. The system combines the economic benefits of mass production with the flexibility of being able to specify a range of materials – metal, plastic, wood, rubber or leather – to suit individual projects. That approach was explored again for Alessi, which is renowned for its investment in new manufacturing processes. Here, laser-cutting technology was the starting point for a family of objects, starting with a breakfast tray, which is fabricated from folded aluminium sheet and is available in a variety of finishes.

3

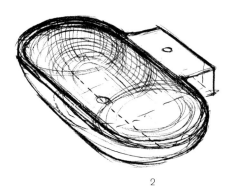

4

1

2

5

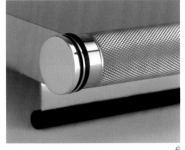

6

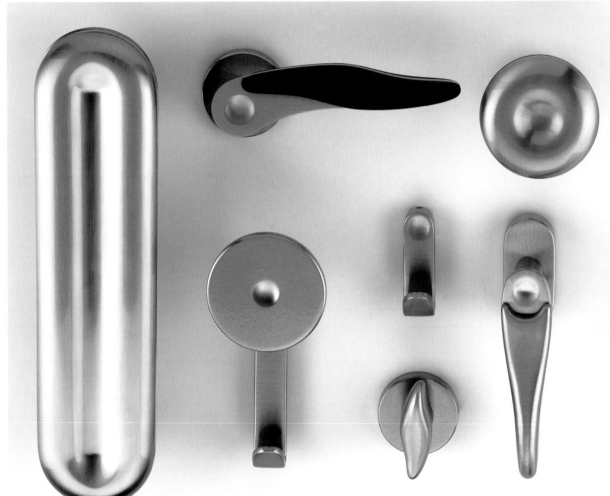

1. A bidet and toilet from the Bathroom Foster series.

2. Norman Foster's design study for a washbasin, which forms part of the same Bathroom Foster series.

3. A detail of the Library Storage System developed for Acerbis.

4. The shelving system in use at the Cambridge Law Faculty Library.

5, 6. Details of the laser-cut aluminium breakfast tray designed for Alessi.

7, 8. The NF 95 Door Handle shown with its family of related objects, and in some of its many 'sandwiched' finishes.

9. One of Norman Foster's early design sketches, indicating the range of materials in which the door handle can be specified.

7

8

wood

leather
plastic

metal
dull/shiny
glass

rubber
plastic

9

Asprey Shops
London, England and New York, USA 2001–2004

Asprey is a long-established, quintessentially British, luxury goods brand with a worldwide reputation. The company's new owners sought to expand the brand in a way that would build on the best of Asprey's heritage, while projecting a bold vision for the future. They commissioned two separate projects on two of the most famous shopping streets in the world – New Bond Street in Mayfair and Fifth Avenue in Manhattan – with a mandate to promote the timelessness, values and craftsmanship associated with Asprey's goods through contemporary design.

Asprey has been based in New Bond Street since 1846. However, over the years, behind its original premises the company had expanded to occupy five listed buildings. The challenge was to link this disparate group to create a coherent sequence of retail spaces, together with associated offices and workshops. The back of these buildings was an undiscovered world. By clearing previous roof structures, restoring the Georgian facades, and covering the space with a delicate steel and glass roof, a new courtyard was created at the heart of the store. Here the complex is made legible with a sweeping spiral stair that connects levels and offers changing perspectives of the old and the new. The interiors are characterised by a limited palette of rich materials – Venetian plaster, stone, hardwood and leather – and products are displayed in purpose-designed bronze-framed display cases.

Asprey's New York store occupies three floors alongside the main entrance to the Trump Tower. The facade, with its strong vertical emphasis, is a contemporary reinterpretation of Asprey's iconic London shopfront. Brilliant white lacquered recesses behind the glass contrast with the dividing black band of the company's sign. The entrance is flanked by sleek, curved glass windows, which echo bow-fronted Victorian shops, but are of a scale unimaginable in a nineteenth-century street. Inside, luxury and authentic British style are the keynotes. The entrance opens into a three-storey atrium that expresses a mix of tradition and modernity. The pale floors of British limestone and Wilton carpet, the grand marble staircases with their glass balustrades and bronze handrails, and the translucent lifts together create a feeling of ease, opulence, light and space.

1

2

3

Previous pages, left: Norman Foster's sketch for the New York storefront. Right: Detail of the main entrance to the Fifth Avenue store.

1. The Fifth Avenue store seen from 57th Street.

2-4. The second and third floors of the Fifth Avenue store and the broad limestone staircase that connects them.

5, 6. Custom-designed display cabinets seen in the ladies fashion and silverware departments in the New Bond Street shop.

7, 8. Asprey's London shop comprises five historical buildings. A newly roofed courtyard and spiral staircase provide points of continuity.

9. Norman Foster's sketch of the staircase and courtyard.

10. The restored New Bond Street shopfront.

11. Norman Foster's sketch indicates the changes made to the original shopfront.

4

5

6

7

8

NF 9

10

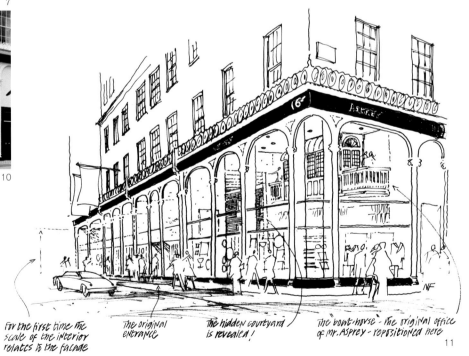

For the first time the scale of the interior relates to the facade

The original entrance

The hidden courtyard is revealed!

The "boat-house" - the original office of Mr. Asprey - repositioned here

NF 11

House in Kawana

Japan 1987–1992

The design of a house, perhaps more than any other building type, brings together the client and the architect in a unique and interdependent relationship. The Kawana house, with its adjoining guesthouse, is one of several projects undertaken with the same client over a number of years. Early discussions focused on traditional Japanese architecture and were latterly distilled into a modern response. The result is a fusion of two traditions: the Japanese love of harmony and respect for nature and the Western refinement of a dematerialised architecture of steel and glass.

Sited on a dramatic stretch of volcanic coastline where long, inaccessible fingers of lava jut into Sagami Bay, the change in levels across the site and the views out to sea are central to the project's design. Set on a raised platform, the house is positioned so that the main living areas have uninterrupted views out to sea. Services and storage areas are arranged around the perimeter, allowing the central accommodation to be configured as one continuous, open and flowing space. The framed structure creates seven rectangular bays defining the main spaces. These toplit spaces can be subdivided by means of sliding screens, while adjustable louvres control the quality of natural light through the glazed roof. Full-height glazed sliding doors line the perimeter, allowing the living spaces to open out on to adjoining terraces, thus eroding divisions between inside and out. The surrounding landscape combines new elements with existing features. Mature trees line the cliff top, while newly planted camphor trees provide privacy from the road. Stone lanterns, some dating from the eighth century, are positioned around the house and a small teahouse of the late Edo period, brought from Shimane Prefecture, completes the overall composition.

As a precursor to several future projects for the same client, including most recently the Kamakura house, the Kawana house laid the foundations for an enduring relationship that has enabled a profound exploration of traditional Japanese architecture in a modern context. The enlightened and intrepid spirit of this body of work has spearheaded an intense and expansive investigation – an attempt to conceive a humane architecture rooted in essential traditions from East and West.

1

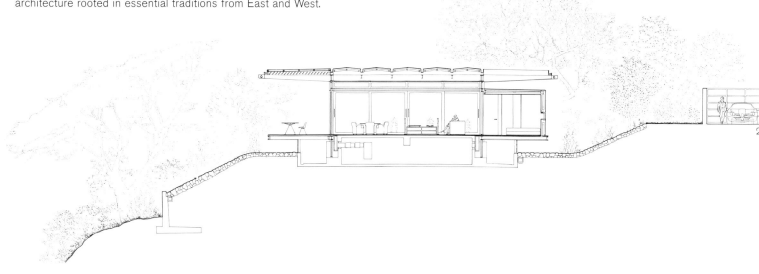

2

1. View of the south-facing terrace and pool of the guesthouse, built around a mature cherry tree.

2. Cross-section through the guesthouse. Like the main house, the toplit living space opens out on to a shaded terrace, with long views out to sea.

3

4

5

6

3. Looking across the garden towards the main house.

4. The living space in the main house can be opened up to form a single volume, or subdivided by means of sliding screens.

5. The master bedroom in the main house.

6. The vista from the master bedroom along the length of the living space.

House in Corsica
France 1990–1993

Poised on the southern tip of Corsica, the location for this house is spectacular – a dramatic, south-facing site high above a rocky bay and commanding long views out to sea. The client is an imaginative patron and the brief was ambitious – living and dining spaces, together with seven bedrooms, a study, and guest and staff accommodation. The challenges of brief and site were compounded by strict planning regulations, which stipulated that the house should be built of timber, in keeping with its neighbours.

Approached from the landward side, the house is discreet, dug into the contours of the site and sheltered by a monopitch roof that spreads out like a protective bird's wing. Organised on a single level, the house is wedge-shaped in both plan and section. Ancillary functions are confined to the northern edge of the plan, where the roof is lowest, while the grander communal spaces, main bedrooms and study are placed on the southern side to take advantage of the soaring double-height volume created by the monopitch as it rises. Closed to the north, the house opens up dramatically to the south to take advantage of the light and breathtaking views. The plan is bisected on the short cross axis by a circulation core, which separates the children's bedrooms from the communal spaces and extends northwards to create a ceremonial sequence of approach and entry. On the southern side, this route culminates in a broad shaded terrace.

Glazed on three sides, with sliding doors that dematerialise the boundary between house and terrace, the outdoors becomes a natural and fluid extension of the interior, in the Mediterranean tradition. Responding to the Spérone context, the house is timber-framed. The most prominent structural members are the long, laminated beams that support the cedar shingle roof. These tapering, rib-like beams extend on the southern side to form a brise-soleil canopy that attenuates the entire roof into a supple, aerodynamic curve.

1

2

1. Looking out to sea over the rising plane of the roof.

2. The view out from the master bedroom across the timber deck of the swimming pool.

3. A cross-section through the house and the steps that lead down from the arrival level.

Right: The timber roof structure cantilevers out to shade the terrace that lines the southern facade.

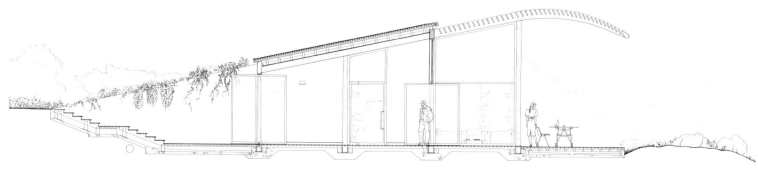

3

House in Kamakura
Japan 2000–2004

Designed for a prominent collector of Buddhist art, this house was conceived as a modern retreat with distinctly Japanese influences. Located in a quiet residential neighbourhood of Kamakura, a coastal town one hour south of Tokyo, the house occupies a site with rich historical associations. These include a Shinto shrine and caves, carved by hand into the cliff-face, which formed part of an eleventh-century workshop for crafting samurai swords. The house is one of three buildings on the site alongside a pavilion, with a gallery for displaying art works, a large function space, and specialised storage. The overall composition ties these buildings together in a harmonious arrangement, informed by the Japanese belief that nature is at its most beautiful when considered in relation to the man-made.

A series of parallel structural walls organises the interior spaces of all three buildings, which are further articulated by perpendicular infill walls that carry the service functions. Special attention has been paid to the subtle use of colour throughout the interiors, with muted tones and dark grey ceilings that add a degree of intimacy. The design team developed a number of specialised materials for the project. The primary walls are clad with a custom-manufactured reconstructed stone, while glass blocks made from recycled television tubes provide diffuse light. Hand-sculpted terrazzo elements are used throughout. The floor surfaces are covered in part with antique Chinese tiles, and the indoor pool is finished in glazed volcanic stone tiles.

The house is planned around the rugged landscape and focuses on a mature cherry tree. Circulation through the building is organised around a sequence of views that progressively move from darkened to fully lit rooms, revealing the house's natural surroundings and the client's extensive antique and modern art collection. A comprehensive integrated lighting system, which includes fibre-optic installations, dedicated spotlights, and naturally backlit glass blocks, further emphasises major individual art works. The attention to the play of light and shadow, created through a combination of materials and artificial and natural light, is fundamental to the design of the house and evokes the quietude of traditional Japanese architecture.

1

2

1. View from the first floor terrace looking towards the Shinto shrine.

2. A night-time view into the living room.

3. East-west cross-section, from the Shinto shrine to the left, down through the pavilion and main house.

4. A view of the Shinto shrine, which occupies an elevated position at the rear of the house.

5. Looking towards the house across the terraced garden.

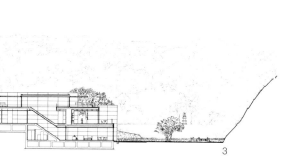

3

6. View across the gardens towards the indoor pool and bedroom areas of the house.

7. Looking down towards the house from the shrine, with Kamakura and the coast in the far distance.

4

5

6

7

Riverside Apartments and Studio
London, England 1986–1990

Riverside is a pioneering example of a building that combines living and working in one location. There are few contemporary examples of this idea in Britain, and where they exist they break with traditional planning guidelines, which typically create separate zones for residential, commercial and industrial uses. Located on the south bank of the Thames, close to Albert Bridge, the site previously existed only as a scene of urban dereliction. The strategy for its renewal involved creating a new network of pedestrian routes and the rehabilitation of the adjacent dock. The effect has been to make this stretch of the riverside accessible to the public and to create connections to neighbouring streets, where a new café culture has evolved.

The building itself has eight storeys, with Foster and Partners' studio occupying the lower three levels and apartments located on the upper floors, all of which share spectacular views of the river. A private courtyard provides separate access and security for those who live in the building, while at the rear of the site a two-storey pavilion accommodates additional studio space and a print shop. The main studio, at first-floor level, is entered via steps through a toplit galleried space and forms a 60-metre-long, double-height volume. Along its southern edge a mezzanine contains meeting and presentation spaces together with a library and image bank, while below is a state-of-the-art model shop.

Everyone in the studio, whatever their job description, has a place at one of the long work benches; the arrangement is very fluid with no division between design and production. Open twenty-four hours a day, seven days a week, the building is animated by its young and cosmopolitan staff (the average age is about thirty and as many languages are spoken). Most offices keep visitors at arm's length. The Foster studio, by contrast, is completely open. Visitors can enjoy the bar – the social focus of the office – while meetings, whether formal or informal, occur in the midst of the creative process itself.

1

2

3

1. The view from one of the upper level apartments.

2. Approaching the building through the rejuvenated dock area to the south.

3. Cross-section showing the main riverside building with its galleried entrance, and the pavilion to the right.

4. The building seen from Chelsea Embankment.

Albion Riverside

London, England 1999–2003

The development of Albion Wharf reinforces a growing new community on the south bank of the Thames, alongside the Foster studio between Battersea and Albert Bridges. A mixed-use development, its ingredients are designed to promote a lively urban quarter where people can live, work and enjoy life in the heart of the city. The scheme comprises three separate buildings linked by new public spaces and routes. Shops, business spaces, cafés and leisure facilities are grouped at ground level, with parking below and residences, including low-cost housing, above.

The principal building on the waterfront is eleven storeys high. Its massing is designed to respect the heights of neighbouring buildings and to frame the view of the river from the opposite bank. Arcing back from the water's edge, the building forms an asymmetrical crescent to create a public space alongside the river walk. The facades are principally of glass, the faceted panels sparkling according to prevailing light conditions and changing viewpoints. Facing the river, curved balconies with clear glass balustrades are accessed through full-height sliding glazed panels, which allow the apartments to open out on to the water. The strong horizontal line of the balconies reinforces a sense of visual order, allowing the clutter of inhabitation to proliferate but not dominate. The southern facade, in contrast, is veiled, clad in a fine net of aluminium rods, and pierced by recessed balconies and windows. The roof continues the building's curving form, wrapping over and around in a single sweep.

A typical floor in the main building contains twenty-six apartments, arranged around four service cores. In total there are 183 apartments, ranging from one to four bedrooms, and twelve duplex penthouses. The apartments are designed to allow a high degree of flexibility. Sliding partitions permit spaces to be opened up or divided for different uses, while balconies offer an extension of living spaces and are deep enough for outdoor dining. The apartments are air-conditioned, with independent central heating, and pre-wired for smart technology, enabling main services to be controlled remotely, either on the internet or by mobile phone.

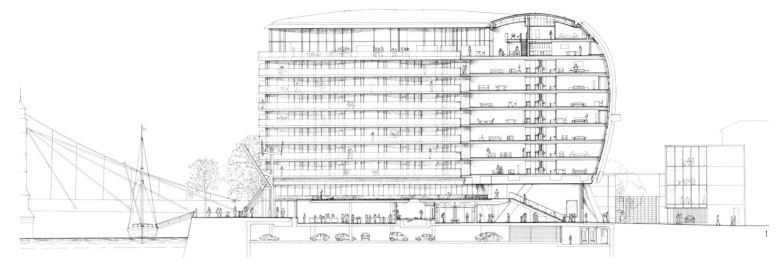

1

Previous pages, left: Design sketch by Norman Foster. Right: The building seen at low tide from Albert Bridge. The snaking balconies catch the light and optimise views.

1. Cross-section through the building from the riverside walk and Albert Bridge on the left, to Hester Road on the right. Nine apartment floors are arranged above galleries and commercial spaces at street level.

2. Looking up at the fluid form of the northern facade. Balconies with glazed balustrades run continuously along the river frontage.

3. A small private garden for residents is laid out on the roof of the commercial accommodation – a detail reminiscent of the Willis Faber building.

4. Looking east along the landscaped riverside walkway – one of the few publicly-accessible riverside spaces in the capital.

4

Chesa Futura
St Moritz, Switzerland 2000–2002

The Chesa Futura apartment building in the Engadin Valley fuses
state-of-the-art computer design tools with centuries-old construction
techniques to create an environmentally sensitive building. Although
its form is novel, the building is framed and clad in timber – one of the
oldest and most sustainable building materials. In Switzerland, building in
timber is particularly appropriate in that it follows indigenous architectural
traditions. The larch shingles will respond naturally to exposure to the
elements, changing colour slowly over time to a silver-grey, and will last
for a hundred years without the need for maintenance. Furthermore,
timber is a renewable resource; the trees absorb carbon dioxide as they
grow; felling older trees reinforces the foresting practice of harvesting
to encourage regeneration; and by using locally cut timber, little energy
is consumed in its transportation.

The building consists of three storeys of apartments and an
underground level for car parking, plant and storage. Although small,
the site is spectacularly located on the edge of a slope, looking down
over the village of St Moritz towards the lake. Responding to this location
and to local weather patterns, the building's bubble-like form allows
windows and balconies on the southern side to open up to the sunlight
and panoramic views, while the colder, north facade is more closed,
punctuated with deep window openings in the Engadin tradition. In
Switzerland, where snow lies on the ground for many months of the
year, there is a long tradition of elevating buildings to avoid the danger
of wood rotting due to prolonged exposure to moisture. That tradition
is reinterpreted here by raising the building on eight pilotis and allowing
the ground plane to continue untouched beneath it – a move that has
the added advantage of allowing the apartments to enjoy views that
would otherwise be denied.

Taken overall, Chesa Futura (literally, 'house of the future') might be
regarded as a mini manifesto for architecture, not just here but in other
parts of the world. Contrary to the pattern of sprawl that disfigures the
edges of so many expanding communities, it shows how new buildings
can be inserted into the existing grain at increased densities, while
sustaining indigenous building techniques and preserving the natural
environment.

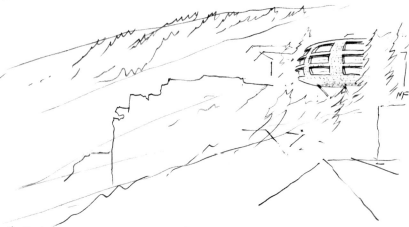

lightly touching down ... perched on the slope ...

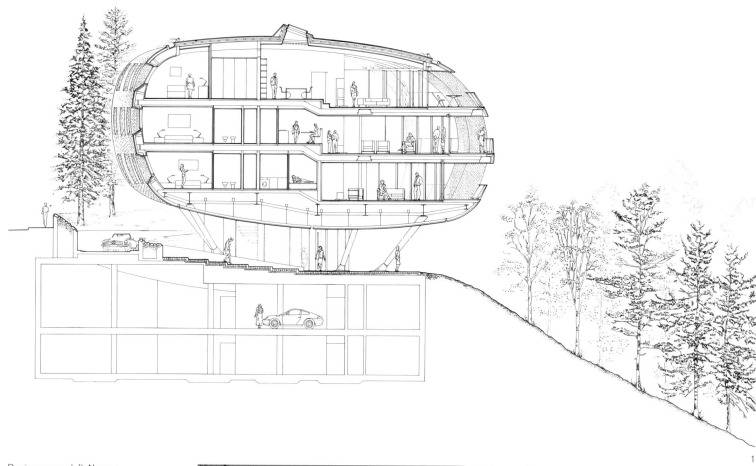

1

Previous pages, left: Norman Foster's sketch emphasises how the building 'touches down lightly'. Right: Detail of the southern facade with its recessed balconies.

1. Cross-section through the apartments. The building is elevated above two levels of subterranean parking.

2. The building seen from the west.

3. Seen from higher up the mountain, the building nestles into the dense fabric of St Moritz.

4. Looking out across St Moritz from one of the deeply recessed balconies.

5, 6. Extracts from a series of sketches by Norman Foster depicting the building in its context.

Overleaf: The building takes its place within St Moritz.

2

3

4

CONTEXT   The Town Square - St Moritz
High density - urban - everything
within walking distance.

5

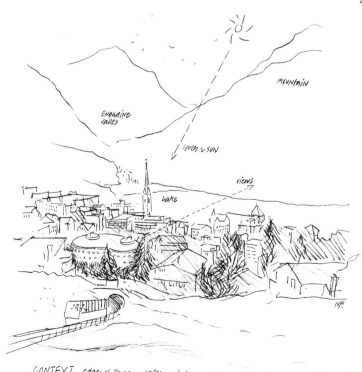

CONTEXT   edge of town ... valley ... lake ... mountains ... views ... sun terraces

6

Hongkong and Shanghai Bank Headquarters
Hong Kong 1979–1986

Conceived during a sensitive period in the former colony's history, the brief for the Hongkong and Shanghai Bank Headquarters was a statement of confidence: to create 'the best bank building in the world'. Through a process of questioning and challenging – including the involvement of a feng shui geomancer – the project addressed the nature of banking in Hong Kong and how it should be expressed in built form. In doing so it virtually reinvented the office tower.

The requirement to build in excess of one million square feet in a short timescale suggested a high degree of prefabrication, including factory-finished modules, while the need to build downwards and upwards simultaneously led to the adoption of a suspension structure, with pairs of steel masts arranged in three bays. As a result, the building form is articulated in a stepped profile of three individual towers, respectively twenty-nine, thirty-six and forty-four storeys high, which create floors of varying width and depth and allow for garden terraces. The mast structure allowed another radical move, pushing the service cores to the perimeter so as to create deep-plan floors around a ten-storey atrium. A mirrored 'sunscoop' reflects sunlight down through the atrium to the floor of a public plaza below – a sheltered space that at weekends has become a lively picnic spot. From the plaza, escalators rise up to the main banking hall, which with its glass underbelly was conceived as a 'shop window for banking'.

The 'bridges' that span between the masts define double-height reception areas that break down the scale of the building both visually and socially. A unique system of movement through the building combines high-speed lifts to the reception spaces with escalators beyond, reflecting village-like clusters of office floors. From the outset, the Bank placed a high priority on flexibility. Interestingly, over the years, it has been able to reconfigure office layouts with ease, even incorporating a large dealers' room into one floor – a move that could not have been anticipated when the building was designed.

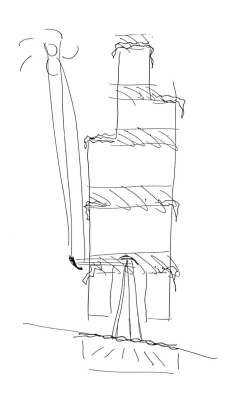

1

Previous pages, left: Norman
Foster's concept sketch
showing how the sunscoop
reflects sunlight down
through the atrium. Right:
Looking into the atrium.

1. The north facade as seen
from Statue Square.

2. A cross-section through
the atrium. The division
between the banking hall
and the ground level plaza
is provided by the minimal
intervention of the glass
underbelly.

3. In a city where public
space is rare, the plaza
beneath the Bank provides
a welcome moment of calm,
and a place to shelter from
the heat of the sun.

4. Hong Kong's Fillipino
community has adopted
the plaza as a favourite
weekend picnic spot.

5. Looking down through
the atrium into the main
banking hall.

6. Escalators lead from the
plaza up to the banking hall.

7. An early design sketch
by Norman Foster.

Overleaf: A detail of the
Bank's stepping form
on the skyline.

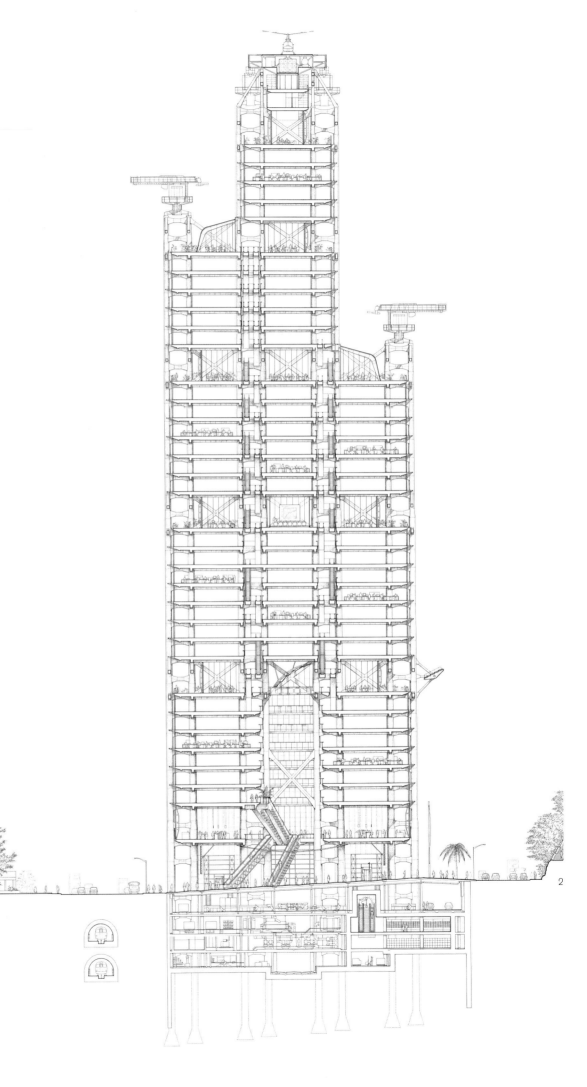

2

3

4

5

6

7

Century Tower

Tokyo, Japan 1987–1991

Century Tower grew from a belief that the commercial realities of speculative offices could be reconciled with an architecture of quality and distinction. Although it advances ideas first explored in the Hongkong and Shanghai Bank, Century Tower is not a corporate headquarters but a prestige office block with a wide range of amenities, including a health club and museum.

Located in Bunkyo-ku, in the heart of Tokyo, the building occupies a site subject to complex zoning regulations. The design response was to divide the tower into two blocks, nineteen and twenty-one storeys high, linked by a narrow atrium. The outer form of the blocks is defined by eccentrically braced frames, responding to seismic engineering requirements in a city where earthquakes and typhoons are very real threats. Inside, the floors are spaced at double height with suspended mezzanines between them, allowing office spaces to be column-free and to enjoy natural light and views. Narrow bridges span the atrium, enabling tenants to lease entire floors. Previously it had been prohibited in Japan to combine open office atria with open-access floor space, due to fire regulations. These were overcome through the pioneering use of smoke-activated baffles – reminiscent of the flaps on aircraft wings – which, in the event of fire, descend from the main and mezzanine floors to accelerate air-flow from the atrium into the affected floor. Fans then draw smoke across the floor and out of the building to avoid smoke migration.

Beyond its technological innovations, Century Tower also sought to harmonise Eastern and Western aesthetic sensibilities, particularly through the use of water. At the foot of the atrium, polished black granite water tables overflow to feed water walls, which in turn frame a staircase that leads to a museum for the client's collection of Oriental antiquities. The juxtaposition of light and dark and the calming effect of the water prepare the visitor for the cave-like museum with its precisely lit objects. Other facilities include a tea house, a restaurant and a health club and pool sheltered beneath a glazed catenary roof.

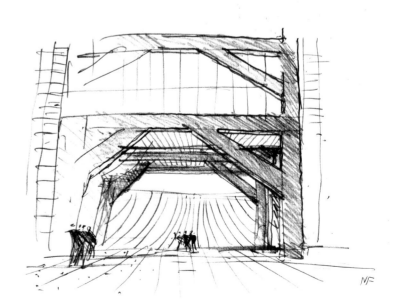

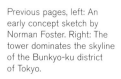

Previous pages, left: An early concept sketch by Norman Foster. Right: The tower dominates the skyline of the Bunkyo-ku district of Tokyo.

1. A glazed catenary roof shelters a swimming pool and health club at the foot of the tower.

2, 3. A staircase leads down from the office lobby to a museum of Japanese art and artefacts.

4, 5. Two views of the atrium that runs the full height of the building. Bridges link across this space and the office floors are double-height with suspended mezzanines in between.

6. Cross-section through the atrium.

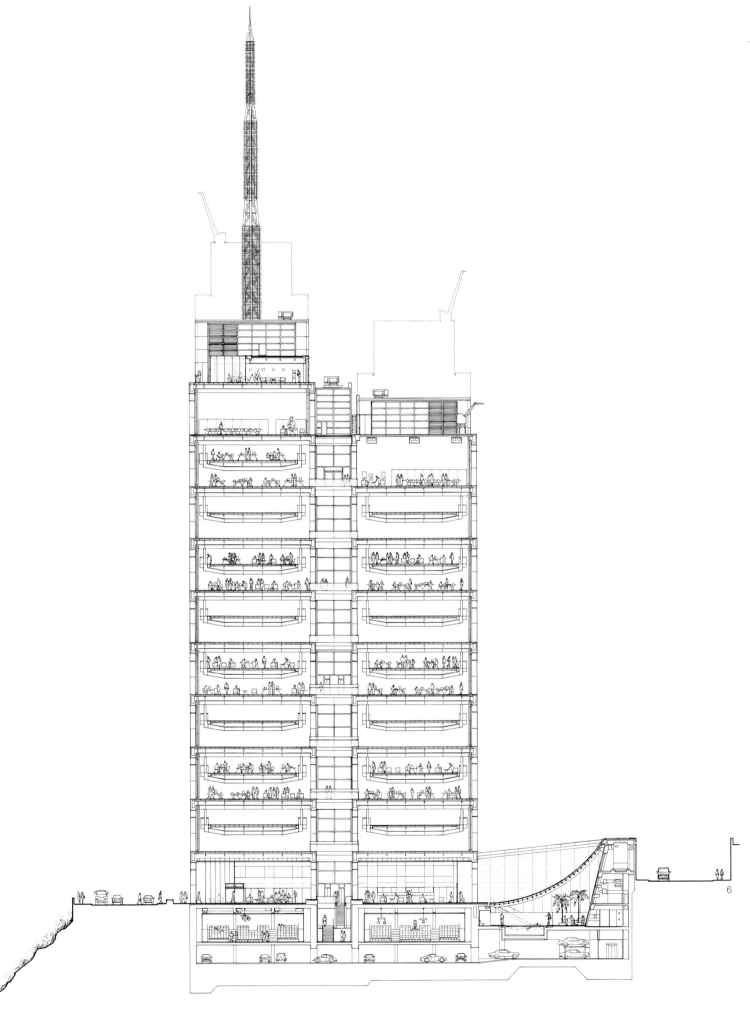

6

257

Torre de Collserola
Barcelona, Spain 1988–1992

In anticipation of the communications requirements of the 1992 Olympic Games, Barcelona was facing an explosion of transmission masts on the neighbouring Tibidabo mountainside. Sensing the environmental impact this would have, Mayor Pasqual Maragall decided that the communications infrastructure for the region should be coordinated. He convinced the three primary players – national and Catalan television and Telefonica – to build a shared telecommunications tower. The competition brief posed the problem as a balancing act between operational requirements and the desire for a monumental technological symbol. The solution reinvents the telecommunications tower from first principles.

A conventional reinforced-concrete tower would have required a shaft with a 25-metre-diameter base in order to achieve the 288-metre height required. Following an analysis of precedents, including bridges and shipbuilding techniques, a new structural concept emerged: a hybrid concrete and steel-braced tube, with a base diameter of only 4.5 metres, which dramatically minimises the tower's impact on the mountainside. In order to meet a programme of just twenty-four months the construction of shaft, equipment decks and mast was overlapped. As the shaft was poured, the steel-framed decks and public viewing platform were assembled on the ground ready to be jacked, inch by inch, into position. In a final flourish, the steel radio mast was telescoped up inside the hollow shaft.

The equipment decks are suspended from the shaft by three primary trusses and braced by Kevlar cables, which are transparent to broadcasting signals. Equipment is installed by lift, and a crane at the top of the mast hoists antennae into place. Inherent flexibility ensures that the tower is able to respond to a rapidly evolving telecommunications future.

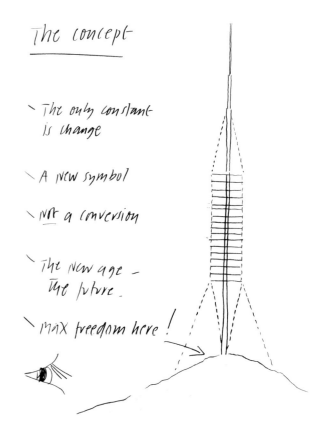

1

2

3

8

9

10

11

4 5 6 7

Previous pages, left: Norman Foster's concept sketch emphasises how the structure should touch the ground lightly. Right: View of the tower from below. The triangulated decks maximise space and optimise stability and aerodynamic efficiency.

1. A sketch by Norman Foster, indicating the tower's symbolic importance as a landmark on the Barcelona skyline.

2-7. As this sequence suggests, the tower's distinctive profile is visible from all across the city.

8. The 288-metre tower seen across the wooded slopes of Collserola.

9-11. Not only is the tower a focal point, it is also a vantage point. This sequence follows the public route up the tower, which culminates in a public viewing gallery.

12, 13. An elevation and cross-section, showing how the twelve floors of accommodation are supported on the central stayed mast. Two servicing levels are buried into the hillside at the foot of the tower.

12

13

Millennium Tower

Tokyo, Japan 1989

Tokyo is among the 'megacities' forecast to exceed populations of fifteen million by 2020. The Millennium Tower challenges assumptions about such future cities. It presents a timely solution to the social challenges of urban expansion on this scale and to the particular problems of Tokyo, with its acute land shortages. Commissioned by the Obayashi Corporation, it provides one million square metres of commercial development, stands 170 storeys high and is the world's tallest projected building.

Rising out of Tokyo Bay, the tower is capable of housing a community of up to 60,000 people, generating its own energy and processing its own waste. With its own transportation system, this vertical city quarter would be self-sustaining and virtually self-sufficient. The lower levels accommodate offices, light manufacturing and 'clean' industries such as consumer electronics. Above are apartments, while the topmost section houses communications systems and wind and solar generators, interspersed with restaurants that exploit the spectacular views.

A high-speed 'metro' system – with cars designed to carry 160 people – tracks both vertically and horizontally, moving through the building at twice the rate of conventional express lifts. Cars stop at intermediate 'sky centres' at every thirtieth floor; from there, individual journeys may be completed via lifts or escalators. This continuous cycle reduces travel times – an important factor in a vertical city, no less than a horizontal one. The five-storey sky centres have different principal functions – one might include a hotel, another a department store. Each is articulated with mezzanines, terraces and gardens to encourage a sense of place. The project demonstrates that high-density or high-rise living does not mean overcrowding or hardship; it can lead to an improved quality of life, where housing, work and leisure facilities are all close at hand.

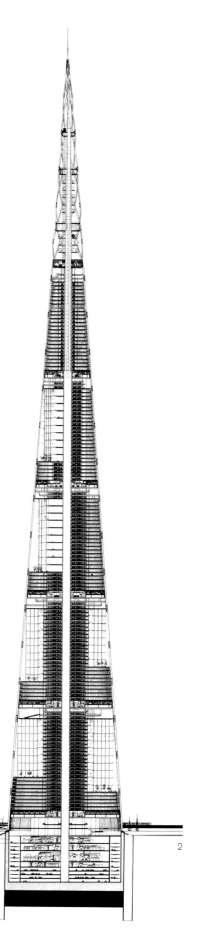

1. Extracts from Norman Foster's concept sketches.

2. Cross-section through the tower. Punctuated at regular intervals by five-storey sky centres, the tower can absorb a wide variety of deep and shallow plan accommodation, from new technology industrial spaces to restaurants, hotels and apartments. Communications and energy infrastructure occupies the upper levels.

Right: Visualisation showing the 170-storey tower located 2 kilometres offshore in Tokyo Bay.

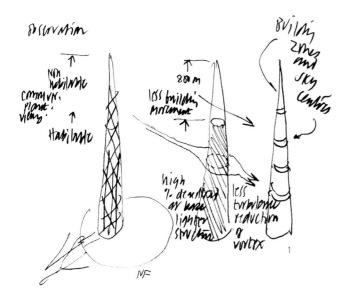

Commerzbank Headquarters
Frankfurt, Germany 1991–1997

At fifty-three storeys, the Commerzbank is the world's first ecological office tower and the tallest building in Europe. The project explores the nature of the office environment, developing new ideas for its ecology and working patterns. Central to this concept is a reliance on natural systems of lighting and ventilation. Every office is daylit and has openable windows, which – external conditions permitting – allows occupants to control their own environment. The building is naturally ventilated for 80 per cent of the year and as a result has energy consumption levels equivalent to half those of conventional, sealed office towers.

The plan form is triangular, comprising three 'petals' – the office floors – and a 'stem' formed by a full-height central atrium. Four-storey gardens are set at different levels on each of the three sides of the atrium, forming a spiral of gardens that winds up around the building. The gardens become the visual and social focus for village-like clusters of offices. They play an ecological role, bringing daylight and fresh air into the central atrium, and they are also places to relax during refreshment breaks, bringing richness and humanity to the workplace. From the outside they give the building a sense of transparency and lightness. Depending on their orientation, planting is from one of three regions: North America, Asia or the Mediterranean.

The tower has a distinctive presence on the Frankfurt skyline but it is also anchored into the lower-scale city fabric. It rises from the centre of a city block alongside the original Commerzbank building. Through restoration and sensitive rebuilding of the perimeter structures, the traditional scale of this block has been reinforced. The development at street level provides shops, car-parking, apartments and a banking hall, and forges links between the Commerzbank and the broader community. At the heart of the scheme a public galleria with restaurants, cafés and spaces for social and cultural events forms a popular new route cutting across the site. Interestingly, on the day the Commerzbank opened, the *Financial Times* adopted it as the symbol of Frankfurt, just as it features Big Ben and the Eiffel Tower as symbols of London and Paris.

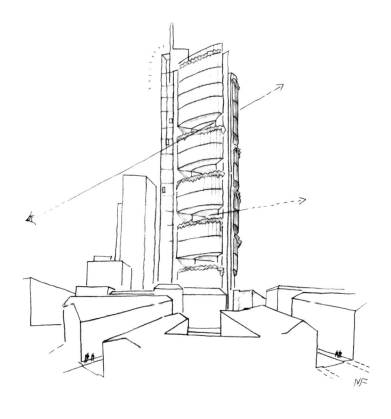

1

2

3

4

5

6

7

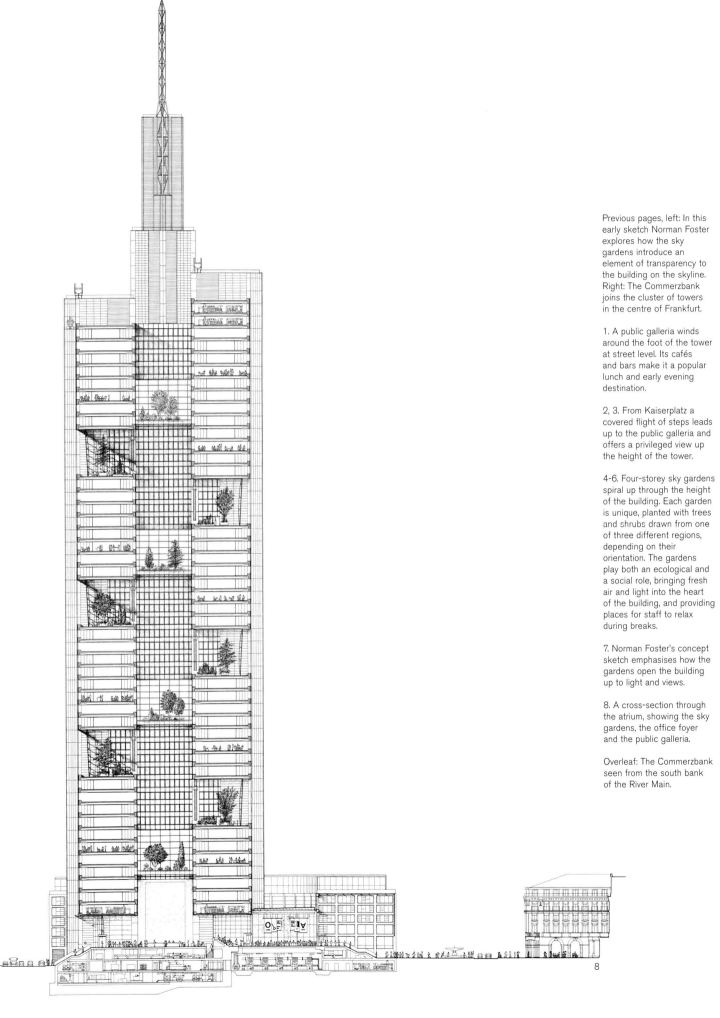

Previous pages, left: In this early sketch Norman Foster explores how the sky gardens introduce an element of transparency to the building on the skyline. Right: The Commerzbank joins the cluster of towers in the centre of Frankfurt.

1. A public galleria winds around the foot of the tower at street level. Its cafés and bars make it a popular lunch and early evening destination.

2, 3. From Kaiserplatz a covered flight of steps leads up to the public galleria and offers a privileged view up the height of the tower.

4-6. Four-storey sky gardens spiral up through the height of the building. Each garden is unique, planted with trees and shrubs drawn from one of three different regions, depending on their orientation. The gardens play both an ecological and a social role, bringing fresh air and light into the heart of the building, and providing places for staff to relax during breaks.

7. Norman Foster's concept sketch emphasises how the gardens open the building up to light and views.

8. A cross-section through the atrium, showing the sky gardens, the office foyer and the public galleria.

Overleaf: The Commerzbank seen from the south bank of the River Main.

8

Jiushi Corporation Headquarters
Shanghai, China 1995 2001

Shanghai is a city that has undergone a dramatic transformation over the last decade. Large areas that previously contained only traditional low-rise buildings now feature thickets of office towers. The Jiushi Corporation is the Chinese company responsible for providing the inward investment for the wave of development that has transformed the South Bund area. As the first major new building in Shanghai to be designed by a Western architect, this forty-storey headquarters tower for Jiushi marked a turning point in recent Chinese construction history, establishing benchmarks for subsequent building in the city and setting new environmental standards.

The essential strategy was to provide a world class building that could be realised largely by local means. The result is a simple, elegant structure, built to the highest specifications and oriented to exploit the strengths of its exceptional site. In response to the spectacular views, the building's services and circulation core is positioned away from the Huangpu River to create an open, flexible floor-plate, free of internal columns, which enjoys a panoramic outlook across the historical Bund and the Pudong. The floor-plates step back at three points over the height of the tower to form sky gardens that arc dramatically across the facade. The six-storey high sky garden at the top of the building comes as a particular surprise in a city where most towers are capped by services installations. This dramatic penthouse space forms the backdrop to Jiushi's own offices. The tower's transparent skin is a sophisticated triple-glazing system that incorporates automatically controlled natural ventilation and allows maximum light penetration without any attendant solar gain in the office spaces.

A transcontinental collaboration, the Jiushi project benefited from a global team that spanned the UK, Japan and China, with materials sourced both locally and from Italy. Consequently, it provides office space completed to international standards yet it is absolutely sensitive to, and rooted in, its context. Its adherence to local architectural tradition is expressed particularly clearly at street level, where a six-storey block at the base of the tower provides shops, restaurants and bars. This building follows the line of the street and incorporates a double-height colonnade evocative of nineteenth-century Shanghai shopping arcades.

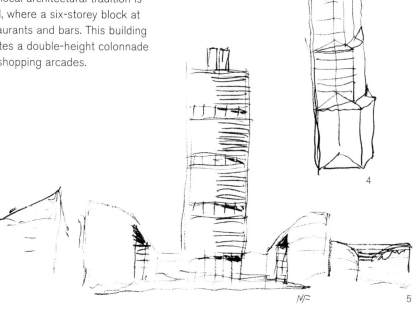

1. The building is punctuated at regular intervals by triple-height sky gardens that arc across the facade.

2. Looking up through the level 36 sky garden.

3-5. Concept sketches by Norman Foster exploring the building's elliptical plan form, and the location of the sky gardens.

Right: The tower is oriented to maximise views across the historical Bund and the Huangpu River.

4

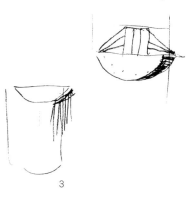

3

5

Swiss Re Headquarters

London, England 1997–2004

London's first ecological tall building and an instantly recognisable addition to the city's skyline, Swiss Re's headquarters at 30 St Mary Axe is rooted in a radical approach – technically, architecturally, socially and spatially. It rises forty-one storeys and provides 76,400 square metres of accommodation, including offices and a shopping arcade accessed from a newly created public plaza. At the very top of the building – London's highest occupied floor – is a club room that offers a spectacular 360-degree panorama across the capital.

Generated by a radial plan, with a circular perimeter, the building widens in profile as it rises and tapers towards its apex. This distinctive form responds to the constraints of the site: the building appears more slender than a rectangular block of equivalent size; reflections are reduced and transparency is improved; and the slimming of its profile towards the base maximises the public realm at ground level. Environmentally, its profile reduces the amount of wind deflected to the ground compared with a rectilinear tower of similar size, helping to maintain pedestrian comfort at street level, and creates external pressure differentials that are exploited to drive a unique system of natural ventilation.

Conceptually, the tower develops ideas explored in the Commerzbank and before that in the Climatroffice, a theoretical project with Buckminster Fuller that suggested a new rapport between nature and the workplace, its energy-conscious enclosure resolving walls and roof into a continuous triangulated skin. Here, the tower's diagonally braced structural envelope allows column-free floor space and a fully glazed facade, which opens up the building to light and views. Atria between the radiating fingers of each floor link together vertically to form a series of sky gardens that spiral up the building. These spaces are a natural social focus – places for refreshment points and meeting areas – and function as the building's 'lungs', distributing fresh air drawn in through opening panels in the facade. This system reduces the tower's reliance on air conditioning and, together with other sustainable measures, means that the building is expected to use only half the energy consumed by air-conditioned office towers.

Previous pages, left: Norman
Foster's sketch explores
how the building sits within
the close urban grain of the
City of London. Right: The
building approached from
Leadenhall Street.

1. Cross-section through the
tower showing the spiralling
sky gardens and upper level
restaurant and bar spaces.

2. The club room at the top
of the building offers 360-
degree panoramic views
across London.

3. Sketch by Norman Foster
exploring the design of
the club room.

4, 5. The external skin is
a triangulated geodetic
structure, clad entirely
in glass panels.

6. Norman Foster's early
sketch exploring different
colour options for the
horizontal and vertical
cladding members.

7, 8. Looking into the main
entrance and lobby space.

Overleaf: The tower seen
on the City skyline at night.

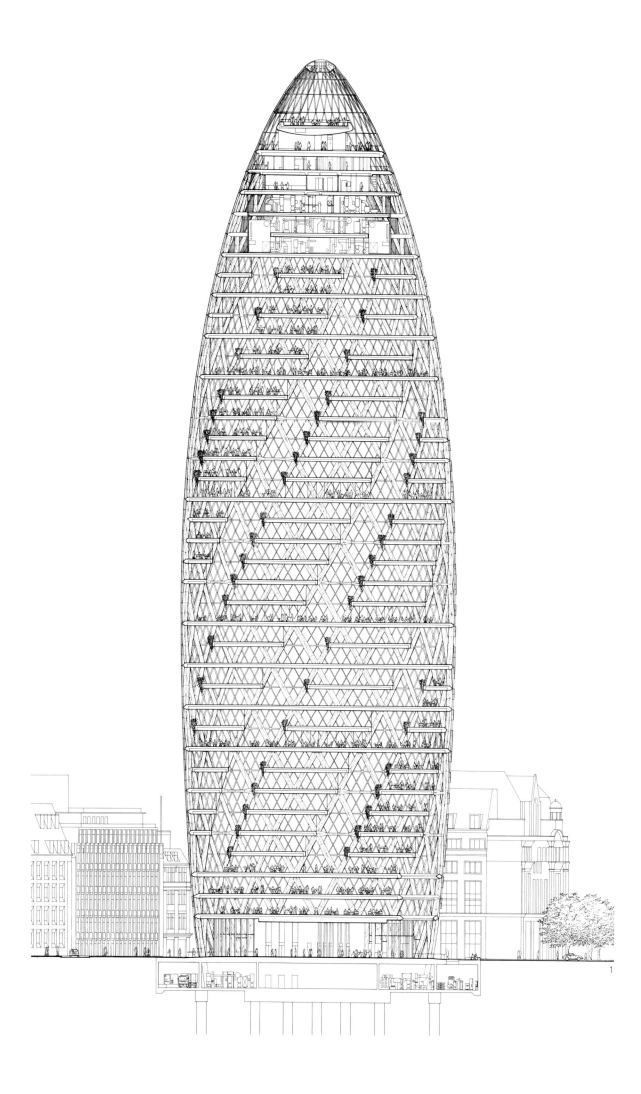

1

2

3

4

5

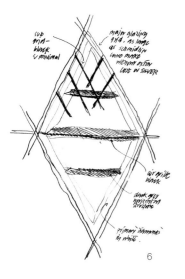

6

7

8

World Trade Center Redevelopment
New York, USA 2002

The rebuilding of the World Trade Center site is one of the most important urban planning and architectural challenges of recent times. It is about memory, but equally it is about rebirth, demonstrating to the world the continuing strength and faith in the future that has traditionally shaped the New York skyline. Following the events of September 11 2001 the practice commissioned an expert multidisciplinary team to conduct an in-depth study into safety in tall buildings. The lessons from that study informed this proposal, which celebrated New York's positive spirit with a unique twinned tower, designed to be the safest, the greenest and the tallest in the world.

The tower's crystalline form was based on triangular geometries – cross-cultural symbols of harmony, unity and strength. The two parts of the tower 'kissed' at three intervals over its 500-metre height, creating strategic links – escape routes in case of emergency – which corresponded with public levels containing observation decks, exhibition spaces and cafés. The tower was thus articulated vertically as village-like clusters, each with its own tree-filled atrium – effectively a 'park in the sky'. The building was naturally ventilated through its multi-layered, 'breathing' facade, and the atria played an environmental role, performing as its 'lungs', the trees oxygenating the circulating air.

In urban terms, the redevelopment was identified as a catalyst for the regeneration of the whole of Lower Manhattan, an opportunity to repair the street pattern that was eradicated in the 1960s and to bring new life to an area suffering economic decline. In place of a barren plaza, it envisaged green parks and streets on a human scale lined with shops, restaurants and bars. Connections further afield were strengthened by integrating public transport networks in an interchange below ground – a new gateway into Manhattan celebrated by a soaring glass canopy. The footprints of the World Trade Center towers were preserved as sanctuaries for remembrance and reflection. Ramps led visitors down into an ambulatory lining an open volume where each tower once stood. Here, the city would be hidden from view, the sky above empty.

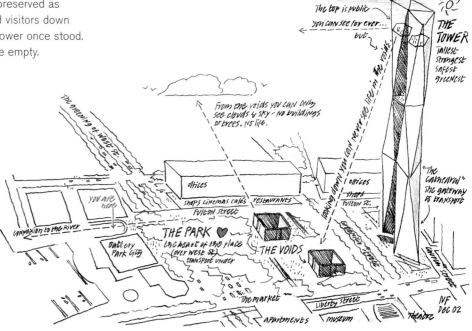

2

Previous pages, left: Norman Foster's concept sketch describes how the new towers are integrated into the fabric of Downtown Manhattan. Right: A visualisation showing the crystalline form of the new towers illuminated on the New York skyline.

1. Visualisation looking south from Midtown Manhattan and the Empire State Building towards the new 500-metre towers.

2, 3. Renderings depicting the landscaped public park at the base of the towers.

4. The footprints of the destroyed towers are preserved as a memorial to those who lost their lives on September 11. A ramp leads vistors down into the ambulatory running around the site of the south tower.

1

3

4

The Studio

Norman Foster:

'It is self-evident that if we suggest that an environment can influence the quality of our lives then it is inevitable that we should try to set an example in the environment that we create for ourselves as architects ...'

'... Two key characteristics of the studio and the way that we work are the democracy and freedom of communication that we enjoy. The studio has no partitions or separate rooms and meetings tend to take place informally, often around the computer screen ...'

'… Every member of the office, whatever his or her role, has an identical workspace at one of the long benches that span the width of the room. You might describe that as democracy in the workplace …'

'… The entrance to the studio dispenses with the traditional waiting area. Instead, visitors can enjoy the bar, which is the social focus of the office, have a coffee, read a newspaper or make a phone call if there is any need to wait …'

'… Although design is centralised in London and management flows out from there, it is impossible to think of the practice in isolation from the network of project offices around the world. The dynamic of Riverside owes much to the interaction and movement between these different places and cultures …'

'… The office is open twenty-four hours a day, seven days a week. There are no pressures or rewards for working antisocial hours; preferences and attitudes vary between individuals and this is reflected in a degree of choice – the important thing is that people are together when they need to be. Riverside is virtually a self-contained world with its own printing shop and photographic studio. For me, it is a rare combination of a wonderful team and a great place to work.'

The Practice
Norman Foster

1

As a practice we have always been guided by a belief that the quality of our surroundings has a direct influence on the quality of our lives, whether that is in the workplace, at home or in the public realm. Allied to that is an acknowledgement that architecture is generated by the needs of people, which are both material and spiritual, and a concern for the physical context and sensitivity to the culture and climate of place. That holds true whether we are creating a new building or making interventions within a historic structure.

As professionals we have dual responsibilities — first to the clients we serve but also to the public domain and the many users involved. A high degree of personal service coupled with a commitment to respect the precious resources of cost and time has always characterised our client relationships. Another resource is 'creative flair' — perhaps the most precious of all. This is equally true in the pursuit of beauty as it is in adding value — the two do not have to be in conflict. Excellence of design and its successful execution are central to our approach.

Over the past four decades, the quest for excellence has embraced not only architecture but also infrastructure and products. Many works have become landmarks — symbols of their place. These may be parliament buildings, centres of culture, towers or bridges. In each case, the social agenda will have been a strong generator; this particularly applies to the workplace, schools, universities, libraries, residential and medical research buildings.

In the past, the practice was responsible for some emblematic one-off residences. More recently we have enjoyed the challenge of producing higher density housing which combines quality and relatively low cost — albeit in a limited context. We are now examining the potential to push these boundaries much further. Other current challenges include the creation of larger scale communities and destinations with an emphasis on mixed use and leisure. The scale, diversity and global reach of our new projects have never been so exciting. These expanding opportunities have led recently to the further evolution of the way in which the practice is structured, building on the best traditions of its past.

To undertake consistently, in a decade, some of the biggest projects in the world, needs depth of resources. In that sense, 'size matters'. At the time of writing the practice is around 650 strong, with a highly talented and dedicated team drawn from more than fifty nations, and with an average age of thirty-two. However, creativity and personal service are best nurtured by the compact group where 'small is beautiful'. The resolution of these apparently conflicting ideals is mirrored in the practice's structure.

The practice is led by myself as chairman with Spencer de Grey and David Nelson as deputy chairmen, and Graham Phillips as chief executive. This core group has worked closely together for more than thirty years. Together we form the executive board, which is responsible for the strategic direction of the practice. Alongside this group, the office is organised into six design groups each with a senior partner as leader and a partner as deputy. All of these individuals have been chosen for their proven track record over many years in the practice — a combination of creativity, attention to detail, delivery and management skills. The group leaders are: Grant Brooker, Nigel Dancey, Brandon Haw, Paul Kalkhoven, Mouzhan Majidi and Andy Miller. The deputies, each with the capabilities of a leader, are: Andy Bow, John Drew, Gerard Evenden, Michael Jones, David Summerfield and Armstrong Yakubu.

The groups are not shaped by specialisation of building type or geographical location. Each group has a rich cross-section of projects, large and small, around the world. That may range from an office building in London, to a research facility on an American campus or a university in a clearing in the Malaysian jungle. This diversity is good for creativity, innovation and motivation. The tight-knit nature of the groups also ensures personal service and close contact between the design team and the client throughout a project, from the first meetings to the hand-over of the finished building and beyond. As part of this process, key members of the design team will move with the project to the building site, wherever that is in the world, and will maintain a local office until the project is complete.

The six groups are complemented by a range of specialist teams, including communications, environmental research, graphics, interior design, materials, model making, product design, space planning and 3D computer modelling. Leadership of research and development, specialist management and contract administration, and IT and computer modeling is provided by Stefan Behling, Mark Sutcliffe and Iain Godwin respectively, all of whom are senior partners. The day-to-day running of the practice is steered by the management board, chaired by Graham Phillips with representation from each of the six groups and the practice's support services.

5   6   7

8   9   10

2   3   4

1. Norman Foster
2. Spencer de Grey
3. David Nelson
4. Graham Phillips

The design of each new project is reviewed regularly, both formally and informally. This process takes place under the direction of the design board, which has been created in the spirit of 'challenging and being challenged' and has executive responsibility for design across the office. The board balances the greater spread of responsibility in the groups with a broader overview of shared values, coupled to a process that can initiate design as well as review it. Alongside myself, the board comprises Spencer de Grey, David Nelson, Graham Phillips and Stefan Behling, with Narinder Sagoo as its advisor.

Until recently, Spencer de Grey and David Nelson were focused on their own projects, both in the London studio and on sites around the world. Now they are able to range much wider, engaging through the design board with every new project as well as sharing creative sparks directly with the leaders, deputies and teams. Graham Phillips, who has also led many of the practice's projects, combines a strategic involvement in design through the design board with his primary responsibilities for the management of the practice.

Stefan Behling, who has worked on a range of projects over the past eighteen years, brings to bear a particular expertise in ecology and sustainability. A key member of the design board, he is also responsible for research on an office-wide basis and balances these roles with that of Professor of Architecture at Stuttgart University. Narinder Sagoo offers another perspective. A younger architect, he is also responsible for graphic visualisations across selected projects. The composition and leadership of the design board will develop and rotate over time, with the potential for mobility between groups and the board.

In developing and communicating the design concept, the project teams are supported by a broad spectrum of in-house disciplines. The advent of digital technologies has allowed us to design and build structures with complex geometric forms that would not have been feasible as little as twenty years ago. The practice's in-house specialist modelling group has introduced a highly advanced three-dimensional computer modelling capability that allows architects both to explore design solutions rapidly and to communicate data to consultants and contractors. While new technologies have transformed the way the practice works, traditional model-making still plays a key role and our sophisticated model shop can produce everything from sketch models to full size mock-ups.

The practice also has an information centre with a comprehensive materials research centre that helps architects to select materials and products and initiates the use of new materials, ensuring that we have the knowledge base to create inspirational as well as sustainable buildings. Beyond that, we have developed a number of tools to implement the design of sustainable buildings. The practice's ambition is to establish an individual sustainability profile for every project. This ongoing development tool allows each team to determine appropriate targets and methods at the beginning of each project. In doing so, our aim is to provide a system to monitor the sustainability agenda of individual projects, and to promote a strong sustainable ethic. Each design team is encouraged to record its sustainable design methods, regardless of the project's size, location, climate, or type. This information is collated in a database that can be accessed throughout the practice to inform and enrich subsequent projects.

We recognise, however, that as architects we are only as powerful as our advocacy. We understand that not every project will be able to meet all the desired criteria. But equally we believe that we have a responsibility to try to persuade clients and developers to adopt sustainable strategies – even small steps in the right direction are better than none at all. The practice's sustainability forum was established to raise the level of environmental awareness throughout the office, and promote the use of sustainable technologies and methods. The forum is part of the research and development group, whose role is to ensure that the practice remains at the forefront of architectural innovation. It is an interdisciplinary working group, with representatives from the six design groups, the information centre, communications, training, and research departments. These representatives provide the crucial link between the forum's resources and knowledge and the individual design teams.

This sustainability methodology is augmented by providing formal and informal training to the practice's staff on a range of issues, including renewable energy sources, sustainability criteria and assessment, environmental analysis, and visualisation techniques. By maintaining a commitment to internal and external research, we are not only up-to-date with new knowledge and techniques, but are also able to evaluate their relevance and appropriateness for individual projects. These measures ensure that environmental awareness is an integral part of the practice's culture as it evolves to meet the challenges of the next forty years.

5. Grant Brooker
6. Brandon Haw
7. Mouzhan Majidi
8. Paul Kalkhoven
9. Andy Miller
10. Nigel Dancey
11. Stefan Behling
12. Mark Sutcliffe
13. Iain Godwin

11   12   13

The Team

Founder and Chairman
Norman Foster

Deputy Chairmen
Spencer de Grey
David Nelson

Chief Executive
Graham Phillips

Senior Partners
Stefan Behling
Grant Brooker
Nigel Dancey
Iain Godwin
Brandon Haw
Paul Kalkhoven
Mouzhan Majidi
Andy Miller
Mark Sutcliffe

Partners
Andy Bow
Simon Bowden
Angus Campbell
Chris Connell
John Drew
Gerard Evenden
Matteo Fantoni
D'Arcy Fenton
Jason Flanagan
Pedro Haberbosch
Christian Hallmann
Katy Harris
Richard Hawkins
Darron Haylock
Ken Hogg
Mike Jelliffe
David Jenkins
Iwan Jones
Michael Jones
Jan Landolt
Paul Leadbeatter
Robert McFarlane
Nikolai Malsch
Max Neal
Anthony O'Donovan
Sven Ollmann
Ross Palmer
Jonathan Parr
Charles Rich
Giles Robinson
Narinder Sagoo
Dan Sibert
John Small
David Summerfield
Huw Thomas
Brian Timmoney
Juan Vieira-Pardo
Hugh Whitehead
Michael Wurzel
Armstrong Yakubu

Associate Partners
Bob Ashworth
Mark Atkinson
John Ball
Cara Bamford
Gamma Basra
Stephen Best
Toby Blunt
John Blythe
Chris Bubb
Jan Coghlan
Bruce Curtain
Philipp Eichstadt
Luke Fox
Mike Gardner
Michael Gentz
Russell Hales
Lee Hallman
Robert Harrison
Thouria Istephan
Reinhard Joecks
Arjun Kaicker
Josef Kaps
Anton Khmelnitskiy
David Kong
Stuart Latham
Alistair Lenczner
Muir Livingstone
Jun Luo
James McGrath
Neil MacLeod
Luis Matania
Bobbie Michael
Kate Murphy
Antoinette Nassopoulos
Divya Patel
Tom Politowicz
David Rosenberg
Paul Smith
Hugh Stewart
Neil Vandersteen
Jeremy Wallis
Colin Ward
Chris West
Ian Whitby
Miriam White
Tracey Wiles
Edson Yabiku

Associates
Stefan Abidin
Francis Aish
Bob Atwal
James Barnes
Alexander Barry
Mike Bass
Aike Behrens
Jonathan Bell
Matthew Blackstaffe
Kimberley Boon
Arthur Branthwaite
Fiona Bruce-Smythe
William Castagna
Martin Castle
Marie Clarke
David Crosswaite
Nigel Curry
Chloé di Vittorio
James Edwards
Iain Fairbairn
Colin Foster
Juan Frigerio
Stanley Fuls
Marco Gamini
Anna Garreau
Ulrich Hamann
Peter Han
Darryn Holder
Mike Holland
John Jennings
Jeremy Kim
Edmund Klimek
Angelika Kovacic
Andreas Krause
Jurgen Kuppers
Loretta Law
Darren Lawson
Chris Lepine
Nicholas Ling
Sarah Lister
Ricardo Mateu
Martina Meluzzi
Joon Paik
Nadine Pieper Bosch
Ingo Pott

Tony Price
Catherine Ramsden
Mark Read
Austin Relton
Martin Rolfe
Filo Russo
Margaret Saunders
Roland Schnizer
Richard Scott-Wilson
Michael Sehmsdorf
Danny Shaw
Neville Smith
Silvia Soh
Diane Teague
Damian Timlin
Dara Towhidi
John Walden
Vincent Westbrook
Jessica Wood
Richard Wotton
Nigel Young

Group One
Grant Brooker
John Drew

Katja Ackerman
Jason Alderson
Volkan Alkanoglu
Sofia Arraiza
Matthew Austen
Thomas Austerveil
Aike Behrens
Jonathan Bell
Doretta Bevilacqua
Tobias Bloemeke
Thomas Brune
Peter Buche
Hon Kong Chee
Shin Hyung Cho
Graham Collingridge
Svetlana Curcic
Bruce Curtain
Nerea Feliz
D'Arcy Fenton
Manuel Fernandez
Michaela Fuchs
Ingo Glatsch
Monika Goebel
Igor Gottschalk
Ashman Goyal
Fenna Haakma Wagenaar
Andreas Hammer
Christopher Hammerschmidt
Isabel Hannig
Robert Harrison
Timothy Kemp
David Kong
Angelika Kovacic
Hideo Kumaki
Jurgen Kuppers
Ashley Lane
Siuwai Law
Paul Leadbeatter
Randy Liekenjie
Andrew Lister
Sarah Lister
Peter McLaughlin
Milena Marucci
Gregor Milne

Antoinette Nassopoulos
Max Neal
Kristine Ngan
Ricardo Ostos
Misza Ozdowski
Joon Paik
Nicholas Paterson
Damon Pearce
Daniel Poehner
Damiano Rizzini
Martin Rolfe
Ricky Sandhu
Luis Santos
Anne-Marie Saul
Orsolya Say
Owe Schoof
Jonathan Scull
Dan Sibert
Viktorie Smejkalova
Neville Smith
Robert Smith
Laura Stecich
Hugh Stewart
Cesar Tarancon
Caroline Tarling
Sanja Tiedemann
Xing-Yu Tong
Hiroko Uchino
Jerry van Veldhuizen
Oliver Voss
Paul West
Ian Whitby
Miriam White
Sam Wilson
See Teck Yeo
Kevin Yiu

Group Two
Brandon Haw
Armstrong Yakubu

Paul Allen
Sandor Ambrus
Susanne Bauer
Francesca Becchi
Rafe Bertram
Ian Blaney
Stephanie Brendel
Chris Bubb
Dominic Choi
Chris Connell
Neil Crawford
Nigel Curry
Federico D'Angelo
Juan Diaz-Llanos Garcia
Mandy Edge
James Edwards
Philipp Eichstadt
Matteo Fantoni
Tommaso Fantoni
Kathleen Feagin
Marco Ferri
Will Freeman
Sabrina Friedl
Marco Gamini
James Goodfellow
Roland Grube
Robert Hall
Ulrike Hammerschmidt
Peter Han
Andrew Holt
Mike Jelliffe
John Jennings
Nasrin Kalbasi
Sofia Karim
Agnieszka Klak
Edmund Klimek
Johanna Knaak
Beata Kniec
Michaela Koster
Andreas Krause
Jai Krishnan
Julia Kruger
Jan Landolt
Christian Lange

Tillmann Lenz
Bob Leung
Supriya Gokhale Mankad
Consuelo Manna
Declan O'Donnell
Emma Penttinen
Laura Pullicino
Gareth Pywell
Martin Reichel
David Rosenberg
Pia Salin
Dorothea Schulz
Ben Scott
Kirsten Scott
Cristina Segni
Paul Smith
Ingrid Solken
Robin Tandavanit
Damian Timlin
Chris West
Michael Wurzel

Group Three
Mouzhan Majidi
Andy Bow

Stefan Abidin
Mark Atkinson
Zak Ayash
Rubens Azevedo
John Ball
Cara Bamford
Angus Campbell
Stefano Cesario
Alan Chan
Olson Chan
Steven Chiu
Young Wie-Yang Chiu
Alan Chung
Gunnar Dittrich
Wulf Duerrich
Andrea Etspueler
Tie Fan
Colin Foster
Kristin Fox
Luke Fox
Juan Frigerio

Michael Gentz
Richard Hawkins
Jorge Hernandez
Gabriel Ho
Ken Hogg
Darryn Holder
Anton Khmelnitskiy
Jeremy Kim
Hernan Kraviez
Phyllis Fat Yin Lam
Lorotta Law
Alistair Lenczner
Da Chun Lin
Jun Luo
Andrew McMullen
Mathis Malchow
Tony Miki
Carlo Negri
Jonathan Parr
Rodrigo Pereira
Sean Roche
Riko Sibbe
Pearl Tang
Vincent Thiry
Huw Thomas
Brian Timmoney
Tsvetan Toshkov
Wing Sai Tsui
William John Walshe
Joyce Wang
Colin Ward
Vincent Westbrook
Irene Wong
Shyue-Jiun Woon
Dion Young
Zheng Yu
Jean Wenyan Zhu

Group Four
Paul Kalkhoven
Michael Jones

Alex Barry
Paul Bavister
Eleanor Baxter
Scott Beaver
Marco Belcastro
Simona Bencini
Robin Blanchard
Simon Bowden
Philippe Brysse
Armin Buchbinder
Sebastian Busse
William Castagna
Carmen Chan
Jan Coghlan
Laurens Costeris
Eike Danz
Gennaro di Dato
Aaron Davis
Gilles Delage
Hugo D'Enjoy
Chloé di Vittorio
Ben Dobbin
Dagmar Eisenach
Leslie Epking
Iain Fairbairn
Anne Fehrenbach
Jon Fielding
Jason Flanagan
Morgan Fleming
Simone Gauss
Anthony Guma
Darron Haylock
Reinhard Joecks
Chris Kallan
Graeme Laughlin
Stuart Macalister
James McGrath
Luis Matania
Peter Matcham
Jakob Mcvcs
Kate Murphy
Yat Lun Ng
Luigi Orioli
Mathis Osterhage

Laszlo Pallagi
Silvia Paredes
Pritesh Patel
Michael Pelken
Raphael Petit
Bjorn Polzin
Susanne Popp
Catherine Ramsden
Austin Relton
Katherine Ridley
Carsten Saelzer
Maddalena Sanvito
Gaby Schneider
Gordon Seiles
Philip Smith
Julius Streifeneder
Diego Suarez
Colm Tamney
Anja Tassotto
Jane Tily
Robbie Turner
Leonhard Weil
Richard Yates

Group Five
Andy Miller
Gerard Evenden

Ana Agag Longo
Bob Atwal
Andreas Becker
Toby Blunt
John Blythe
Florian Boxberg
Arthur Branthwaite
Marco Callegaro
Martin Castle
Ho Ling Cheung
Hayley Cross
David Crosswaite
Glenis Fan
Ramses Frederickx
Stanley Fuls
Juan Gabriel La Mafda
Giulia Galiberti
Sandra Glass
Pedro Haberbosch

Christian Hallmann
Ulrich Hamann
Klaus Heldwein
Ingeborg Kurte
Stuart Latham
Luca Latini
Giulia Leonie
Muir Livingstone
Paolo Longo
Robert McFarlane
Emanuele Mattutini
Martina Meluzzi
Tom Mival
Virginia Mommens
Laura Morales
Michael Ng
Sven Ollmann
Dele Olubodun
Gary Owen
Erkin Ozay
Ross Palmer
Yan Pan
Emily Phang
Nadine Pieper Bosch
Daniel Pittman
Tom Politowicz
Ingo Pott
Bernardo Sanchez
Roland Schnizer
Richard Scott-Wilson
Michael Sehmsdorf
Marilu Sicoli
Sylvia Soh
Sunphol Sorakul
Julia von Sponeck
George Stowell
Iwona Szwedo
Matthew Tan
Roderick Tong
Dara Towhidi
Karsten Vollmer
Jin Watanabe
Wing Kei Wong
Edson Yabiku
Chin Len Yao
Akay Zorlu

Group Six
Nigel Dancey
David Summerfield

Shiri Achu
Daniel Aisenson
James Barnes
Daniel Baukus
Stephen Best
Stephan Birk
Jennifer Bonner
Marie Christoffersen
Miguel Costa
Luciano Di Domenico
Katerina Dionysopoulou
Cyrille Druart
David Drummond
Berend Frenzel
Marija Gonopolsjaja
Roland Haehnel
Henriette Hahnloser
Russell Hales
Lee Hallman
Dominik Hauser
Christine Heil
Liza Heilmeyer
Joost Heremans
Alessandro Isola
Iwan Jones
Josef Kaps
Nina Krause
Andries Kruger
Louis Lafargue
Annabel Langen
Nicholas Ling
Abel Maciel
Gil Madeira
Nikolai Malsch
Carlos Martin Mendez
Ricardo Mateu
Carsten Mundle
Michael Oades
Florian Oelschlager
Lorena Prieto
Peter Ridley
Giles Robinson
Filo Russo
Stephan Schaefer

Danny Shaw
Carlos Sole Bravo
Laurent Tek
Roberto Timpano
Guvenc Topcuoglu
Gloria Tsai
Stefan Unnewehr
Jonas Upton-Hansen
Juan Vieira-Pardo
Paul Wang
Tracey Wiles
Pietje Witt
Corina Woolls-King
Raza Zahid

Graphics
Narinder Sagoo
Matthew Blackstaffe

Gregory Gibbon
Andrea Goecke
William Ings
Sarah Kelly
Carl Murphy
Neryhs Phillips
Jenny Vernon

Modelshop
Neil Vandersteen

Richard Brown
Alexandra Carr
Bryan Cory
John Dixon
Edward Hiscock
Sam Morgan
Benjamin Mullaert
Joe Preston
Paul Pritchard
Diane Teague
Robert Turner
Gareth Verbiest
John Walden
Richard Wotton

Product Design
John Small

Mike Holland
Todd Hutton
Werner Sigg
Stefano Tonelli
Dmitri Warner

Specialist Modelling Group
Hugh Whitehead

Francis Aish
Chris Lepine
Mirco Becker
Xavier De Kestelier
Karen Fiano
Brady Peters
Raquel Viola

Visualisation
Gamma Basra

Chris Glew
Michael Haley
Dimitar Karanikolov
Naveed Mughal
Joshua Newman
Tsvetan Toshkov

Workplace
Arjun Kaicker

Harriet Gillham
Martin Glover
Francesca Jack
Peggy Kan

In addition to these groups, the
Foster studio is supported by
a further 170 administrative
colleagues.

Complete Works

Banks

HSBC World Headquarters,
London, England 1997–2002

Citibank Headquarters,
London, England 1996–2000

Emirates Bank Headquarters,
Dubai, UAE 1995
Credit du Nord Headquarters,
Paris, France 1993
World Trade Centre, Berlin,
Germany 1992
Commerzbank Headquarters,
Frankfurt, Germany 1991–1997
Hongkong and Shanghai Bank
Headquarters, Hong Kong
1979–1986

Bridges

Millennium Bridge, London,
England 1996–2000
Arsta Bridge, Stockholm,
Sweden 1995
Millau Viaduct, Gorges du Tarn,
France 1993–2004
Oresund Bridge,
Sweden, Denmark 1993
Spandau Bridge, Berlin,
Germany 1992
Viaduct, Rennes, France
1991

Pont de la Fourvière, Lyon,
France 1991
Pont du Medoc, Bordeaux,
France 1991
Pont d'Austerlitz, Paris,
France 1988

Civic Realm

World Squares for All: Parliament
Square and Environs, London,
England 2005
World Squares for All: Trafalgar
Square and Environs, London,
England 1996–2002
World Squares for All Masterplan,
London, England, 1996
National Police Memorial, London,
England 1993–2004

Porte Maillot Masterplan, Paris,
France 1993
Masterplan, Lüdenscheid,
Germany 1992
Masterplan, Berlin, Germany 1990
Masterplan, Nîmes, France 1990
Statue Square Masterplan,
Hong Kong 1980

Communication

NTT Broadcasting Centre, Nagano,
Japan 1995
Multimedia Centre, Hamburg,
Germany 1995–1999

Telecommunications Facility,
Santiago de Compostela,
Spain 1994

Torre de Collserola, Barcelona,
Spain 1988–1992
ITN Headquarters, London,
England 1988–1990

Bunka Radio Station, Tokyo,
Japan 1987
Televisa Headquarters, Mexico
City, Mexico 1986
BBC Radio Centre, London,
England 1982–1985

Conference

National Scottish Arena, Glasgow,
Scotland 2004–
Convention Centre, Perth,
Australia 2000
Scottish National Exhibition Centre,
Glasgow, Scotland 1995–1997

Congress Centre, Valencia,
Spain 1993–1998
Convention and Exhibition Centre,
Hong Kong 1993
Villepinte Exhibition Halls, Paris,
France 1993
Congress Hall, San Sebastian,
Spain 1990
Trade Fair Centre, Berlin,
Germany 1990
Congress Hall, Toulouse,
France 1989
Knoxville Energy Expo,
USA 1978

Culture and Arts

Smithsonian Institution Courtyard,
National Portrait Gallery,
Washington DC, USA 2004–
Zenith, Saint-Etienne,
France 2004–
Avery Fisher Hall, Lincoln Center,
New York, USA 2003–
Lenbachhaus, Munich,
Germany, 2003–
National Museum, Beijing,
China 2003–
New Globe Theater, New York,
USA 2003–
Regent Theatre Development,
Sydney, Australia 2003–
Walter Benjamin Foundation,
Portbou, Spain 2003–
Winspear Opera House, Dallas,
USA 2002–
Museum of Fine Arts, Boston,
USA 1999–
Musée Quai Branly, Paris,
France 1999
'Modern Britain 1929–1939'
Exhibition, Design Museum,
London, England 1999
Anthony D'Offay Gallery
Redevelopment, London,
England 1998–2001
Uffizi Redevelopment, Florence,
Italy 1998
Cultural Centre, Dubai, UAE 1998
Feasibility Study for the
Roundhouse, London,
England 1997
The Sage Gateshead,
Gateshead, England
1997–2004
Prado Museum Extension, Madrid,
Spain 1996

Cardiff Bay Opera House, Cardiff,
Wales 1994
Centre de la Mémoire,
Oradour sur Glanes,
France 1994
The Great Court at the British
Museum, London,
England 1994–2000
Imperial War Museum, Hartlepool,
England 1993
National Gallery of Scottish Art,
Glasgow, Scotland 1993
Musée de Préhistoire des Gorges
du Verdon, Quinson,
France 1992–2001
Addition to Joslyn Art Museum,
Omaha, USA 1992–1994
Clore Theatre, Imperial College,
London, England 1992
Design Centre, Essen,
Germany 1992–1997
Houston Museum of Fine Arts
Redevelopment, Houston,
USA 1992
Crescent Wing, Sainsbury Centre
for Visual Arts, Norwich,
England 1988–1991
Sackler Galleries, Jerusalem,
Israel 1988

American Air Museum, Duxford,
England 1987–1997
Salle de Spectacles, Nancy,
France 1986
Sackler Galleries, Royal Academy
of Arts, London,
England 1985–1991
Carré d'Art, Nîmes,
France 1984–1993
Whitney Museum Development
Project, New York, USA 1978
Sainsbury Centre for Visual Arts,
Norwich, England 1974–1978
Floating Theatre, London,

England 1972
Samuel Beckett Theatre,
St Peter's College, Oxford,
England 1971

Education and Health
Arizona State University, Arizona
USA 2004–
Corby Academy, England 2004–
Folkestone Academy, England
2003–
Saga-Kings Academy, Folkestone,
England 2003–
Thomas Deacon Academy,
Peterborough,
England 2003–
Centre for Advanced Studies
in the Social Sciences,
University of Oxford,
England 2002–
Djanogly City Academy,
Nottingham,
England 2002–2005
London Academy, London,
England 2002–
The West London Academy,
London, England 2002–
The Business Academy, Bexley,
England 2001–2003
Capital City Academy, London,
England 2001–2003
Petronas University of Technology,
Kuala Lumpur, Malaysia
1998–2004
Free University of Berlin, Germany
1997–2005
Economics Department Building,
Faculty of Social Sciences,
University of Oxford, England
1996–2000

ASPIRE National Training Centre,
London, England 1995–1998

Faculty of Management, Robert
Gordon University, Aberdeen,
Scotland 1994–1998

British Library of Political and
Economic Science, LSE,
London, England 1993–2001

Forth Valley Community Care Village,
Larbert, Scotland 1993–1995

Marine Simulator Centre,
Rotterdam, The Netherlands
1992–1993
School of Physiotherapy,
Southampton,
England 1992–1994
Lycée Albert Camus, Fréjus,
France 1991–1993
Institute of Criminology,
University of Cambridge,
England 1991

Faculty of Law,
University of Cambridge,
England 1990–1995
Cranfield University Library,
Cranfield, England 1989–1992

Students' Union Building,
University College London,
England 1980
Palmerston Special School,
Liverpool, England 1974–1975
Special Care Unit, London,
England 1971–1973
Newport School, Newport,
Wales 1967

Government
Palace of Peace, Astana,
Kazakhstan 2004–
Milan Regional Government
Headquarters, Italy 2004–
UN Headquarters, New York,
USA 2003
New Supreme Court,
Singapore 2000–2005
City Hall, Greater London Authority
Headquarters, London,
England 1998–2002
Her Majesty's Treasury
Redevelopment, London,
England 1996–2002
New German Parliament,
Reichstag, Berlin,
Germany 1992–1999
Police Academy, New York,
USA 1992
EEC Parliament, Brussels,
Belgium 1991
Hôtel du Département, Marseilles,
France 1990

Industry

HACTL Freight, Superterminal,
Chek Lap Kok,
Hong Kong 1992–1998
High Bay Warehouse, Lüdenscheid,
Germany 1992
Tecno Headquarters Factory,
Valencia, Spain 1992
Billingsgate Fish Market, London,
England 1981
Renault Distribution Centre,
Swindon, England 1980–1982
IBM Technical Park, Greenford,
England 1975–1980

Cincinnati Milacron, Cincinnati,
USA 1974
German Car Centre, Milton Keynes,
England 1973–1974
Modern Art Glass Warehouse,
Thamesmead,
England 1972–1973
Factory for SAPA, Tibshelf,
England 1972–1973
Computer Technology Factory,
Hemel Hempstead,
England 1970–1971
Pirelli Warehouse Study 1970
Factory Systems Study 1969–1972
Reliance Controls Electronics
Factory, Swindon,
England 1965–1966
(with Team 4)

Leisure and Sport

Faustino Winery, Gumiel de Hizan
in Ribera del Duero,
Spain 2004–
Hotel Puerta Americana, Madrid,
Spain 2004–
Silken Hotel, London,
England 2004–
Beijing Swimming Pool, Beijing,
China 2003
Bilbao Athletic Club, Bilbao,
Spain 2003–
Pelham Square, Hastings,
England 2003
Sentosa Resort,
Singapore 2003–
Yacht Club de Monaco,
2003–
Dolder Hotel, Zurich,
Switzerland 2002–
Elephant House, Copenhagen Zoo,
Copenhagen, Denmark 2002–
London City Racecourse, London,
England 2000–
Sitooterie, Belsay Hall,
England 2000

Grandstand, Newbury Racecourse,
England 1999–2000

Wembley National Stadium,
London, England 1996–
Clubhouse, Silverstone Racetrack,
Silverstone, England 1995
Great Glasshouse, National
Botanic Garden of Wales,
Llanarthne, Wales 1995–2000

Science World, Bristol,
England 1995
Stadium, Oita, Japan 1995
Casino-Kursaal, Ostend,
Belgium 1994
Grand Stade, Paris, France 1994
Sealife Centre, Blankenberge,
Belgium 1994
Space Discovery Museum, Tokyo,
Japan 1994
Medieval Centre, Chartres,
France 1993
Tennis Centre, Manchester,
England 1993
Volcano Theme Park, Euro Disney,
Paris, France 1992
Holiday Inn, The Hague,
The Netherlands 1988
Stage Set for Paul McCartney
1988
Hotel for La Fondiaria, Florence,
Italy 1987
Royal Thames Yacht Club, London,
England 1987
Marina, Battery Park, New York,
USA 1986
Athletics Stadium, Frankfurt,
Germany 1981–1986

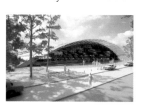

Granada Entertainment Centre,
Milton Keynes, England 1979
London Gliding Club,
Dunstable Downs, England 1978
Country Club and Marina for Fred
Olsen, Vestby, Norway 1974
Pavilion Leisure Centres, Knowsley,
England and Badhoevedorp,
The Netherlands 1972

Masterplans

Canadian Court Masterplan,
Orlando, USA 2004–
La Altura, Havana, Cuba 2004–
Santa Giulia, Milan, Italy 2004–
Milan Fair, Milan, Italy 2004
Sovereign Bay, Gibraltar 2003–
FC Barcelona Masterplan,
Barcelona, Spain 2003–
Boavista, Lisbon, Portugal 2002–
Croydon Gateway, London,
England 2002–
Turin University Masterplan, Turin,
Italy 2002–
World Trade Center Masterplan,
New York, USA 2002
West Kowloon Masterplan,
Hong Kong 2001–
Montecity, Milan, Italy 2000–
Elephant and Castle, London,
England 2000–
'Quartermile' Royal Infirmary,
Edinburgh, Scotland 2000
More London, London Bridge,
England 1998–

The Point, 'Golden Mile,' Durban,
South Africa 1997
Eurogate, Vienna, Austria 1997
Getafe Masterplan, Madrid,
Spain 1997
Linz Solar City, Linz, Austria 1995
Regensburg Solar City,
Germany 1995
Lisbon Expo '98, Portugal 1993
Planning Studies, Corfu,
Greece 1993
Albertopolis, London,
England 1993
Atrium Business Park, Berlin,
Germany 1992
Imperial College, London,
England 1992

Freising Business Park, Freising,
 Germany 1992
Yokohama Harbour, Yokohama,
 Japan 1992
Inner Harbour and City Centre,
 Duisburg, Germany 1991–2003
Sagrera Station Masterplan,
 Barcelona, Spain 1991

Wilhelminapier, Rotterdam,
 The Netherlands 1991–
Cannes Masterplan, France 1990
Centre d'Affaires, La Bastide,
 Bordeaux, France 1990
Gerland Business Park, Lyon,
 France 1990
City of Cambridge, England 1989
Paternoster Square Competition,
 London, England 1989
Microelectronic Park, Duisburg,
 Germany 1988–1996
King's Cross Railway Land,
 London, England 1987
St Helier Harbour, Jersey,
 Channel Islands 1976–1977
Regional Planning Study Gomera,
 Canary Islands 1975

Mixed-Use
Avic Plaza, Shenzhen,
 China 2004–
1 Central Park, Dubai, UAE 2004-
Vancouver Tower, Vancouver,
 Canada, 2004–
The Murezzan, Mixed-Use
 Development, St Moritz,
 Switzerland 2003–
Spinningfields, Manchester,
 England 2003–
Liverpool Ark, Fourth Grace,
 Liverpool, England 2002

Apartments and Hotel Extension,
 Zuoz, Switzerland 1999
Millennium Tower, London,
 England 1996
Gerling Ring-Karree, Cologne,
 Germany 1995–2001

Retail and Office Development,
 Zhongshan Guangzhou,
 China 1994
Al Faisaliah Complex, Riyadh,
 Saudi Arabia 1993–2000

Shinagawa Mixed-Use
 Development, Tokyo, Japan1990
Millennium Tower, Tokyo, Japan 1989
Riverside Apartments and Studio,
 London, England 1986–1990
Open House Community Project,
 Cwmbran, Wales 1978
Fred Olsen Amenity Centre,
 London, England 1968–1970

Offices
Bucklersbury House, London,
 England 2004–
Electricity Building, Milan,
 Italy 2004–
Hines, Hamburg, Germany 2004–
Convention Center Site
 Redevelopment, Washington DC,
 USA 2003
Ranhill Headquarters, Kuala
 Lumpur, Malaysia 2003–
Camomile Street, London,
 England 2002

Drentestaete III, Amsterdam,
 The Netherlands 2002–
6 More London Place, London,
 England 2002–2003
Repsol Headquarters Madrid,
 Spain 2002–
Bishops Square, Spitalfields
 Redevelopment, London,
 England 2001–
51 Lime Street, London,
 England 2001
Scottish Gas Headquarters,
 Customer Contact Centre,
 Edinburgh, Scotland 2001–2003

Hearst Headquarters, New York,
 USA 2001–
France Avenue, Paris,
 France 2000–
1 More London Place,
 Ernst and Young Headquarters,
 London, England 2000–2003
2 More London Riverside, London,
 England 2000–2003
Cisco Systems Office Campus,
 Munich, Germany 2000
Demag Headquarters, Düsseldorf,
 Germany 2000
Farnborough Business Park
 Offices, Farnborough,
 England 2000–2001
The Walbrook, London,
 England 1999
The Metropolitan, Warsaw,
 Poland 1998–2003

J C Decaux International
 Headquarters, Brentford,
 England 1997–2000

Electronic Arts European
 Headquarters, Chertsey,
 England 1997–2000
50 Finsbury Square, London,
 England 1997–2000

Moorhouse, London,
 England 1997–2004
Parkview Offices, Singapore 1997
Swiss Re Headquarters, London,
 England 1997–2004
100 Wood Street, London,
 England 1997–2000
Bath Road Offices, Slough,
 England 1996–1998
Green Park Offices, Reading,
 England 1996–1999
10 Gresham Street, London,
 England 1996–2003
Kingswood Park Offices, Ascot,
 England 1996–1998

126 Phillip Street, Sydney,
 Australia 1996–
Daewoo Electronics Headquarters,
 Seoul, South Korea 1995
IG Metall Headquarters, Frankfurt,
 Germany 1995

Jiushi Corporation Headquarters, Shanghai, China 1995–2001
LIFFE Offices, London, England 1995
21 Moorfields, London, England 1995
Murr Tower, Beirut, Lebanon 1995
Samsung Motors Office and Showroom, Seoul, South Korea 1995–1998
World Port Centre, Rotterdam, The Netherlands 1995–2000

Criterion Place, Leeds, England 1994
Visions for Europe Offices, Düsseldorf, Germany 1994
ARAG Headquarters, Düsseldorf, Germany 1993–2001

33 Holborn Place, London, England 1993–2000

Timex Headquarters, Middlebury, USA 1993
Agiplan Headquarters, Mülheim, Germany 1992–1996

British Gas Offices, Thames Valley Park, Reading, England 1992–1998

Electricité de France Regional Headquarters, Bordeaux, France 1992–1996
1 London Wall, London, England 1992–2003

Tower Place, London, England 1992–2003
Bosch Headquarters, Frankfurt, Germany 1991
Gateway Building for Spitalfields Masterplan, London, England 1991
Obunsha Corporation Headquarters, Tokyo, Japan 1991–1993
St George's Court, London, England 1991
Sanei Corporation Headquarters, Makuhari, Japan 1991
Britannic House Refurbishment, London, England 1990
DS-2 Tower, London, England 1990
Fonta Offices, Toulouse, France 1990
Alpha Building, London, England 1989
Chiswick Park Offices, London, England 1989
Jacob's Island Offices, London, England 1989

Business Promotion Centre, Duisburg, Germany 1988–1993
Microelectronic Centre, Duisburg, Germany 1988–1996
Telematic Centre, Duisburg, Germany 1988–1993
Century Tower, Tokyo, Japan 1987–1991
Stockley Park Offices, Uxbridge, England 1987–1989

IBM London Computing Centre, London, England 1985
Humana Headquarters, Louisville, USA 1982
Fred Olsen Gate Redevelopment, Oslo, Norway 1975
Fred Olsen Offices, Vestby, Norway 1974
Willis Faber & Dumas Headquarters, Ipswich, England 1971–1975
Climatroffice study, 1971
IBM Pilot Head Office, Cosham, England 1970–1971
Air-Supported Office for Computer Technology, Hemel Hempstead, England 1969–1970

Products and Furniture
Forward Desk System for Steelcase 2004
Place Kitchen Furniture for Dada 2004
Foster 500 Furniture for Walter Knoll 2001
Focus Outdoor Lighting for DZ Licht 2001
Saturn Lighting for iGuzzini 2000

Pylons for ENEL, Italy 1999–2000

NF 98 Door Handles for Fusital 1998
A900 Seating and Table for Thonet 1997–1999
Airline Seating System for Vitra 1997–1999
Helit Foster Series Desktop Furniture 1997–2000
Oto Track Lighting System for Artemide 1997–1999
Ra Lighting System for Artemide 1997
Room Control Device for Weidmüller 1997
Duravit and Hoesch 1996–2001
Taps for Stella 1995–1999
Cladding System for Technal 1995
Cambridge Shelving System for Acerbis 1997
NF 95 Door Furniture for Fusital 1994–1995
Tray for Alessi 1994–1998
E66 Wind Turbine for Enercon 1993
Street Lighting for J C Decaux 1993
Tabula Table System for Tecno 1992–1993
Airport Desking System 1989–1991
Street Furniture for J C Decaux 1989
Contract Carpet and Tile Design for Vorwerk 1988
Kite! Chair for Tecno 1987–1997
Nomos Desking System for Tecno 1985–1987
Systems Furniture for Foster Associates 1981

Research

Leslie L Dan Pharmacy Building,
University of Toronto,
Canada 2002–

Faculty Building, Imperial College,
London, England 2001–2004

James H Clark Center, Stanford
University, USA 1999–2003

McLaren Technology Centre,
Woking, England 1998–2004

Flowers Multi-Disciplinary
Research Building, Imperial
College, London,
England 1997–2001

Center for Clinical Science
Research, Stanford University,
Stanford, USA 1995–2000

Sir Alexander Fleming Building,
Imperial College, London,
England 1994–1998

Napp Laboratories, Cambridge,
England 1991

Technology Centres, Edinburgh
and Glasgow, Scotland 1989

Residential

Alassio Apartments, Alassio,
Italy 2004–

Santa Giulia Housing, Milan,
Italy 2004–

Akasaka House, Tokyo,
Japan 2003–

Antilia Residence, Mumbai,
India 2003–

Chalet, Gryon, Switzerland 2003–

Hampton House, London,
England 2003

Leedon Park House,
Singapore 2003–

Madison Avenue residential tower,
New York, USA 2003–

Nottingham residential tower,
Nottingham, England 2003–

Project Lateral apartments,
London, England 2003–

Regent Theatre Development,
Sydney, Australia 2003–

Stornoway House refurbishment,
London, England 2003–2004

Budenberg Haus, Altrincham,
England 2000–

House in Kamakura,
Japan 2000–2004

Chesa Futura, St Moritz,
Switzerland 2000–2002

Albion Riverside, London,
England 1999–2003

Housing 'NF1', Duisburg,
Germany 1997–2001

Private House, USA 1995

Private House, Germany
1992–1994

Refurbishment of Mendelsohn
and Chermayeff House, London,
England 1992–1993

House in Corsica, 1990–1993

House in Kawana,
Japan 1987–1992

Autonomous House 1982–1983

Bean Hill Housing, Milton Keynes,
England 1973–1975

Housing for Wates, Coulsdon,
England 1965 (with Team 4)

Skybreak House and High-Density
Housing, Radlett,
England 1965–1966
(with Team 4)

Creek Vean House and Retreat,
Feock, England 1964–1966
(with Team 4)

Forest Road Annexe, East Horsley,
England 1966 (with Team 4)

Murray Mews Houses, London,
England 1965 (with Team 4)

Waterfront Housing, Feock,
England 1964 (with Team 4)

Retail

Peek & Cloppenburg,
Germany 2004–

767 Fifth Avenue, New York,
USA 2003–

Asprey, London, England
2001–2004

Asprey, New York, USA
2002–2003

Selfridges, London,
England 1999–2007

Selfridges, Glasgow,
Scotland 1997

Repsol Service Stations,
Spain 1997

Cacharel Shops and Franchises,
Europe 1991–1992

Esprit, London, England 1988

Katharine Hamnett, London,
England 1987

Joseph, London, England 1978

Fred Olsen Travel Agency, London,
England 1974

Transport

Beijing Capital International
Airport, Beijing, China 2003–

Yacht *Dark Shadow* 2003

TAV Station, Florence,
Italy 2003–2008

Bilbao Metro Line 2, Spain 2001–

Transport Interchange, Paramatta,
Australia 2000

Motorway Signage System,
England 1998

Expo Station,
Singapore 1997–2001

Dresden Station Redevelopment,
Dresden, Germany 1996–2005

North Greenwich Transport
Interchange, London,
England 1995–1998

Bangkok Airport, Thailand 1994

Ground Transportation Centre,
Chek Lap Kok, Hong Kong
1993–1998

Platform-Edge Screens,
Signage and Furniture for
Mass Transit Railway,
Hong Kong 1993–1997

Hong Kong International Airport,
Chek Lap Kok,
Hong Kong 1992–1998

Kowloon-Canton Railway Terminal,
Hong Kong 1992–1998

Solar-Electric Vehicle, London,
England 1992–1994

Canary Wharf Underground
Station, London,
England 1991–1998

Motor Yacht *Izanami* 1991–1993

Passenger Concourse Building
for British Rail, King's Cross
Station, London, England 1989

Metro System, Bilbao,
Spain 1988–1995

City of London Heliport, London,
England 1988

Turin Airport, Turin, Italy 1987

Stansted Airport, Stansted,
England 1981–1991

Hammersmith Centre, London,
England 1977–1979

Fred Olsen Passenger Terminal,
London, England 1969–1970

Project Credits

Albion Riverside
London, England 1999–2003
Client
Hutchison Whampoa Property
Area
30,000m²
Team
Arup
Davis Langdon & Everest
Exterior International plc
CM International
Jolyon Drury Consultancy
Townshend Landscape
Architects

American Air Museum, Duxford
Duxford, England 1987–1997
Client
Imperial War Museum at Duxford
American Air Museum in Britain
Area
7,400m²
Team
Arup
Roger Preston & Partners
Davis Langdon & Everest
Aerospace Structural and
Mechanical Engineering
Hannah Reed and Associates
Rutherford Consultants

Asprey
London and New York
2001–2004

London
2001–2004
Client
Asprey & Garrard
Area
5,000m²
Team
Alan Baxter Associates
Troup Bywaters & Anders
Davis Langdon & Everest
David Mlinaric
Kondos Roberts

New York
2002–2003
Client
Asprey and Gardener
Area
3,000m²
Team
Cantor Seinuk
Fiskaa Engineering
Gardiner and Theobald
Kondos Roberts

BBC Radio Centre
London, England 1982–1985
Client
British Broadcasting Corporation
Area
52,000m²
Team
Arup
YRM Engineers
David Belfield & Everest
Tim Smith Acoustics

Beijing Airport
Beijing, China 2003–
Client
Beijing Capital International
Airport
Area
420,000m²
Team
Arup
NACO Netherlands Airport
Consultants
Beijing Institute of
Architectural Design
Michel Desvigne
Landscape Concept
Speirs and Major
Architectural Lighting

Bexley Business Academy
2001–2003
Client
Bexley Business Academy Ltd
(Garrard Education Trust,
DfES and 3Es Enterprises)
Area
11,800m²
Team
Davis Langdon & Everest
Buro Happold
Harris Grant Associates
Halcrow
Osprey
Montagu Evans
Second London Wall
Exterior International plc

Bilbao Metro
Bilbao, Spain 1988–2004
Line One
1988–1995
Client
Basque Government
IMEBISA
Length
61km
Team
Sener
TYPSA
Saitec
Arup
Büro Aicher
Weiss Design Asociados
Line Two
1997–2004
Client
Basque Government
IMEBISA
Length
20.5km
Team
Sener
TYPSA
Atelier Weidner
IMEBISA

Boston Museum of Fine Arts
Boston, USA 1999–
Client
Museum of Fine Arts, Boston
Area
51,0000m²
Team
George B H Macomber
Childs Bertman Tseckares Inc
Buro Happold
SEI Companies
Weidlinger Associates Inc
George Sexton Associates
Acentech
Gustafson Guthrie Nichols Ltd
Hughes Associates Inc

British Museum Great Court
London, England 1994–2000
Client
British Museum
Area
19,000m²
Team
Buro Happold
Northcroft
Mace Ltd
Giles Quarme Associates
Claude and Danielle Engle
Lighting
EPP
FEDRA
Sandy Brown Associates

Canary Wharf Underground Station
London, England 1991–1998
Client
Jubilee Line Extension Project
Area
31,500m²
Team
Posford Duvivier
Jubilee Line Extension Project
Arup
Claude and Danielle
Engle Lighting
Davis Langdon & Everest
De Leau Chadwick

Carré d'Art
Nîmes, France 1984–1993
Client
Ville de Nîmes
Area
18,000m²
Team
Arup
OTH
Thorne Wheatley
Claude and Danielle
Engle Lighting
Commins
Jolyon Drury Consultancy
Casso Gaudin
Algoe

CCSR Stanford University
Stanford, USA 1995–2000
Client
Stanford University School
of Medicine
Area
21,000m²
Team
Fong & Chan Architects
Arup
Research Facilities Design
Peter Walker and Partners

Century Tower
Tokyo, Japan 1987–1991
Client
Obunsha Corporation
Area
26,590m²
Team
Arup
Roger Preston & Partners
Northcroft Neighbour
& Nicholson
Claude and Danielle Engle
Lighting
Richard Chaix
Arup Acoustics
Tim Smith Acoustics

Chesa Futura
St Moritz, Switzerland
2000–2002
Client
Sisa AG
Area
4,650m²
Team
Arup
Davis Langdon & Everest
Edy Toscano AG
Peter Walker & Partners
Emmer Pfenninger
Partner AG
EN/ES/TE AG
R & B Engineering GmbH

City Academy, Brent
2000–2003
Client
The Capital City Academy Trust
(Sir Frank Lowe and DfES)
Area
10,500m²
Team
Buro Happold
Davis Langdon & Everest

City Hall
London, England 1998–2002
Client
CIT Group
Area
18,000m²
Team
Arup
Davis Langdon & Everest
Mott Green & Wall
Claude R Engle Lighting

Commerzbank Headquarters
Frankfurt, Germany 1991–1997
Client
Commerzbank AG
Area
100,000m²
Team
Arup
Krebs & Kiefer
Roger Preston & Partners
Pettersen & Ahrends
Schad & Holzel
Jappsen & Stangier
Davis Langdon & Everest
Quickborner Team
Ingenieur Büro Schalm
Lichtdesign
Sommerland
Per Arnoldi

Congress Centre
Valencia, Spain, 1993–1998
Client
City of Valencia
Area
16,000m²
Team
Arup
Roger Preston & Partners
Davis Langdon & Everest
Arup Acoustics
Theatre Projects Consultants
Ingenieria Diez Cisneros
Claude and Danielle
Engle Lighting

Dresden Station
Dresden, Germany 1996–2005
Client
Deutsche Bahn AG
Station & Service
DB ProjektBau GmbH
Area
34,000m²
Team
AYH Homola GmbH & Co KG
Schmitt Stumpf Frühauf
& Partner
Buro Happold

Schmidt Reuter & Partner
adb Denkmalpflege
und Bauforschung
Kaiser BRB
Zibell Willner & Partner
Brandschutz-Consult Leipzig
Speirs and Major Associates

Duisburg Inner Harbour
Duisburg, Germany 1991–2003

Steiger Schwanentor
1993–1994
Client
LEG, Düsseldorf
Pier length
62m
Promenade length
300m
Team
Hans Kolbeck Ingenieur
Büro Klement

Hafenforum
1995–1996
Client
THS, Essen
Area
1,150m²
Team
Architekturbüro Dieter Müller
Ingenieur Büro Cosanne
Glamo GmbH

Canals
1996–1998
Client
IDE, Duisburg
Length and width
175m long
10m wide
Team
ABDOU GmbH
TUV
Ingenieur Büro R Knoke
B-Plan

Housing
  1996–1998
Client
  THS, Essen
Area
  7,000m²
Team
  Ingenieur Büro Cosanne
  Ingenieur Büro Dr Meyer

Duisburg Microelectronic Park
  Duisburg, Germany 1988–1996

Telematic Centre
  1988–1993
Client
  GTT
  Kaiser Bautechnik
Area
  3,500m²
Team
  Ingenieur Büro Dr Meyer
  Kaiser Bautechnik
  ROM
  Oskar Anders GmbH

Microelectronic Centre
  1988–1996
Client
  GTT
Area
  12,000m²
Team
  Ingenieur Büro Dr Meyer
  Kaiser Bautechnik
  Ebert Ingenieur
  Emmer Pfenninger Partner AG
  ITA GmbH
  Höhler & Partner

Business Promotion Centre
  1988–1993
Client
  GTT
  Kaiser Bautechnik
Area
  4,000m²
Team
  Ingenieur Büro Dr Meyer
  Kaiser Bautechnik
  Roger Preston & Partners
  Oskar Anders GmbH

E66 Wind Turbine
  1993
Client
  Enercon GmbH
Height
  100m
Team
  Engineering by Enercon

Electricité de France Regional Headquarters
  Bordeaux, France 1992–1996
Client
  Electricité de France
Area
  7,000m²
Team
  Arup
  SERETE
  MDA France
  Kaiser Bautechnik

Electronic Arts European Headquarters
  Chertsey, England 1997–2000
Client
  Electronic Arts
  P+O Developments
Area
  24,000m²
Team
  Whitby Bird and Partners
  Oscar Faber
  Wheelers
  Land Use Consultants
  Mark Johnson Consultants

Recording Architecture
Tricon
Jeremy Gardner Partnership
Claude and Danielle Engle
Lighting
Schumann Smith Ltd
Rowney Sharman
Exterior International Ltd

Elephant House
  Copenhagen, Denmark 2002–
Client
  Foundation Realdania
  for Copenhagen Zoo
Area
  2,500m²
Team
  Buro Happold
  Ramboll
  Stig L Andersson Architects
  Davis Langdon & Everest

Expo Station
  Singapore 1997–2001
Client
  Land Transport Authority
Area
  7,164m²
Team
  Arup
  Cicada Private Ltd
  Claude and Danielle Engle
  Lighting
  Davis Langdon & Seah
  Singapore Pte Ltd
  Land Transport Authority
  PWD Consultants Pte Ltd

Faculty of Law, University of Cambridge
  Cambridge, England
  1990–1995
Client
  University of Cambridge
Area
  8,500m²
Team
  Anthony Hunt Associates
  YRM Engineers

Davis Langdon & Everest
Sandy Brown Associates
Emmer Pfenninger
Partner AG
Cambridge Landscape
Architects
Arup
Halcrow Fox

Florence Station
  Florence, Italy 2003–
Client
  TAV-RFI
Area
  47,000m²
Team
  Arup
  Davis Langdon & Everest
  Land Use Consultants
  Claude Engle Lighting
  ETA

Free University of Berlin
  Berlin, Germany 1997–2005
Client
  Free University of Berlin
  Berlin Senate Administration
  for Urban Development
Team
  Schmidt Reuter Partner
  Pichler Ingenieure
  Institut für Fassadentechnik
  Höhler & Partner
  Büro Peters
  Büro Noack
  Kappes & Scholtz
  Hosser Hass & Partner
  Ingenieur Büro Lankau
  Moers
  Akustik-Ingenieurbüro
  Moll GmbH

Furniture

A900 Seating
1997–1999
Client
Thonet, Germany

Airline Seating System
1997–1999
Client
Vitra, Switzerland

Foster 500 Series
2001–2002
Client
Walter Knoll, USA

Kite! Chair
1987–1997
Client
Tecno spa, Italy

Tabula Table System
1992–1993
Client
Tecno spa, Italy

Great Glasshouse, National Botanic Gardens of Wales
Llanarthne, Wales 1995–2000
Client
National Botanic Gardens
of Wales
Area
5,800m²
Team
Gustafson Porter
Anthony Hunt Associates
Max Fordham & Partners
Symonds Ltd
Colvin and Moggridge
Schal International

10 Gresham Street
London, England 1996–2003
Client
Standard Life Investments
Area
34,224m²
Team
Davis Langdon & Everest
Waterman Partnership
Roger Preston & Partners
Buro Four Project Services
Bovis Lend Lease

HACTL Superterminal, Chek Lap Kok
Hong Kong 1992–1998
Client
Hong Kong Air Cargo
Terminal Ltd
Area
260,000m²
Team
Arup
Levett & Bailey

Hearst Tower
New York, USA 2001–
Client
Hearst Corporation
Area
79,500m²
Team
Adamson Associates
Cantor Seinuk Group
Flack & Kurtz
George Sexton
Cerami
VDA
Ira Beer
Tishman Speyer Properties

H M Treasury Redevelopment
London, England 1996–2002
Client
Exchequer Partnership
Stanhope Bovis and Chesterton
Area
50,000m²
Team
Waterman Partnership
JBB
Hanscomb Partnership
BDSP
Speirs and Major
Gustafson Porter
Arup
Feilden and Mawson
Per Arnoldi

Hongkong and Shanghai Bank Headquarters
Hong Kong 1979–1986
Client
Hongkong and Shanghai
Banking Corporation
Area
99,000m²
Team
Arup
Roger Preston & Partners
Levett & Bailey
Northcroft Neighbour
& Nicholson
Claude and Danielle
Engle Lighting
Tim Smith Acoustics
Technical Landscapes Ltd
Quickborner Team
Jolyon Drury Consultancy
Corning Glass
Humberside Technical Services
Project Planning Group
R J Mead & Company

Hong Kong International Airport, Chek Lap Kok
Hong Kong 1992–1998
Client
Hong Kong Airport Authority
Area
516,000m²
Team
BAA
Mott Connell Ltd
Arup
Fisher Marantz Renfro Stone
O'Brien Kreitzberg &
Associates Ltd
Wilbur Smith Associates

House in Corsica
Corsica 1990–1993
Area
450m²
Team
Arup
Roger Preston & Partners
Davis Langdon & Everest

House in Kamakura
Kamakura, Japan 2000–2004
Area
1,700m²
Team
Obayashi Corporation
Northcroft
Arup Facade Engineering
Roger Preston & Partners

House in Kawana
Kawana, Japan 1987–1992
Area
6,946m²
Team
Obayashi Corporation
Arup
Claude and Danielle Engle
Lighting
Northcroft Neighbour
& Nicholson
Roger Preston & Partners
Tim Smith Acoustics

Imperial College Sir Alexander Fleming Building
London, England 1994–1998
Client
Imperial College and
South Kensington
Millennium Commission
Area
25,000m^2
Team
Schal Construction Management
Claude and Danielle Engle
Lighting
Research Facilities Design
Sandy Brown Associates
Warrington Fire
WSP
Waterman Partnership
Per Arnoldi

Imperial College Faculty Building
London, England 2001–2004
Client
Imperial College
Area
4,000m^2
Team
Buro Happold
Gardiner and Theobald
Management Services
Davis Langdon & Everest
Jenkins and Potter
Warrington Fire Research
Sandy Brown Associates
Lerch Bates Associates
Per Arnoldi
Exterior International plc

Imperial College Tanaka Business School
London, England 2000–2004
Client
Imperial College
Area
6,250m^2
Team
Buro Happold
Gardiner and Theobald
Jenkins and Potter
Davis Langdon & Everest
Warrington Fire Research
Sandy Brown Associates
Hyder Consulting
Halcrow Group
Per Arnoldi

James H Clark Center, Stanford University
Stanford, USA 1999–2003
Client
Stanford University
Area
8,240m^2
Team
MBT Architecture
Peter Walker & Partners
Hathaway Dinwiddie
AlfaTech
Middlebrook + Louie
Cupertino Electric
Therma
RLS
Charles Salter & Associates
Brian Kangas Faulk
Wilson Ihrig & Associates
Claude and Danielle Engle
Lighting
Davis Langdon & Everest

Jiushi Corporation Headquarters
Shanghai, China 1995–2001
Client
Jiushi Corporation
Area
62,000m^2
Team
Obayashi Corporation
Design Department
East China Architectural
Design Institute (ECADI)
Claude and Danielle Engle
Lighting

Joslyn Art Museum Addition
Omaha, USA 1992–1994
Client
Joslyn Art Museum
Area
5,800m^2
Team
Henningson Durham
and Richardson
Davis Langdon & Everest
Claude and Danielle Engle
Lighting
R F Mahoney and Associates

Lycée Albert Camus
Fréjus, France 1991–1993
Client
Ville de Fréjus
Area
14,500m^2
Team
Arup
Roger Preston & Partners
Davis Langdon & Everest
Desvigne & Dalnoky
Claude and Danielle Engle
Sandy Brown Associates

McLaren Technology Centre
Woking, England 1998–2004
Client
TAG McLaren Holdings
Area
60,000m^2
Team
Arlington Securities
Arup
Schmidt Reuter Partner
Davis Langdon & Everest
Terence O'Rourke
WSP
Intec Management
Claude and Danielle Engle
Lighting
Atelier Dreiseitl

Milan Fair Masterplan
Milan, Italy 2004
Client
Risanamento SpA; IPI SpA
Fiat Engineering SpA
Astaldi SpA
Chelsfield plc
Langdale Consulting
Area
340,000m^2
Team
Gehry Partners
Estudio Moneo
Cino Zucchi
Urbam
Enterprise LSE Cities
Olin Partnership
Battle McCarthy
BMS Progetti Srl
Halvorson Kaye
Studio Ermanno Casasco
Studio TRM Srl
Systematica SpA
Technion Srl

Millau Viaduct
  Gorge du Tarn, France
  1993–2004
Client
  French Ministry of Equipment,
  Transport, Housing, Tourism
  and Sea
Length
  2.5km
Team
  Chapelet-Defol-Mousseigne
  Europe Etudes Gecti
  Sogelerg
  SERF
  Agence TER
  Compagnie Eiffage du Viaduc
  de Millau

Millennium Bridge
  London, England 1996–2000
Client
  Millennium Bridge Trust
  London Borough of Southwark
Length
  320m
Team
  Arup
  Sir Anthony Caro
  Davis Langdon & Everest
  Claude R Engle Lighting
  Monberg & Thorsen/
  McAlpine

Millennium Tower
  Tokyo, Japan 1989
Client
  Obayashi Corporation
Area
  1,040,000m²
Height
  840m
Team
  Obayashi Corporation

Motor Yacht *Izanami*
  1991–1993
Length
  58.5m
Team
  Gerhard Gilgenost
  Dr Lurssen Werfl

Musée de Préhistoire des Gorges du Verdon
  Quinson, France 1992–2001
Client
  Département Alpes de
  Hautes Provence
Area
  4,500m²
Team
  Bruno Chiambretto
  Olivier Sabran
  SEV Ingenierie
  Davis Langdon & Everest

New German Parliament, Reichstag
  Berlin, Germany 1992–1999
Client
  Bundesrepublik Deutschland
Area
  61,166m²
Team
  Kuehn Bauer und Partner
  Davis Langdon & Everest
  Kaiser Bautechnik
  Fischer Energie und
  Haustechnik
  IKP Professor Dr Georg Plenge
  Müller BBM GmbH
  Claude and Danielle
  Engle Lighting
  Leonhardt Andrä und Partner
  Planungsgruppe Karnasch-
  Hackstein
  Acanthus
  Amstein & Walthert

Nomos Table
  1985–1987
Client
  Tecno spa, Italy

126 Phillip Street
  Sydney, Australia 1996–
Stage 1
Client
  Bankers Trust
Area
  67,370m²
Team
  Hassell Pty Ltd
  Arup
  Roger Preston/Lincolne
  Scott Australia Pty
  Rider Hunt Sydney Pty Ltd
  Lerch Bates & Associates
  JBA Urban Planning
  Godden Mackay Logan

Stage 2
Client
  Principle/Investa Property Group
Area
  67,370m²
Team
  Hassell Pty Ltd
  CGP Management Pty Ltd
  Bovis Lend Lease Pty Ltd
  Norman Disney & Young
  Arup Facade
  Stephen Grubits & Associates
  Pty Ltd
  LHO Group Hydraulic & Fire
  Protection Consultants
  Masson Wilson Twiney
  Pty Ltd
  JBA Urban Planning
  Godden Mackay Logan

Petronas University of Technology
  Malaysia 1998–2004
Client
  Universiti Teknologi Petronas
Site Area
  450 hectares
Team
  GDP Architects
Arup
  Roger Preston & Partners
  Majutek Perunding
  Research Facilities Design
  Schumann Smith Ltd
  Sandy Brown Associates
  Majid & Associates
  BDG McColl
  HSS Integrated
  Jurukur Bahan Malaysia
  KPK
  KLCCB
  Ranhill Bersekutu
  Shah P K & Associates
  Vision Design
  Marshall Day Acoustics

Product Design

NF 95 Door Furniture
  1994–1995
Client
  Fusital (Valli & Valli)

Tray for Alessi
  1994–1998
Client
  Alessi spa, Italy

Bathroom Foster
  1996–2001
Client
  Duravit and Hoesch

Cambridge Shelving System
  1997
Client
  Acerbis

Renault Distribution Centre
Swindon, England 1980–1982
Client
Renault UK Ltd
Area
25,000m²
Team
Arup
Davis Belfield & Everest
Tim Smith Acoustics
Technical Landscapes Ltd
Quickborner Team

Repsol Headquarters
Madrid, Spain 2002–
Client
Repsol YPF
Area
56,000m²
Team
Halvorson Kaye
Structural Engineers
Aguilera Ingenieros
Alatec
Emmer Pfenninger
Lerch Bates
XCO2 conisbee

Repsol Service Stations
Spain 1997
Client
Repsol
Height
8m
Team
Arup
Davis Langdon & Everest
Roger Preston & Partners
Claude and Danielle Engle
Lighting

**Riverside Apartments
and Studio**
London, England 1986–1990
Client
Petmoor Development
Area
13,000m²
Team
Arup
Roger Preston & Partners
Schumann Smith Ltd
Tim Smith Acoustics
Claude and Danielle Engle
Lighting
Emmer Pfenninger
Partner AG
O & H Construction

**Sackler Galleries,
Royal Academy of Arts**
London, England 1985–1991
Client
Royal Academy of Arts
Area
312m²
Team
Anthony Hunt Associates
James R Briggs
George Sexton Associates
Julian Harrap Architects
Davis Langdon & Everest

The Sage Gateshead
Gateshead, England 1997–2004
Client
Gateshead Council
Area
17,500m²
Team
Arup
Mott MacDonald
Buro Happold
Davis Langdon & Everest
Theatre Projects Consultants
Equation Lighting Design Ltd
Lerch Bates & Associates Ltd
Burdus Access Management
Winton Nightingale

Desvigne & Dalnoky
WSP
Laing Ltd
Space Syntax Laboratories

**Sainsbury Centre for
Visual Arts**
Norwich, England 1974–1978
Client
University of East Anglia
Area
6,186m²
Team
Anthony Hunt Associates
Hanscomb Partnership
Tony Pritchard

Smithsonian Institution
Washington, USA 2004–
Client
The Smithsonian Institution
Area
2,800m²
Team
Smith Group
Buro Happold
Battle McCarthy
Emmer Pfenninger
Davis Langdon & Everest
Sandy Brown Associates
George Sexton Associates
Lerch Bates

Stansted Airport
England 1981–1991
Client
BAA
Area
85,700m²
Team
Arup
BAAC
Beard Dove
Currie & Brown
Claude and Danielle
Engle Lighting
ISVR Consultancy Services
University of Bristol

Supreme Court
Singapore 2000–2005
Client
The Supreme Court Singapore
Area
77,609m²
Team
CPG Consultants PTE Ltd
TID Associates PTE Ltd
Arup Facade Engineering
Tierra Design
Lighting Planners Associates Inc
CCW Associates PTE Ltd
Colt International Ltd

Swiss Re Headquarters
30 St Mary Axe, London, England
1997–2004
Client
Swiss Reinsurance Company
Area
76,400m²
Team
Arup
Gardiner & Theobald
Hilson Moran Partnership Ltd
RWG Associates
Van Densen & Associates

Torre de Collserola
Barcelona, Spain 1988–1992
Client
Torre de Collserola SA
Area
Tower platforms 5,800m²
Height
288m
Team
Arup
Davis Langdon & Everest
MC-2
BMT Fluid Mechanics Ltd
Oxford University Wind
Tunnel Laboratory
Telecommunications Facility

Tower Place
London, England 1992–2003
Client
Tishman Speyer
Properties Ltd
Marsh & McLennan
Companies Inc
Area
42,000m^2
Team
Arup
E C Harris
Claude and Danielle
Engle Lighting
Townshend Landscape
Architects
MACE

Trafalgar Square
London, England 2002–2003
Client
Transport for London
Commission
The Greater London Authority
Steering Group
Westminster City Council
The Department for Culture,
Media and Sport
The Parliamentary Works
Directorate
English Heritage
The Royal Parks Agency
London Transport Buses
Area
48,000m^2
Team
W S Atkins
Feilden & Mawson
Speirs & Major
GMJ Data Presentation
TPS Schal
Davis Langdon & Everest
Fitzpatrick

Wembley Stadium
London, England 1996–
Client
Wembley National
Stadium Ltd
Area
170,000m^2
Team
HOK Sport+Venue+Event/
LOBB
Mott Stadium Consortium
Franklin & Andrews
Nathaniel Lichfield & Partners
Steer Davies Gleeve

West Kowloon Cultural District
Hong Kong 2001–
Client
Dynamic Star International
Area
1,300,000m^2
Team
Arup
Rocco Design Ltd
Davis Langdon & Everest
MVA Hong Kong Ltd
Fisher Marantz Stone
Theatre Project Consultants
Michel Desvigne Paysagiste
ADI Limited
Bartlett School of Planning
BMT Asia
CPG
Maunsell Consultants Asia
Parsons Brinckerhoff Asia Ltd
Shankland Cox Asia Ltd
WT Partnership

Willis Faber & Dumas
Ipswich, England 1971–1975
Client
Willis Faber & Dumas Ltd
Area
21,000m^2
Team
Anthony Hunt Associates
John Taylor & Sons
Davis Belfield & Everest
Sound Research Laboratories
Martin Francis
Adrian Wilder
J A Storey & Partners

**World Squares for
All Masterplan**
London, England 1996–2002
Client
City of Westminster
Department for Culture,
Media and Sport
English Heritage
Government Office for London
The Houses of Parliament
London Transport
The Royal Parks Agency
Area
19,000m^2
Team
Halcrow Fox
Civic Design Partnership
Davis Langdon & Everest
Space Syntax Laboratory
W S Atkins
Feilden and Mawson
Schal Construction Management
Speirs & Major
GMJ
Ricky Burdett

World Trade Center
New York, USA 2002
Client
Lower Manhattan
Development Corporation
Area
17,600,000m^2
Team
Anish Kapoor
Cantor Seinuk, Israel Seinuk
Roger Preston & Partners
Lerch Bates Associates Ltd
Davis Langdon & Everest
Space Syntax

Yacht Club de Monaco
Monaco 2003–
Client
Service Des Travaux Publics
de Monaco
Area
14,000m^2
Team
OGER International
Iori & Giraldi Architectes

Project Awards

2004

Business Academy,
Bexley, England
    Civic Trust Commendation
    RIBA Award

Capital City Academy,
Brent, England
    Civic Trust Commendation

Chesa Futura, St Moritz,
Switzerland
    Holzbaupreis Graubünden,
    Commendation

Forth Quarter Masterplan,
Edinburgh, Scotland
    RICS Awards, Joint Winner,
    Regeneration

Foster 500/5 Series
    Red Dot Design Award

10 Gresham Street, London,
England
    Civic Trust Award

Hong Kong International Airport,
Chek Lap Kok, Hong Kong
    Skytrax Airport of the Year

James H Clark Center,
Stanford University, USA
    AISC Engineering Awards of
    Excellence, Merit Award
    R&D Magazine Laboratory
    of the Year Award
    SEAONC Award of Excellence
    in Structural Engineering

Metropolitan, Warsaw, Poland
    Construction Investment Journal
    Awards, Best Overall Project
    MIPIM Award, Winner of the
    'Business Centres' Category
    RIBA Worldwide Award

More London Plot 1,
London, England

British Council for Offices,
London Commercial Workplace
Award for 1 More London Place
Structural Steel Design Award
The Sage Gateshead, England
    ICE North Robert Stephenson
    Award for Concept and Design

Scottish Gas Headquarters,
Edinburgh, Scotland
    British Council for Offices,
    National and Scotland
    Commercial Workplace Award

Swiss Re Headquarters, 30 St
Mary Axe, London, England
    Emporis Skyscraper Award
    IAS/OAS Awards, Best Central
    London Development
    International Highrise Award,
    Honourable Mention
    London Architecture Biennale,
    Best New London Building
    RIBA Award
    RIBA Stirling Prize

Tower Place, London, England
    Civic Trust Commendation

World Squares for All: Trafalgar
Square, London, England
    Civic Trust Special Award,
    Hard Landscaping
    RIBA Award
    RIBA London/English Heritage
    Award for a Building in a
    Historic Context

2003

City Hall, London, England
    Institution of Civil Engineers
    London Association Merit
    Award

Expo Station, Singapore
    Architecture+ Cityscape
    Awards, Winner of the Public
    Arts and Culture Category

Gerling Ring-Karree,
Cologne, Germany
    Kölner Architekturpreis

Great Court, British Museum,
London, England
    ECCS European Steel
    Design Award
    RIBA Award

Great Glass House, National
Botanic Garden of Wales,
Llanarthne, Wales
    The Dewy-Prys Thomas Prize

HM Treasury, London, England
    British Construction Industry
    Awards, Major Project Category,
    High Recommendation
    British Council for Offices,
    National and London
    Refurbished Workplace Award
    Public Private Finance Award,
    Best Design Project

Millennium Bridge,
London, England
    RIBA Award

Swiss Re Headquarters, 30 St
Mary Axe, London, England
    AR/MIPIM Future Project Prize,
    Best of Show joint winner
    ECCS European Steel
    Design Award

Tower Place, London, England
    Construct Award for Innovation
    and Best Practice

World Squares for All: Trafalgar
Square, London, England
    European Union Prize for
    Cultural Heritage/Europa Nostra
    Awards, Diploma in the Cultural
    Landscape Category

2002

British Library of Political and
Economic Science, London School
of Economics, England
    Civic Trust Commendation

Yacht *Dark Shadow*
    Show Boats Awards, Best
    Sailing Yacht under 38 Metres

Electronic Arts European
Headquarters, Chertsey, England
    Concours des Plus Beaux
    Ouvrages de Construction
    Metallique

Expo Station, Singapore
    Singapore Construction
    Excellence Award,
    Civil Category

Foster 500 Series
    Red Dot Design Award

Great Court, British Museum,
London, England
    Camden Design Award
    Civic Trust Award
    National Heritage Museum of
    the Year Award 2000/2001

Hong Kong International Airport,
Chek Lap Kok, Hong Kong
    ARCASIA Award for
    Architecture 2001/2002, Gold
    Medal in category B-4

Jiushi Headquarters,
Shanghai, China
    Lu Ban Prize

Millau Viaduct, Gorges du Tarn,
France
    Singapore Construction
    Excellence Award,
    Civil Category

Newbury Racecourse Grandstand,
Newbury, England
    Structural Steel Design Awards,
    Commendation

2001
Bathroom Foster for Duravil
and Hoesch
    Innovationspreis Architektur
    und Technik, Sanitaryware
    Category, Commendation

Canary Wharf Underground
Station, London, England
    World Architecture Awards,
    Best Transport/Infrastructure
    Building

Citigroup Headquarters,
London, England
    British Council for Offices,
    National and South and East
    London Corporate Workplace
    Building Award

Electronic Arts European
Headquarters, Chertsey, England
    Civic Trust Award

Great Court, British Museum,
London, England
    British Construction Industry
    Awards, Major Project Category,
    Highly Commended
    DuPont Benedictus Awards,
    Special Recognition
    Institution of Civil Engineers,
    'Special Award' with Buro
    Happold (and Mace)

Great Glasshouse, National
Botanic Garden of Wales,
Llanarthne, Wales
    Civic Trust Award
    D&AD Silver Award
    for Environmental Design
    & Architecture
    H&V News Awards,
    Environmental Initiative

of the Year Award
Helit Foster Series
Desktop Furniture
    iF Product Design Award

Hong Kong International Airport,
Chek Lap Kok, Hong Kong
    Architectural Ironmongery
    Specification Awards
    2000/2001, Winner of
    the Overseas Public
    Buildings Category

Kingswood Technical Park,
Ascot, England
    Civic Trust Award

Willis Faber & Dumas
Headquarters, Ipswich, England
    Concrete Society Award,
    Certificate of Excellence in
    the Mature Structures Category
    for Corporate Headquarters

2000
A900 Seating for Thonet
    Baden-Württemberg
    International Design Award,
    Focus Working Environment
    Red Dot Design Award

American Air Museum, Duxford,
England
    Celebrating Construction
    Achievement Award

ASPIRE National Training Centre
    Civic Trust Commendation

Canary Wharf Underground
Station, London, England
    AIA UK Chapter Design
    Awards, Commendation
    British Construction Industry
    Awards, Special Award for the
    Pursuit of Engineering and
    Architectural Award
    Civic Trust Award
    Excellence in Public Transport

Railway Forum/Modern Railways
Industry Innovation Award
Royal Fine Art Commission Trust
Building of the Year Award,
High Commendation
RIBA Award

Electronic Arts European
Headquarters, Chertsey, England
    RIBA Award
    Runnymede Borough
    Council Design Award,
    Commercial Category
    The Times/Gestetner Digital
    Office Collection Award,
    Third Prize
    Whitby Bird and Partners'
    Structural Award

Expo Station, Singapore
    Institution of Engineers Australia,
    High Commendation
    Metal Roofing and Cladding
    Association of Australia Special
    Achievement Award
    NRCA Gold Circle Award
    for Innovation

Great Glasshouse, National
Botanic Garden of Wales
Llanarthne, Wales
    Architecture in Wales Eisteddfod
    Gold Medal in Architecture
    The Concrete Society
    Building Award
    The Leisure Property
    Awards, Finalist for
    Best National Scheme
    RIBA Award
    Royal Institute of
    Chartered Surveyors
    Building Efficiency Award.
    Structural Steel Design Award

Helit Foster Series
Desktop Furniture
    Architektur und Office,
    Architecture and Industry
    in Partnership

Imperial College, Sir Alexander
Fleming Building
    Civic Trust Commendation

J C Decaux International
Headquarters, Brentford, England
    The Concrete Society and British
    Precast Concrete Federation
    Award for Excellence in
    Precast Concrete
    RIBA Award
    RIBA Crown Estate
    Conservation Architecture Award

New German Parliament,
Reichstag, Berlin, Germany
    Architekturpreis des BDA Berlin
    MIPIM Special Jury Prize
    Preis des Deutschen Stahlbaues

North Greenwich Transport
Interchange, London, England
    Civic Trust Award
    National Lighting Design
    Awards, Distinction

Room Control Device
for Weidmuller
    iF Product Design Award

Saturn Lighting for iGuzzini
    iF Product Design Award

World Port Centre, Rotterdam,
The Netherlands
    Corus Construction Award
    for the Millennium

1999
American Air Museum,
Duxford, England
    Civic Trust Award
    Concrete Society Award
    Design Council Millennium
    Product Award
    FX International Interior Design
    Award, Best Museum

Hong Kong International Airport,
Chek Lap Kok, Hong Kong
    Best Architecture in Hong Kong,
    Second Prize, voted by the
    people of Hong Kong
    Construction Quality Awards
    International Project of the Year
    Design Council Millennium
    Product Award
    Institute of Structural Engineers
    Structural Award, Commendation
    International Lighting Design
    Award of Excellence
    Structural Steel Design Award
    Travel & Leisure Magazine
    Critics' Choice Award for
    Best Airport

Hongkong and Shanghai Bank
Headquarters, Hong Kong
    Best Architecture in Hong Kong,
    First Prize, voted by the people
    of Hong Kong

Imperial College, Sir Alexander
Fleming Building, London, England
    R&D Magazine Laboratory of
    the Year Award, High Honours
    RIBA Regional Award

New German Parliament,
Reichstag, Berlin, Germany
    Architects' Journal and Bovis
    Europe Grand Award for
    Architecture at the Royal
    Academy Summer Exhibition
    Design Council Millennium
    Product Award
    Deutscher Architekturpreis
    DuPont Benedictus Award,
    Special Recognition
    ECCS European Award for
    Steel Structures
    Eurosol Preis für Solares Bauen
    RIBA Regional Award
    RIBA Conservation Award

North Greenwich Transport
Interchange, London, England
    Aluminium Imagination Award
    Structural Steel Design Awards,
    Commendation

Repsol Service Stations, Spain
    City Planning, Architecture and
    Public Works Award, Madrid,
    First Prize

Robert Gordon University
Faculty of Management,
Aberdeen, Scotland
    Civic Society Award
    RIBA Regional Award

Room Control Device for
Weidmuller
    Design Plus Award

Valencia Congress Centre,
Valencia, Spain
    RIBA Regional Award

Willis Faber & Dumas
Headquarters, Ipswich, England
    British Council for Offices Test
    of Time Award, Commendation

1998
Agiplan Headquarters,
Mülheim, Germany
    Bund Deutscher Architekten
    Ruhr Area, 'Gute Bauten' Award,
    Commendation

American Air Museum, Duxford,
England
    RIBA Regional Award
    RIBA Stirling Prize
    Royal Fine Art Commission
    BSkyB Building of the Year
    Award

ASPIRE National Training Centre,
Stanmore, England
    Harrow Heritage Trust
    Observer Award

Bath Road Offices,
Slough, England
    Business & Industry Agents
    Society Award

Bilbao Metro, Bilbao, Spain
    Brunel Award, Madrid
    RIBA Regional Award
    Veronica Rudge Green Prize
    in Urban Design

British Gas Offices, Thames Valley
Park, Reading, England
    British Council for Offices
    Award, Commendation
    RIBA Regional Award

Carré d'Art, Nîmes, France
    Veronica Rudge Green Prize
    in Urban Design

Commerzbank Headquarters,
Frankfurt, Germany
    Bund Deutscher Architekten,
    Martin-Elsaesser-Plakette
    RIBA Regional Award

Duisburg Microelectronic Centre,
Duisburg, Germany
    Bund Deutscher Architekten
    Nordrhein-Westfalen Area Award

Great Glasshouse, National
Botanic Garden of Wales
Llanarthne, Wales
    BIAT Open Award for
    Technical Excellence

Hong Kong International Airport,
Chek Lap Kok, Hong Kong
    British Construction Industry
    International Award
    HKIA Silver Medal

Kingswood Technical Park,
Ascot, England
    Business & Industry Agents
    Society Award

Kowloon-Canton Railway Terminal,
Hong Kong
    HKIA Certificate of Merit

Motorway Signage System
    Design Council Millennium
    Product Award

Wind Turbine for Enercon
    Design Council Millennium
    Product Award

1997
American Air Museum,
Duxford, England
    AIA London Chapter Excellence
    in Design Commendation
    British Construction Industry
    Awards, High Commendation
    British Guild of Travel Writers
    Silver Unicorn Award

Bilbao Metro, Bilbao, Spain
    Manuel de la Dehesa Award,
    Commendation

Cambridge University Faculty of
Law, Cambridge, England
    David Urwin Design Awards,
    Commendation

Commerzbank Headquarters,
Frankfurt, Germany
    British Construction Industry
    International Award

Duisburg Microelectronic Centre,
Duisburg, Germany
    RIBA Regional Award

1996
Duisburg Microelectronic Centre,
Duisburg, Germany
    Bund Deutscher Architekten
    Rechter Niederrhein Area,
    'Gute Bauten' Award

Linz Solar City, Linz, Austria
  International Academy of
  Architecture Medal and
  Honorary Diploma

Solar-Electric Vehicle
  ID Design Distinction Award
  in Concepts

1995
Bilbao Metro, Bilbao, Spain
  Premio Radio Correo Award

Cranfield University Library,
Cranfield, England
  Civic Trust Award

Duisburg Inner Harbour
Masterplan, Duisburg, Germany
  Disabled Access Award for
  Steiger Schwanentor

Joslyn Art Museum Extension,
Omaha, USA
  American Concrete Institute
  (Nebraska) Award of Excellence
  AIA Regional and State
  Architecture Award

Solar-Electric Vehicle
  Design Review Minerva Award,
  Commendation
  Design Week Award for
  Product Design

1994
Century Tower, Tokyo, Japan
  Intelligent Building Promotion
  Award
  The Society of Heating, Air
  Conditioning and Sanitary
  Engineers of Japan Award

Cranfield University Library,
Cranfield, England
  British Steel Colorcoat Award,
  Runner Up

Duisburg Business Promotion
Centre, Duisburg, Germany
  Bund Deutscher Architekten
  Bezirksgruppe Ruhr Award

Marine Simulator Centre,
Rotterdam, The Netherlands
  Architectural Review Best
  European Interior Lighting
  Scheme Highlight Award
  Interiors (USA) Award

Stansted Airport, Stansted,
England
  BBC Design Awards Finalist

1993
Torre de Collserola
Telecommunications Tower,
Barcelona, Spain
  The Architecture FAD
  Award, Barcelona
  The Architecture and Urbanism
  Award of the City of Barcelona
  Cultural Foundation of
  Madrid Award
  The Opinion FAD Award,
  Barcelona

Carré d'Art, Nîmes, France
  Interiors (USA) Award

Cranfield University Library,
Cranfield, England
  Bedfordshire Design Award,
  Special Award
  British Construction Industry
  Building Award
  British Construction Industry
  Supreme Award
  Concrete Society Award,
  Highly Commended
  Design Review Minerva
  Award, Commendation
  Eastern Electricity Commercial
  Property Award, Best
  Architectural Project
  Eastern Electricity Commercial
  Property Award, Best Public

Development
  Eastern Electricity Commercial
  Property Award, Building
  Services System, Special
  Commendation
  Eastern Electricity Commercial
  Property Award, Building
  of the Year
  Financial Times Architecture
  Award, Commendation
  Interiors (USA) Award
  Lighting Design Award,
  Highly Commended
  RIBA Regional Award

Crescent Wing, Sainsbury Centre
for Visual Arts, Norwich, England
  International Association
  of Lighting Designers
  Awards, Citation

Sackler Galleries, Royal Academy
of Arts, London, England
  Design Review Minerva Award
  Marble Architecture Award,
  Special Mention
  RIBA Best Building of the
  Year Award

Stansted Airport, Stansted,
England
  Benedictus Award, USA,
  for Innovative Use of
  Laminated Glass
  Financial Times Architecture
  Award, Commendation

Stockley Park Offices, Uxbridge,
England
  British Council for Offices Award

1992
Torre de Collserola
Telecommunications Tower,
Barcelona, Spain
  Premio Alcantara Award
  for Public Works in Latin
  American Countries

Century Tower, Tokyo, Japan
  BCS Award, Tokyo
  Lightweight Metal Cladding
  Association Award
  Nikkei Business Publications
  Award for New Technology

Crescent Wing, Sainsbury Centre
for Visual Arts, Norwich, England
  Civic Trust Award
  Design Review Minerva Award,
  Commendation
  RIBA Regional Award

ITN Headquarters, London,
England
  British Council for Offices Best
  Building Award
  Design Review Minerva Award,
  Commendation
  RIBA Regional Award

Sackler Galleries, Royal Academy
of Arts, London, England
  British Construction Industry
  Award, High Commendation
  Design Review Minerva Award,
  Commendation
  Institution of Civil Engineers
  Merit Award
  Interiors (USA) Award
  Mansell Refurbishment Award
  National Dryline Wall Award
  RIBA National Award
  RIBA Regional Award
  The Royal Fine Art Commission
  and Sunday Times Building of
  the Year Award
  Structural Steel Design Award

Stansted Airport,
Stansted, England
  Architects' Journal Hilight
  Lighting Award, Commendation
  Brunel Award, Madrid, for
  British Rail Station
  Civic Trust Award
  Concrete Society Award
  Design Review Minerva Award,

Commendation
RIBA National Award
RIBA Regional Award
Royal Institute of Chartered
Surveyors Energy Efficiency
Award
Structural Steel Design Award

1991
Century Tower, Tokyo, Japan
    Institution of Structural
    Engineers Special Award

ITN Headquarters,
London, England
    Aluminium Imagination Award

Stansted Airport, Stansted,
England
    Aluminium Imagination Award
    British Association of Landscape
    Industries Award
    British Construction Industry
    Supreme Award
    British Gas Energy
    Management Award
    Business and Industry Panel
    for the Environment Award
    Mies van der Rohe Pavilion
    Award for European Architecture
    National Childcare Facilities
    Award
    Royal Town Planning Institute
    Silver Jubilee Award

Stockley Park Offices,
Uxbridge, England
    Aluminium Imagination Award

1990
Willis Faber & Dumas
Headquarters, Ipswich, England
    RIBA Trustees Medal

1989
Stockley Park Offices,
Uxbridge, England
    British Construction Industry
    Award

1988
Esprit Shop, London, England
    Interiors (USA) Award

Hongkong and Shanghai Bank
Headquarters, Hong Kong
    PA Innovations Award
    Quaternario Award for Innovative
    Technology in Architecture

1987
Nomos Desking System for Tecno
    Design Centre Award Stuttgart
    Premio Compasso d'Oro Award

1986
Hongkong and Shanghai Bank
Headquarters, Hong Kong
    Institution of Structural
    Engineers Special Award
    Marble Architectural Award
    R S Reynolds Memorial Award
    Structural Steel Award

Renault Distribution Centre,
Swindon, England
    First Prize, European Award for
    Industrial Architecture

1984
Renault Distribution Centre,
Swindon, England
    Civic Trust Award
    Financial Times Architecture
    at Work Award
    Structural Steel Design Award

1983
Hongkong and Shanghai Bank
Headquarters, Hong Kong
    Premier Architectural Award
    Royal Academy of Arts, London

1981
IBM Technical Park,
Greenford, England
    Financial Times Industrial
    Architecture Award,
    Commendation

1980
IBM Technical Park,
Greenford, England
    Structural Steel Design Award

Sainsbury Centre for Visual Arts,
Norwich, England
    Ambrose Congreve Award
    Museum of the Year Award
    Sixth Eternit International Prize
    for Architecture, Brussels

1979
Sainsbury Centre for Visual Arts,
Norwich, England
    British Tourist Board Award
    R S Reynolds Memorial Award

1978
Sainsbury Centre for Visual Arts,
Norwich, England
    RIBA Award

1977
Palmerston Special School,
Liverpool, England
    RIBA Award

Willis Faber & Dumas
Headquarters, Ipswich, England
    RIBA Award

1976
Palmerston Special School,
Liverpool, England
    Eternit International Prize
    for Architecture, Brussels

Willis Faber & Dumas
Headquarters, Ipswich, England
    Business and Industry Panel
    for the Environment Award
    R S Reynolds Memorial Award

1974
Modern Art Glass Warehouse,
Thamesmead, England
    Financial Times Industrial
    Architecture Award

1972
IBM Pilot Head Office,
Cosham, England
    RIBA Award
    Structural Steel Design Award

1971
Air-Supported Office
    Financial Times Industrial
    Architecture Award,
    Commendation

1970
Fred Olsen Amenity Centre,
London, England
    Financial Times Industrial
    Architecture Award

1969
Creek Vean House, Feock, England
    RIBA Award

Fred Olsen Amenity Centre,
London, England
    Architectural Design Project
    Award

1967
Reliance Controls Electronics
Factory, Swindon, England
    Financial Times Industrial
    Architecture Award

1966
Reliance Controls Electronics
Factory, Swindon, England
    Architectural Design Project
    Award

1965
Housing for Wates
    Architectural Design Project
    Award

1964
Waterfront Housing
    Architectural Design Project
    Award

Practice and Personal Awards

2005
Norman Foster
  Great Britons Award for
  Outstanding Achievement
  in the Creative Industries

2004
Norman Foster
  Prince Philip Designer's Prize
  Transatlantic Bridge Award

2003
Norman Foster
  City of Rome Lifetime
  Achievement Award and
  Medaglia di Roma
  Werkstatt Deutschland, 'die
  quadriga' prize for Vision,
  Courage and Responsibility

2002
Norman Foster
  Member of the Order 'Pour le
  mérite' for Sciences and Arts
  Praemium Imperiale Award
  for Architecture
  International Union of Architects,
  Auguste Perret Prize

2001
Norman Foster
  South Bank Show Award
  for Visual Arts

1999
Norman Foster
  Laureate of the 1999 Pritzker
  Architecture Prize
  Life Peerage in the Queen's
  Birthday Honours List
  Commander's Cross of the
  Order of Merit of the Federal
  Republic of Germany
  Le Prix Européen de
  l'Architecture de la Fondation
  Européenne de la Culture
  Special Prize, 4th International
  Biennial of Architecture,
  São Paulo, Brazil

1998
Foster and Partners
  The Building Award, Architectural
  Practice of the Year
Norman Foster
  German-British Forum,
  Special Prize

1997
Foster and Partners
  The Building Award, Large
  Architectural Practice of the Year
  British Construction Industry
  Awards, A Decade of Success
  1988–1997
  International Association of
  Lighting Designers IALD/Hilight
  Excellence in Lighting Award
  European Aluminium Award
  for Architecture

Norman Foster
  Appointed to the Order of
  Merit by the Queen
  Silver Medal of the Chartered
  Society of Designers
  International Academy of
  Architecture Grand Prize 1997
  Cristal Globe
  Prince Philip Designers Prize,
  Special Commendation
  Premi a la millor tasca de
  promocio international de
  Barcelona

1996
Foster and Partners
  The Building Award, Large
  Architectural Practice of the Year
Norman Foster
  American Academy of Arts
  and Sciences Award
  The Building Award,
  Construction Personality
  of the Year
  MIPIM Man of the Year Award
  Honorary Doctorate, Doctoris
  Honoris Causa, Technical
  University of Eindhoven

Honorary Doctorate, Doctor
of Letters, Honoris Causa,
University of Oxford
Honorary Doctorate of
Literature, University of London

1995
Foster and Partners
  The Building Award,
  Architectural Practice of the Year
  Queen's Award for Export
  Achievement

Norman Foster
  Gold Medal, Universidad
  Internacional Menedez Pelayo
  Santander, Spain

1994
Foster and Partners
  CICA CAD Drawing Award

Norman Foster
  American Institute of Architects
  Gold Medal
  Officer of the Order of Arts
  and Letters, Ministry of Culture,
  France

1993
Norman Foster
  Honorary Degree, University
  of Manchester

1992
Norman Foster
  Arnold W Brunner Memorial
  Prize from the American
  Academy and Institute of Arts
  and Letters, New York
  Honorary Degree, University
  of Valencia, Spain
  Honorary Degree, University
  of Humberside

1991
Norman Foster
  Gold Medal of the French
  Academy of Architecture
  Honorary Doctorate, Royal
  College of Art, London

1990
Norman Foster
  The Chicago Architecture Award
  Knighthood in the Queen's
  Birthday Honours List

1989
Norman Foster
  Grosse Kunstpreis Award,
  Akademie der Kunst, Berlin

1988
Norman Foster
  Royal Designer for Industry

1987
Norman Foster
  Japan Design Foundation Award

1986
Norman Foster
  Honorary Doctorate,
  University of Bath

1984
Foster Associates
  Honourable Mention,
  UIA Auguste Perret Prize
  for Applied Technology
  in Architecture

1983
Norman Foster
  The Royal Gold Medal
  for Architecture

1980
Norman Foster
  Honorary Doctorate,
  University of East Anglia

Index